Mental Health Professionals, Minorities, and the Poor

Mental Health Professionals, Minorities, and the Poor

Michael E. Illovsky, Ph.D.

Brunner-Routledge
New York and Hove

Published in 2003 by
Brunner-Routledge
29 West 35th Street
New York, NY 10001
www.brunner-routledge.com

Published in Great Britain by
Brunner-Routledge
27 Church Road
Hove, East Sussex
BN3 2FA
www.brunner-routledge.co.uk

Brunner-Routledge is an imprint of the Taylor & Francis Group.
Printed in the United States of America on acid-free paper.

Cover Design: Pearl Chang
Cover Photo: Corbis

10 9 8 7 6 5 4 3 2 1

Library of Congress Cataloging-in-Publication Data
Illovsky, Michael.
    Mental health professionals, minorities, and the poor / Michael
Illovsky.
        p. cm.
    Includes bibliographical references and index.
    ISBN 0-415-93576-8 (hbk.)
    1. Psychiatry, Transcultural. 2. Cross-cultural counseling. 3. Cultural psychiatry.
I. Title.
    RC455.4.E8 I43 2002
    616.89—dc21

                                                    2002009826

This book is dedicated to the children of the world,
with the fervent hope that their lives will be better.

Contents

Preface

This is not a "how to" do therapy book; instead, it is a "think about what you are doing" and how to provide meaningful approaches to therapy book. Readers are informed of issues in minority mental health. The reader is provided with succinct summaries of what has been written in many areas of minority mental health. Many references are provided to allow the reader to find more information about what has been written. There are critiques of the effectiveness of minority mental health professionals in their interactions with minorities and the poor. The therapist is encouraged to go beyond common beliefs, espoused values, and accepted myths. Solutions that are offered include the exploration of other therapeutic approaches— examples are provided in the chapters on technology and evolution. There is a focus on aspects of the mental health fields that are often overlooked, summarily dismissed, or ignored. Racist, political, and economic aspects of ethnic minority mental health work are explored, and the development of endogenous systems in underdeveloped U.S. minority communities is encouraged. Conditions of ethnic minorities in other parts of the world are explored to gain perspective and to examine what has been done elsewhere. A world perspective makes it clearer that the conditions of minorities are often more a function of social, economic, and political forces and are not necessarily a function of the characteristics of the minority group.

In cross-cultural studies, as we question our assumptions, explore the robustness of our present approaches and techniques, and develop new ones, and as we tailor our services to meet the needs of specific populations, what we learn can be used to cater to the needs of people in the general population with specific needs. It is hoped that scholars and practitioners in ethnic studies will delineate the universal and culturally specific aspects of mental health work.

Note: It is understood that some of the websites listed in this book may be defunct or may have moved by the time of the publication of this book. Many times the website material was from sources that have hardcopies of the Internet version (or were from other websites); therefore, the material can be obtained from these originating sources (e.g., journal articles); or, if the specific web address does not contain the document, the sponsoring organization may be able to provide information on where and how to obtain the material that was on its website. Another way to obtain information from web addresses that no longer exist is to simply type in the author's name or name of the article and do a search on the Internet.

1

◄〇►

Introduction

On September 11, 2001, planes crashed in the World Trade Center and the Pentagon, stridently forcing us to look at the culture, values, perceptions, and behaviors of others. Like it or not, ready or not, we need to deal with people of other cultures. S. Huntington (1996), of the Institute for Strategic Studies at Harvard University, wrote that the world is entering a new phase that enormously affects our national interests and security. He states that the fundamental conflicts in the world will not be ideological or economical. Instead, the conflict will be cultural. He wrote that the conflict will be between Western and non-Western civilizations, with the non-Western nations emerging as primary instead of secondary (or tertiary) forces in world politics and power. These cultures and civilizations are distinguished by such elements as language, history, religion, customs, systems, and subjective and group feelings of identification. These differences are fundamental and are less mutable than politics and economics and thus can lead to conflict. The increasing interactions among the peoples of the earth force us to contend with each other. As one culture's values and systems (e.g., those of the White, Euro-American, middle class) impinge on another culture's, there will be reactions (sometimes violent) from people in the culture that is being impinged upon. Huntington elaborates on the political, economic, social, and national values and perceived differences that can and do result in conflict. Western values such as the rule of law, equality, democracy, the free market, separation of church and state, basic human rights, the individual, and so on, do not necessarily resonate well in some other cultures—instead, there are cultures that may adhere to their own values and way of doing things. He presents a number of suggestions for dealing with non-Western cultures. However, more relevant to this book are his suggestions that the West will need to accommodate itself to people with different values and interests. The West will need to develop a profound understanding of other cultures and of how these cultures view their own interests. Westerners will need to identify commonalties between their cultures and others, and they will need to understand that there is no uni-

1

versal culture to be imposed on others; instead, there are different cultures and each must learn to coexist with the others.

As this country becomes increasingly heterogeneous, and as we increase our interactions with people from cultures throughout the world, as inevitably we must, I hope that increasing our knowledge of people of other cultures will improve our capacity to live harmoniously with others. I also hope that people involved in the provision of mental health services to those of other cultures will not do so in an exploitive fashion; I hope that our interactions will ameliorate the conditions of those who do not have full access to the American dream. The study of the mental health of ethnic groups helps increase our understanding of the psychology, thoughts, feelings, and behaviors of other cultural entities that we interact with. Martin Luther King, Jr., gave a speech at the American Psychological Association's Annual Convention in Washington, D.C., in September 1968. What he said about Negroes still pertains to many non–European American groups and to the poor living in the United States. This book is an attempt to move the social sciences in directions that are relevant to non–European American problems and the problems of the poor. The following are excerpts from his speech:

> White America has an appalling lack of knowledge concerning the reality of Negro life. . . . There are some things concerning which we must always be maladjusted if we are to be a people of good will. We must never adjust ourselves to racial discrimination and racial segregation. . . . We must never adjust ourselves to economic conditions that take necessities from the many to give luxuries to the few. (King, 1999, p. 29)

The studies of cross-cultural psychology and cross-cultural counseling have emerged as fascinating and challenging areas of the social and behavioral sciences and in the helping professions. In this shrinking world, more and more of our interactions entail working with persons and populations that are different. Such interactions occur in daily life, in the workplace, in business, in politics, and in the military—to name but a few of the applications of these areas of study.

Although the study of the mental health of ethnic minorities is relevant to psychology and counseling, other fields can also find it relevant. For example, Vega and Rumbaut (1991) wrote: "Far from being a subject of idiosyncratic interest on the margin of sociological inquiry, the study of the mental health of racial-ethnic minorities addresses issues of core theoretical and empirical concern to the discipline" (p. 352). The authors go on to state that the study of the subjective experience of the individual and the individual in relationship to society is central to the study of minorities—as it is central to many key aspects of sociology. Although the focus of this book is on psychology and counseling, the analysis provided here is based on the literature from such fields of study as psychology, counseling, ethology, ethnology, anthropology, social psychology, comparative animal studies, sociobiology, evolutionary psychology, evolutionary psychiatry, evolutionary biology, cybernetics, game theory, linguistics, physical anthropology, electronic technology, computer science, organizational psychology, organizational sociology, and so on. Such a multidisciplinary approach is critical to the understanding of human behavior (Pawlik & d'Ydewalle, 1996). These fields of study are examined—and processed through the filters of psychology and counseling—to determine how they can be applied to improving the mental health of minorities in the United States. The garnering of information from different areas of knowledge and applying it to psychology is in keeping with calls from the federal government, the American Psychological Association, and numerous groups and authors for greater interdisciplinary sharing and interactions (e.g., Azar, 1998a, b, c, d; Bertenthal, 1998; Bhattacharyya, 1998; Friedman & Rogers, 1998; Pennebaker, 1995; Sechrest & Pion, 1990). The applications of knowledge of cross-cultural human behavior extend far beyond therapeutic interactions in the office. The applications are myriad and can be used in such areas as promoting therapeutic compliance, health education, and disease prevention (Pawlik & d'Ydewalle, 1996).

There are psychological researchers, scholars, and educators in the United States, Europe, Asia, Africa, and South America who have called attention to the culturally narrow focus of psychologists in the United States (Gergen, Gulerce, Lock, & Misra, 1996; Lunt & Poortinga, 1996; Mays, Rubin, Sabourin, & Walker, 1996; Pawlik & d'Ydewalle, 1996). U.S. psychologists' ethnocentric views limit the science and application of psychology throughout the world. If U.S. psychology continues on its present insular, culturally limiting course, it will fail to "meet the psychological needs of its own U.S. population, with its rapidly growing multicultural, multinational, and multiracial population" (Mays, Rubin, Sabourin, & Walker, 1996, p. 486). Psychology needs to become sensitive "to cultural specifics, cultural generalities, and cultural biases possibly inherent in the language of psychological science" (Pawlik & d'Ydewalle, 1996). "To assume Western concepts of the mind, along with its methods of study, not only lends itself to research of little relevance to other cultures, but also disregards and undermines alternate cultural traditions" (Gergen et al., 1996, p. 496). Lunt and Poortinga (1996) wrote that "accusations may be leveled in the practitioner domain in which therapeutic interventions and methods have been dominated mainly by Western and anglophone paradigms" (Lunt & Poortinga, 1966, p. 504). When interacting with other cultures, Berry, Poortinga, Segall, and Dasen (1992) wrote that ethnocentrism in psychology results in cultur-ally inappropriate stimuli or items, the use of instruments and methods that are not suitable, ignorance that conceptualizations are culturally spe-cific and limited, and the selection of topics and applications that may be intended to meet the needs of the subjects, but instead are really meeting the needs of one's own culture.

Though non–European American populations are growing rapidly in the United States and European American counselors and therapists have to interact more and more with people who are ethnically different from themselves, the same theories, models, approaches, and techniques that were developed by and for European Americans continue to be used on all populations. These are of questionable validity when applied cross-culturally. For example, Ramseur (1991) investigated how well universal models of mental health could be applied to African Americans. He chose to exam-ine the models and approaches of Freud, Maslow, and Erikson. He used the following six criteria to determine how well the models could be ap-plied to African Americans: (a) definitions of freedom from illness; (b) defi-nitions of averageness; (c) definitions of ideal personality type; (d) using multiple criteria, definitions of psychological mental health; (e) develop-mental/life-span perspectives; and (f) stress/adaptation approaches. Using these criteria, he found that although universal models of psychological health offer some positive perspectives and ideas, they generally have little to say about the unique social-cultural context of African Americans (Ramseur, 1991, p. 373). He wrote that "theories or models that postulate universal pathology or pathological outcomes are clearly unhelpful and do not fit current findings" (Ramseur, 1991, p. 375). He stated that no existing theory or model addresses the questions of the social and psychological characteristics of psychologically healthy Black adults and how they change over the life span.

We need to examine our theories, models, assumptions, approaches, and techniques. We need to determine which are effective, for whom, for which problems, and under which conditions. It is unlikely that the present White approaches and techniques have a monopoly on transcending all cultures, classes, space, and time. With new populations to be served, and with more students from other cultures being trained as counselors and therapists (it is hoped), it would behoove us to develop better and more effective methods to help new and different clientele. We have the knowl-edge of previous generations of counselors and therapists to draw on. Now we must also draw upon the knowledge and experiences of "minority" peoples to help determine which approaches and techniques transcend culture and which are more apropos to specific cultures. One of the themes of this book is that what is found to be effective for a particular ethnic group can be applied to individuals in all groups—each group has members with characteristics and needs similar to some minority groups; for example, if we find that a particular cultural group places a great deal of emphasis on group cohesion, and we develop techniques to deal with this particular aspect of the cultural group, these techniques can be used to help individuals in other groups who have to deal with group pressure.

A copious amount has been written and spoken about cross-cultural treatment. In these materials it is almost a mantra for authors to tell the reader that one needs to know about the culture one is interacting with, that generalizations should not be made to all members of an ethnic group, that there are enormous variations within each ethnic group, and that the terms used to designate ethnic minority groups are inappropriate and inaccurate. Many, many groups and individuals have provided guidelines and standards for the delivery of services. These are very important, and the reader is encouraged to attend to these problems. However, though references are given in this book to literature that deals with these topics, the focus of this book is on areas that are usually not examined in the mental health literature. The focus is more on the social, political, and economic aspects of the delivery of mental health. To use an analogy (that I stole from someone else—though I do not know who), instead of focusing on how we are to save a drowning person (the clinical approach), we should also examine who is pushing the drowning person into the water. We should examine and correct the slippery ground that facilitates people tumbling into the water. We should focus on teaching potential drowning victims about conditions that are detrimental to them, and we should teach them how to swim and save themselves.

TERMS USED

The mental health workers discussed in this book are master's and doctoral-level service providers trained in counselor education and psychology programs. The terms *counselor, therapist,* and *mental health professional* are used interchangeably. Typically, counselors graduate from colleges of education, and psychologists graduate from psychology departments. Psychology programs often are more affiliated with the sciences, whereas colleges of education are often more affiliated with the arts.

The terms *minorities* and *ethnic,* as used in this book, follow the definitions of those given by writers such as Royce (1982). That is, these terms are more political and social labels that are used to differentiate those in control from those who are considered "outsiders": They are a "minority people if the politically and economically more powerful group perceives and treats them as inferiors" (Axelson, 1993, p. 153). The definition of "ethnic" (as it pertains to this book) is the one offered by Webster's (1990) dictionary: "of or relating to a large group of people classed according to common racial, national, tribal, religious, linguistic, or cultural origin or background" (p. 426). The definition for "minorities" also follows that provided by Webster (1990): "a part of a population differing from others in some characteristics and often subjected to differential treatment" (p. 757). By the previous two definitions, the two terms can reflect populations with intertwining features: The characteristics that are referred to in the "minorities" definition might take the form of cultural differences and, more obviously, often pertain to such overt features such as skin color, shape of eyes, and so on. The differential treatment that they are subjected to often takes the form of discrimination, to the detriment of the ethnic group. This differential treatment often results in lower socioeconomic conditions— being poorer.

Some minority ethnic groups have attained social, political, or economic influence (or any combination of these) in their countries that is disproportionate to their size (e.g., the Parsis of India and the Germans of Argentina). Unless they are discriminated against to their detriment, these groups are not the focus of this book. The focus of this book is on those ethnic groups that live in societies in which they are placed at a disadvantage because of their features and cultural practices. These disadvantages can take the form of unfavorable different treatment in employment and social, political, and economic areas.

The labeling of ethnic groups in this country has posed continuous problems. To name a few of these problems: (a) the labels applied to groups do not necessarily apply to individuals because of the tremendous variation within groups, (b) the labels do not correctly identify the group, (c) the labels change frequently, (d) there is little agreement over which labels are used to designate the groups, (e) there are changes over time, (f) individuals within ethnic groups have different degrees of manifestations of ethnicity, (g) individuals can have multiple ethnicities, and so on.

As a first step toward a more rational way of naming minority groups, the following suggestions are offered:

1. The scientific community should take the lead in the naming of ethnic groups. Its reliance on the media, politicians, and common popular parlance to name groups has resulted in inaccuracies, inconsistencies, and vicissitudes in the labeling of groups. For example, in regard to the vicissitudes in the labeling of those of African American (to use the contemporary term) ethnic heritage, this group has been referred to as Negro, colored, Black, Afro-American, and African American in just

this century alone. Scholars need a more consistent labeling of the group studied.

2. The criteria used in the labeling process should be consistent across groups. Therefore, if one group is referred to as Whites—a skin color designation—the other group should not be referred to as African Americans, a land of origin (or cultural) designation. In applying the same criteria across groups, they should be referred to as Blacks and Whites, or African Americans and European Americans.

3. The nomenclature should indicate cultural differences and not racial and biological differences: Racial differences imply biological differences, and biological differences have been shown to be an invalid method of classifying people. Humans constitute one race. The separation of groups based on biological distinctions has found to be inadequate, inaccurate, and inappropriate. At the very most, biological differences are reflective of clines (that is, gradients) that overlap and are not reflective of quantum differences. If one were to make cultural and biological analyses of ethnic groups, it should be clearly stated that cultural and biological analyses are being made—and not reify the impression that these two separate concepts are the same.

In this book, the terms *minorities, ethnic groups, non-Whites, non-Europeans,* and other terms are used interchangeable to designate non-White/non-European groups from "White," "European" groups. It is understood that these terms are hopelessly inadequate and inappropriate, but it is hoped that the reader will tolerate these terms and understand that I need to use some terms to distinguish the various groups and that all the terms that are used to designate minority/ethnic groups and nonminority/ethnic groups encounter problems.

The chapters, basically, follow this outline:

Chapter 2 looks at some of the factors that might impact ethnic minority–counseling effectiveness. These may be the result of life experience differences between the therapist and the client, as illustrated in demographic differences, as well as such factors as biases in the selection and training of therapists, and the impact of social, political, and economic differences.

Chapter 3 presents information on minority mental health research and factors that might confound the research. The chapter also briefly presents information on some of the abuses of data collection and reporting. This chapter is relevant because our therapeutic approaches, our impressions of minorities and their needs, and the training of therapists depend on the minority mental health research and literature.

Chapter 4 looks at the possible uses of technology to overcome barriers in the delivery of services to minorities and its applications in the education, training, and development of minority communities.

Chapter 5 presents a model and approach that might be useful in providing services to people of different cultures: It examines evolutionary biology and evolutionary psychology and presents explanations of pathology and racism from this perspective.

Chapter 6 provides information on populations that are not usually covered in the ethnic minority literature—groups within minority populations. These include ethnic minorities with different sexual orientation or disabilities, ethnic women, older persons, those who live in rural areas, and the ethnic minority middle class.

Chapter 7 examines the status of domestic minorities and those in other countries. Explanations are provided as to why inequities might exist, as well as solutions.

Chapter 8 provides concluding remarks. The reader is encouraged to take action, explore therapeutic methods and the use of technology, become aware of the contributions of other cultures and use them, and connect the study of ethnic groups in this country with studies in other countries.

2

—◄○►—

Factors to Consider
When Providing Services
to Cross-Cultural Persons

Most psychological approaches and techniques of psychology purport that they transcend culture and that their delineations of solutions to problems are universally applicable (Corsini & Wedding, 1995; Hall, Lindzey, & Campbell, 1998). As mentioned earlier, there are people who question these basic assumptions (e.g., Ramseur, 1991). Helms (1985, 1986) wrote that divergence in attitudes, beliefs, and coping strategies can be a source of dissonance between the mental health professional and the client. What the European American counselor values, considers priorities, defines as problems, and considers relevant may be different from what the non-European client values and considers relevant. It is to the White counselor's advantage to claim that his or her therapeutic approaches transcend culture: This confirms the universality of the European approaches; this allows the therapist to continue using the assumptions, models, and approaches that he or she has previously used; and this diminishes the need to learn more about other cultures and approaches. To admit our limitations would result in exposing the inadequacies of counseling on a therapeutic level, as well as reveal the racist political, economic, and social aspects of counseling that are the result of, and the reasons for, these therapeutic limitations.

DIFFERENCES THAT MIGHT MITIGATE THERAPEUTIC
EFFECTS WHEN COUNSELING MINORITIES

Demographic Data

It is generally posited that differences between peoples can be a source of dissonance and misunderstanding—this can apply to the relationships between the therapist and client as well. The literature on minorities delves into "cultural differences" as an explanation of differences between "mainstream" society, as represented by the therapist, and the ethnic minority member. Some of these differences can be quantified through the demographic data that reveal factors that affect groups. Lefley (1999) wrote that in modern industrialized countries, minorities are particularly vulnerable to the stresses of poverty, economic or political activities, family disintegration, diminished status, and feelings of oppression and attribution of problems to external malevolence. Industrialization can increase the differences between the haves and the have-nots. It can increase social and economic anomie; dislocation might occur; there could be changes in family structure and roles (e.g., females could gain employment outside the family or village and could obtain income); people's worth could be viewed in terms of their labor and not for other aspects of their being; and so on.

Though not all members of an ethnic group may share the same demographic features, the outside community may lump all members of the ethnic group as having the same characteristics, and individual members may be impacted by the demographic factors that affect a group's culture. There are many sources of demographic minority data, including the U.S. Census Bureau (2001); the U.S. Department of Health and Human Service's *Directory of Minority Health and Human Services Data Resources* (2001), and the *U.S. News Coverage of Racial Minorities: A Sourcebook* (Keever, Martindale, & Weston, 1997). The following demographic data from the *New York Times Almanac 2001* (Wright, 2000) illustrate some of the differences between Whites and ethnic minority groups. Compared to Whites, Blacks are more likely to be divorced, to be unmarried, to be in single-parent families, not to own their own homes, to be in prison (417 White males per 1,000,000 resident population are in jail, compared with 3,408 for Black males), to have less money (about half of what Whites have), to live in poverty, to be arrested, and to have HIV.

Cultural Differences

When therapists counsel those from other cultures, questions arise as to whether there are factors that may affect rapport, communications, definitions, understanding of the problem, empathy, priorities, and so forth. These factors may affect the relationship, therapy, and counseling of the client. Many have written that differences between the European American mental health professional and the non–European American client can have an impact on the relationship and on the therapy that is provided (e.g., Ivey, 1981, 1986, 1993; Locke, 1992; Pandered & Casas, 1991; Pedersen, 1985, 1988; Prilleltensky, 1997; Sue, 1990; White & Parham, 1990). The following are some of the reported differences.

White and Parham (1990) described African American culture as having such characteristics as its members being influenced by their African heritage, having greater interdependence and emotional vitality, having oral traditions and a tradition of collective survival, and having a different perception of time.

Marin and Marin (1991) characterized those of Hispanic culture as having high interdependence—especially to the extended family; conformity; willingness to sacrifice for the group; avoidance of interpersonal conflict; more clearly defined gender roles; and more obedience toward those of authority.

Asian Americans have been characterized by Uba (1994) as having an emphasis on harmony in relationships, placing group interests over those of self, and having a commitment to fulfill responsibilities—especially to the family.

Native Americans have been described by Attneave (1982) as being present-oriented, in harmony with nature, and focused on the welfare of the group over the individual. Bennett (1994) reports Native American tribes as having the themes of valuing generosity, cooperation, community, and family.

Sue (1995a) presented literature demonstrating that Western-bound cultural values that are generic to many counseling schools of thought may conflict with the values of non–European Americans. Western-bound cultural values that are generic to many counseling schools include:

1. *Focus on the individual.* In contrast, members of minority groups are more focused on family and community. When the European American mental health professional interacts with the non–European American, if the non–European American does not focus on the self, negative labels are attached to the non–European American client and his or her behaviors; for example, the client may be described as dependent, immature, enmeshed in the family, having boundary issues, and so forth.

2. *Verbal expression of emotions.* When the European American mental health professional interacts with the non–European American, if the non–European American is not verbal, articulate, emotive, and assertive, then negative labels are attached to the non–European American client and his or her behaviors—for example, inhibited, repressed, uninvolved, and so on.

3. *Openness and intimacy.* For the European American, self-disclosure may be accepted as a natural therapeutic condition. However, for a non–European American client, intimate self-disclosure might be prohibitive because of cultural and sociopolitical factors. If the non–European American does not engage in self-disclosure, then negative labels are attached to his or her behaviors—for example, suspicious, guarded, paranoid, resistant, and so forth.

4. *Insight.* Many counseling approaches regard insight as an important ingredient in therapy and for therapeutic change. But in some non–European American cultures (e.g., Chinese), insight is not viewed as necessary or sufficient for effective therapy to occur. If the non-European client does not engage in insightful exploration, then the client may be defined as being resistant, lacking in the ability to engage in self-exploration, and so on.

5. *Competition versus cooperation.* Competition is valued among many European Americans. But in many non–European American cultures cooperation is valued. If the non–European American does not engage in the European American mental health professional's standards of competition, then negative labels are attached to the U.S. non-European and his or her behaviors—for example, passivity, lack of assertiveness.

6. *Linear-static time emphasis.* European American cultures view time as linear and static; run by clocks. Among some non–European American cultures, time is viewed as circular, dynamically flowing, harmonious, and marked by events rather than the clock. If the non–European American does not abide by the European American mental health professional's perception of time (e.g., is late for a session), then negative labels are attached to the non–European American client, for example, passive-aggressive, irresponsible, resistant, and so on.

7. *Nuclear versus extended family.* The European American mental health professional's definitions of family are often in terms of the nuclear family, whereas many non–European cultures define family to include ancestors, aunts, uncles, and other extended members of the family—definitions of family members may or may not be dependent on genetic commonality.

8. *Locus of responsibility.* Many counseling approaches focus on the resolution to problems through exploring internal conflicts and resolving personal issues. For many European Americans resolution to many problems is gained through resolution of such external factors as racism, discrimination, and prejudice.

9. *Scientific empiricism.* Counseling depends upon symbolic logic, cause and effect, and linear, rationalistic, or reductionist analyses of phenomena, whereas many non–European cultural groups have a nonlinear, wholistic view and approach to the world.

Peng and Nisbett (1999) studied the way people from Chinese cultures and those from European American cultures in the United States dealt with contradictions. They found that people from Chinese cultures were more likely to take a compromising, moderating, "middle of the way" perspective, whereas those from European American backgrounds had a tendency to take polarizing, categorical, extreme perspectives when dealing with contradictions.

Differences with ethnic groups are not necessarily superficial. They have deep roots developed through the ages to help that particular ethnic group's survival (Baldwin, 1991; Nobles, 1991). In the case of many non-European ethnic groups, the development of these behavioral patterns has far deeper roots than that of European cultures. In Europe, the behavioral patterns have evolved around survival within the context of the state (which is a recent phenomena), whereas non–European American ethnic groups have evolved within the context of other, more enduring groups, such as the family and the tribe. Many non–European American peoples have successfully adapted to U.S. society, but in counseling and therapy, the required adaptations entail changing the very essence of many ethnic group members.

The changes and adaptations required by the mental health professional of the non-White client can entail changes in feelings, thoughts, concepts, behaviors, family relations, values, perceptions, and so on. These changes are occurring within the context of the non-White client's social, political, psychological, religious, behavioral, ethnic, and economic milieus. These are milieus that the European American mental health professional is not familiar with when interacting with the non–European American client. Therefore, changes in feelings and thoughts that are gained in interactions with the therapist may fail because they are not maintained and reinforced by the minority's environment.

Learning Styles. Numerous authors (e.g., Baruth & Manning, 1992; Boykin & Toms, 1985; Cushner, McClelland, & Safford, 1992; Hale-Benson, 1986; Irvine & York, 1995; Shade, 1982, 1989a, 1989b) have reported research that indicates that African Americans, Latin Americans, and Native Americans have styles of learning that are different from those of European Americans. Some cultural groups learn better in a cooperative (compared to a competitive) manner; others learn better kinesthetically; through art and music; with the buttress of tradition; through examples relevant to their lives, and so on.

Free Will. "Free will" is a very expedient concept for the dominant group to accept and propagate (McConahay & Hough, 1976; Sears, 1991; Yetman, 1985). It readily explains why the dominant group has resources and power and why others do not. Members of the dominant group can believe that they obtained their positions of power through their own efforts—and not through circumstances, institutional racism, or ethnic privilege. The concomitant corollary to this is that those who are disfranchised, those without power and resources, are in their poorer state and are in less powerful positions because of the lack of personal internal factors. Explanations of these personal shortcomings can include: They are lazy, they lack the will power, they are sabotaged by their value systems, or they have inculcated the "negative" aspects of their culture. This is not to say that the concept of free will is not a good one. As with the case of individualism, to tell minorities that they lack personal choices because they are controlled by external forces is to impart an extremely dysfunctional message. Such a message would absolve the person from taking action, would increase a sense of powerlessness, and would decrease personal locus of control—this would be detrimental to the person and to the minority community. However, the function and ramifications of the concept of free will can have implications. To attribute lack of success to shortcomings in the exercise of free will can help mitigate the reality of racism and place a spurious burden on the victim.

Self-Esteem. The issue of self-esteem has received considerable attention in the past few years (Adler et al., 1992; Edwards, 1995; Fortson, 1997; "High self-esteem . . . ," 1996; Kantrowitz & Wingert, 1992; Krauthammer, 1990; Leo, 1990; Mecca, Smelser, & Vasconcellos, 1989; Sykes, 1995). Researchers have not been able to correlate increased self-esteem with any positive effects (Dawes, 1998; Edwards, 1995). Research has failed to correlate self-esteem with any improvements in such areas as educational performance and psychological improvement (Fortson, 1997; Leo, 1990; Mecca, Smelser, & Vasconcellos, 1989; Sykes, 1995).

It is understandable why self-esteem approaches are used: (a) it is easy to train people in its use as a therapeutic technique, (b) it induces the perception in the mental health professional that he or she is doing something, (c) the concept of self-esteem is easier to grasp than having to deal with the nuances of culture and ethnicity, (d) the client who is the recipient of these strategies is likely to comply because it seems innocuous, (e) it has intuitive appeal and the media have readily embraced it, (f) the mental health professional does not have to deal with the other apparent intractable problems that affect non–European Americans' mental health—such as racism and unemployment, and (h) it is a cheap method of dealing with problems. Misguided strategies to increase self-esteem can lead to contraindications and impractical guidance (Adler et al., 1992; Edwards, 1995; Kantrowitz & Wingert, 1992; Krauthammer, 1990).

It should be noted that we rarely question what self-esteem is predicated on. If self-esteem measures are defined by Whites, and normed on Whites, the results might not be valid when measuring non-Whites on this concept. Also, if a self-esteem scale measures factors that are relevant to European Americans but not to non–European Americans, then the valence of the results are different. For example, a scale may define self-esteem in terms related to individualism and independence (behaviors more valued by Whites), or self-esteem may be measured in terms related to religiousity and commitment to the community/group (behaviors valued by many Mexican Americans). These scales may produce different results, depending on the culture the person is from. It has long been the impression that African Americans have lower self-esteem than Whites (Ramseur, 1991). Studies have indicated that this may not be the case (Edwards, 1974; Heiss & Owens, 1972; Jensen, White, & Galliher, 1982; McCarthy & Yancey, 1971; Taylor, 1976; Veroff, Douvan, & Kulka, 1981). The assumption is that given their lower socioeconomic status, discrimination, the fact they are not White, racism, and so on, African Americans must have lower self-esteem (e.g., Kardiner & Ovesey, 1951). However, African Americans do not necessarily gauge themselves by European American standards and values (Cross, 1985; Gibbs, 1985; Taylor, 1976); consequently, their self-esteem may be intact. They may have developed coping skills to deal with the disadvantages that society forces on them (Barbarin, 1983; Barnes, 1980; Gibson, 1982; Lykes, 1983; McCarthy & Yancey, 1971; Neff, 1985; Neighbors, Jackson, Bowman, & Gurin, 1983). The previous studies are not unique to African Americans; J. Crocker and B. Major (1989) found that ethnic minorities, women, gays, and people with physical disabilities do not have low self-esteem—these groups have developed self-protective attribution strategies to deal with the assaults on their self-esteem.

What I have written here should not be construed as advocating that self-esteem strategies be abandoned. Rather, our basic assumptions should be questioned. Serious consideration should be given in regard to when, where, and for whom we use our approaches and techniques. We may want to consider our methods of improving self-esteem; for example, instead of improving self-esteem through intrapsychic exploration of feelings, another way of promoting self-esteem might be by empowering people to exercise their political and economic skills and change the systems that impact them. Because White, middle-class people already control the political and economic systems, they do not necessarily see the need to examine and manipulate these systems. Although mental health professionals may not see the relevance of these skills in the lives of ethnic minorities (and in the lives of the lumpen proletariat—who are excluded from participating in the economy), it is amazing how they see the relevance of these same entrepreneurial, economic, and political issues in aggrandizing their own professional and legislative self-interests. It is amazing how the manipulation of the economic, political, and social institutions to increase the benefits of the mental health professional can increase their self-esteem—but such manipulation is considered outside the ken of therapeutic approaches to increase the self-esteem of minorities.

This is not to deny the importance and relevance of clinical problems in therapy. Clients do have clinical problems, and therapists need to have clinical skills. But there is a place sometimes in therapy to increase the client's political and economic knowledge and skills because these impact on clinical problems.

Eating Disorders. Garner and Bemis (1985) suggest that anorexia nervosa is culturally syntonic—that is, related to the beliefs, values, and expectations of a particular culture (Garner, Garfinkel, Schwartz, & Thompson, 1980). In regard to bulimia, Schwartz, Barrett, & Saba (1985) wrote that ethnic (sic) families focus on different issues than all-American (sic) families. They state that ethnic families are less preoccupied with mainstream American family values and are more interested in the values of their own cultures. Although ethnics and mainstream American families are both interested in appearance, the ethnic members are more interested in their own traditional roles. The ethnic families are more concerned with their families and show less aversion to fatness. They are less concerned with mainstream interest in achievement and success and more concerned with conforming to their own cultural values (e.g., security and acceptability). Those with bulimia from all-American families show a wider range of behaviors than do ethnic families. All-American families are frequently ambitious, competitive, appearance-conscious, success-driven, and prone to compare self and family to others. On the other hand, Schwartz, Barrerr, and Saba (1985) wrote that ethnic families frequently show only their young, dependent side when they interact with others.

Language. Language is the main modality for counselors and therapists when they interact with their clients. It is through language that therapists obtain information, evaluate information, diagnose, and offer treatment. Yet when it comes to cross-cultural communication, the words, concepts, signs, and symbols that constitute language may have different meanings and impact for different people. We cannot assume that the language a particular group uses necessarily conveys what we want to convey and what we think we are conveying (Russell, 1986). When we use language, we engage in language games (Wittgenstein, 1969)—games originate from our lives and shape our lives. People from different cultures may have different factors that shape their lives; therefore, they may have different language games.

Cognitive Development. In a review of the cognitive development research, Rogoff and Chavajay (1995) report that culture shapes many aspects of cognitive development. Goodnow (1976) finds that the interpretation of problems and methods of solution differ among cultural groups. Definitions of intelligence vary among cultures (Lutz & LeVine, 1982; Serpell, 1982). Responses to questions (e.g., in responses to questions to measure cognitive processes) can also vary across cultures, depending upon the characteristics of the person asking the questions (Irvine, 1978; Mehan, 1979). According to Vygotsky (1978), cognitive activities are related to cultural background—numerous authors substantiate his premise (Hakuta & Garcia, 1989; Heath, 1989; Laosa & Henderson, 1991; Miller-Jones, 1989; Moll, 1990). All these studies support the proposition that there are cognitive differences among groups.

Racism-Stressors. There is no doubt that everyone encounters stressors. However, non–European Americans encounter stressors in addition to the ones common to European Americans—the stressors engendered by racism (Vega & Rumbaut, 1991). The additional stressors induced by racism can impact the physical and mental health of individuals and communities (Armstead, Lawler, Gorden, Cross, & Gibbons, 1989; Bell, 1992; Bullock & Houston, 1987; Chunn, Dunston, & Ross-Sheriff, 1983; Clark, Anderson, Clark, & Williams, 1999; Cooper, 1993; Cornell, Peterson, & Richards, 1999; Cose, 1993; Dovidio & Gaertner, 1986; Feagin & Feagin, 1978; Idson & Price, 1992; Jones & Korchin, 1982; Krieger, 1990; Landrine & Klonoff, 1996; National Institute of Mental Health, 1983). If we look at the mental health morbidity rates among non–European Americans we find that the rates in some of these populations are despairingly higher than those in the average population (Mays & Albee, 1992; National Institute of Mental Health, 1980, 1981; President's Commission on Mental Health, 1978; Sue, 1977). These differences could be attributed in part to the stressors of racism—and the repercussions of racism on social and economic factors such as unemployment and underemployment. At the United Nations Commission of Human Rights, Amnesty International (1999) denounced U.S. violations of the human rights of its people of color—specifically, African Americans, Latinos, and Asian Americans (Comas-Diaz, 2000): "As a human rights violation, racism is pervasive throughout North American society. The human rights of people of color are insidiously violated in the medical and mental health systems" (Gollub, 1999—as cited in Comas-Diaz, 2000, p. 1320).

Racism has an effect on the physical and mental health of those who experience it. Clark, Anderson, Clark, and Williams (1999) examined studies on the effects of racism on physical and mental health. They wrote that racism can increase the reactivity of some African Americans to stress. They report that African Americans with darker skin may experience, indirectly, an increase of negative health outcomes like hypertension. They wrote that the type of discrimination and the rate of reporting may be related to African Americans' socioeconomic status. They suggest that those in higher socioeconomic brackets may experience more subtle forms of racism and racism in the form of institutional racism, although African Americans in the lower socioeconomic brackets may experience more overt racism—hence more measurable and reportable. Responses to racism can include anger, paranoia, anxiety, helplessness, hopelessness, frustration, fear, and resentment. These responses can lead to other responses: anger suppression, aggression, hostility, alcohol use, use of drugs to blunt feelings (Cooper, 1993; Cornell, Peterson, & Richards, 1999); depression, distrust, paranoia (Fernando, 1984; Peterson, Maier, & Seligman, 1993); and passivity, overeating, avoidance, and attempts to gain control over self and environment (Bullock & Houston, 1987).

Stress can also affect physiological systems, such as those involved in immune, neuroendocrine, and cardiovascular functioning (Andersen, Kiecolt-Glaser, & Glaser, 1994; Cacioppo, 1994; Cohen & Herbert, 1996). Stress can lead to the suppression of B- and T-lymphocytes, which can then hinder the body's attempts to counter invasive bacteria and viruses. Stress can prolong respiratory infections and slow healing. Stress can induce neuroendocrine responses such as activating the pituitary-adrenocortical and hypothalamic-sympathetic-adrenal medullary systems. These stress-induced responses can change the release of antidiuretic hormones, prolactin, growth hormone, glucocorticoids, epinephrine, norepinephrine, adrenocorticotropic hormone, cortisol, and B-endophine. Along with these neuroendocrine changes, there can be increases in cardiovascular responses that can include increase in the magnitude and rate of cardiac contraction, skeletal muscluar vasodilation, venoconstriction, splanchnic vasoconstriction, renal vasoconstriction, and so on.

Stress may be linked to low birth weight and infant mortality, depression, breast cancer survival, heart disease, blood pressure, pulmonary disease, upper respiratory infection, and marital problems. Stress, and stress-induced responses, can contribute to psychological and health problems.

Perceptions. A Harris poll ("Poll: Minorities Find . . . ," 1994; "Poll: Minorities See . . . ," 1994) found that African, Latin, and Asian Americans had different perceptions than Whites. Most of the non-Whites believed that Whites are bigoted, bossy, and insensitive to other people; have a long history of bigotry and prejudice; control power and wealth in America; and did not want to share it with non-Whites. The preceding survey was given to adults. Surveys of Black youth (e.g., Loupe & Wright, 1993) also found differences in adolescents' perceptions; among the findings were that Black high school youths were more likely to perceive that there were barriers raised by racism, whereas fewer Whites perceived this to be the case.

In the counseling relationship, there could be differences in perceptions between the European American counselor and the non–European American. As an example, consider the smiles and expressions of warmth and friendliness of the therapist—very fundamental, basic human gestures. Through these modes, the counselor attempts to convey that he or she is caring and friendly and should be trusted. The friendliness and smiles that are the signs of congeniality are not necessarily received with the intended message of sincerity and benevolence. In our society, the façade of friendliness can serve a number of functions (Social Capital Interest Group, 2002). Friendliness and smiles can be taught as part of presenting a façade to facilitate business transactions (Arthur, 1995; Baldry, 1999; Bloomfield & Fairley, 1991; Feldman, 1992; Hogrefe, 1988; Jones, 1997; Judd & Wyszecki, 1975; Knapp & Hall, 1992; Malandro, 1989; Port & Samovar, 1993; Price & Arnould, 1999; Rosier, 1999; Segerstrale & Molnar, 1997; University of Northern Iowa Business Communication, 2002; Vargas, 1986). Computer programs can mimic friendliness (Singularity Institute of Artificial Intelligence, 2001). Friendliness and smiles can be used to mask bigotry (White, 1999; Southern Poverty Law Center, 2002). Kurth (1970) stated that American culture uses friendliness as a mechanism to maintain social distance and avoid self-disclosure, as well as to inhibit deeper involvement, trust, and confidentiality. For the ethnic minority, the appearance of warmth and friendliness on the part of the White therapist could be perceived as superficial. The therapist's good intentions may not compensate for the ignorance and naiveté that may result from the therapist coming from another socioeconomic and cultural background—an insulated, comfortable world that is unrelated to the client's world. The smiles and good intentions could be psychological mechanisms to compensate for the detrimental aspects of the therapist's behavior and to ward off the client's wrath; for example, the therapist may think: How can the client feel I am wrong or be angry at me if I am smiling and convey that I have goodness in my heart? The therapist's good intentions could serve as expressions of denial mechanisms—for example, the therapist may think: I have good intentions; therefore, I must be doing good. The counselor could be seen as another jobholder who obtained this position because of his or her privileged class and ethnic status. The counselor could be seen as someone taking a job from a non–European American. The counselor's superficial warm gestures could be seen as a substitute for not learning more about the client's culture. Thus, the counselor's smiles and good intentions may not convey what is intended.

The counselor might not be aware that the relationship between the European American and the non-European American has had a history of detrimental effects for the non–European. European American therapists may want to deny that they carry the luggage of the past with them; nevertheless, many of the effects, perceptions, and values of the past are still with us. Danieli (1997) and others wrote about the intergenerational affects of trauma. Through experience, education, "racial memory," stories, songs, and oral traditions, the non-European client may know of the detrimental effects of European Americans. There might be such perceptions and memories as the following: European Americans had something to do with the destruction of non-Europeans' values, culture, and political, economic, religious, and social systems; and they exploited the land, spread sickness, disempowered the males, subjugated the females, and rendered non-Europeans to subservient positions. This has always been accompanied by good intentions on the part of the European American—for example, the intention to civilize, to develop the economy, to educate, to serve, to provide leadership, or to confer Christianity. These good intentions are commendable, but many minorities are aware that there were, and are, other processes operating.

Another difference in perception between the therapist and the client may be that of power. The European American mental health professional may be seen as a power figure to a greater extent by non–European American clients than by European American clients (Higginbotham, 1995). One should consider that when a non–European American client interacts with a European American mental health professional, it is almost always under conditions and terms defined by the European American therapist—for example, in terms of location, mode of interaction, content of session, length of interaction, language used, and so forth. It is the mental health professional who defines the relationship. If the client does not cater to the counselor's definitions and parameters, then the counselor may allocate negative labels to the client and to the client's behavior.

Emotions. There may be differences in the significance, value, and function of emotional reactions and expression. For example, African American clients are more frequently characterized by emotions and behaviors dominated by hostility, hopelessness, distrust, tension, fear, and perceptions of discrimination when dealing with the European American mental health professional (Vontress & Epp, 1997).

Although it would be impossible to generalize to the 40 or so different Asian groups in this country, there can be differences in the experiencing and expression of emotions between these groups and their European American counterparts (Sandhu, 1997). Compared to people from Western cultures, those from an Asian cultural heritage can experience shame more intensely and for longer periods of time (Ha, 1995). Those of Asian cultural heritage experience embarrassment issues more and are more concerned with respect (Frijda & Mesquita, 1994). Tsai and Levenson (1997) did an ethnological study comparing the emotional differences between Chinese Americans and European Americans. They report that in the Chinese culture, members often believe that moderation of emotions is a sign of a stable personality. Such individuals are considered to have a characteristic that promotes health and facilitates good interpersonal relationships. The authors found that these differences are not just superficial, but are also evident on physiological/cardiac interbeat interval indices. These same characteristics can be considered by the European American therapist to be the signs of an emotionally stunted people who lack the capacity to emote to the degree necessary to have healthy relationships.

It is interesting that the main approach of counseling is the exploration and emoting of feelings. This is an approach that caters well to White, middle-class women's expectations of therapy and is often the preferred mode of therapy for them and their counselors. Even though our counseling approaches are tailored to this group, do their large numbers as clients reflect the inadequacies of our present approaches to dealing with the problems of even this group of people? For example, Herbert et al. (2001) wrote about the well-intentioned but misguided efforts of mental health professionals to encourage survivors of trauma (e.g., September 11, 2001, World Trade Center victims and their families) to discuss the details of their trauma individually or in groups. This might not only be ineffective, but may even cause problems (i.e., be iatrogenic).

Self-Disclosure. Self-disclosure proclivities vary considerably from culture to culture (Tefft, 1980). Self-disclosure has significant repercussions among the cultures in regard to such factors as privacy, social boundary, status, power, stigma, intimacy, security, adequacy, obligation, vulnerability, sanction, access, inclusion/exclusion, cohesiveness, and a host of other sociological and psychological issues. Not engaging in self-disclosure can serve the function of protecting the person from ridicule, humiliation, gossip, and social and group pressure.

When the non–European American client does not emote to the satisfaction of the European American mental health professional, then the mental health professional may deem the client resistant, lacking in skills, and deficit in the capacity to express feelings. If the non–European American person does not cooperate, avoids eye contact, or does not readily comply with the mental health professional's agenda, then the non–European American person is viewed as resistant, sneaky, and passive-aggressive and is provided with other disparaging labels.

The mental health professional might try to use modeling to elicit the desired behaviors from the client. The mental health professional may show how to be true, genuine, open, and authentic by expressing his or her own thoughts and feelings. Having done this, the mental health professional may get even more annoyed (and attach more negative labels) if the non–European American person does not reciprocate. What the mental health professional may not realize is that the mental health professional is asking the client to engage in behaviors that the mental health professional is better versed at. It is the European American mental health professional's game. It is behavior that the mental health professional has the skills to conduct. Mental health professionals may view this behavior as modeling behavior for clients to emulate, but non–European American clients may interpret these behaviors as self-indulgence; that is, the mental health professionals are getting their own needs met by catering to their thoughts and feelings. Or, if the client is aware of the purpose for the mental health professional modeling these behaviors, the message is conveyed that the client is inadequate (which could be the case) because the counselor has to teach these behaviors to the client. Consequently, we have another situation in which a European American is telling a non–European American how inadequate he or she is. An alternative strategy would be to examine the non–European American's preferred mode of interacting and then work in the non–European American's mode—for example, behavioral cues, subtlety of language, or putting the other person's feelings before your own.

Conflict Resolution Styles. Gabrielidis, Stephen, Ybarra, Pearson, and Villareal (1997) investigated conflict-resolution styles. Their hypothesis was that there were differences in the conflict-resolution styles of collectivistic cultures, which place more emphasis on the group, compared to the individualistic cultures, which place more emphasis on the individual. Asian, African, and Native American cultures are examples of collectivistic cultures, whereas the United States and English cultures can be considered examples of individualistic cultures. To test their theory, they sampled people of Mexican culture as representative of collectivistic cultures and sampled people of the United States as representative of those of individualistic cultures. They found that people of Mexican heritage were more concerned with the effects of the outcome of behaviors on others (e.g., resorting to accommodation and collaboration behaviors), compared with those of United States culture, who were more focused on individual gain. They found that avoidance behaviors of those of Mexican heritage were based on concern for others. U.S. counselors may view this concern for others as a blatant example of lack of assertiveness. This lack of assertiveness may be considered by the counselor to be detrimental to the individual because that person is not getting his or her needs met. The counselor will tell the individual that this lack of assertiveness is also damaging to the other person with whom the individual is interacting; for example, by not expressing one's feelings and thoughts to the other person, the other person is not privy to these thoughts and feelings and thus is at a disadvantage.

The minority group member may withdraw in difficult-to-articulate, affect-mediated interactions because of language limitations (Liem, Lim, & Liem, 2000). Or, the minority group member may react emotionally and engender communication problems. Sata's (1973) studies of Nisei (Japanese Americans) called attention to the dynamics between Nisei and natives of the United States. Those raised in the American culture may be more focused on the cognitive aspects of the interaction. They may overlook the emotional aspects of the interaction. Chang (1994) wrote that this might be one of the sources of interethnic conflict—such as that seen in the 1992 Los Angeles riots.

Life Experiences. Although it is true that from an existential perspective, everyone's life is experienced both uniquely and yet universally, it is also true that many groups share life experiences that are different from others'. There are groups that, as a whole, have more access to work, money, power, and social mobility than other groups. Members of distinct groups can share distinct life experiences due to their language, cultural methods of accomplishing tasks, values, perspectives, and ethnicity. These, and other factors, can result in different life experiences between the European American counselor and the non–European American client.

In a study of Blacks, Whites, Asians, Native Americans, and Latinos (Williams, Yu, Jackson, & Anderson, 1997), researchers found that the minor day-to-day irritations of racism had a more detrimental impact than did major stressful life experiences. They found that discriminatory economic, legal, and political systems; discrimination in hiring, firing, and promotion practices; and the many other forms of differential treatment engender differences in the life experiences of Whites and non-Whites. The researchers concluded by stating that eliminating these disparities would require fundamental changes in social systems.

Religion. In the United States there are increasing numbers of people who are of different religions than the ones from which therapists traditionally come. The peoples from the Middle East are bringing their religion, as are those from Asia. Muslims and Buddhists are present in larger numbers now than in the past. Because most therapists are of Judeo-Christian backgrounds, mental health workers would be able to better serve those of different religions if they knew more about these religions (Richards & Bergin, 2000). Richards and Bergin (2000) warn that having cross-cultural skills does not qualify the therapist for dealing with the client who has religious issues that impact her or his mental health—there is much more that needs to be learned. However, having good skills in cross-cultural counseling provides a good foundation upon which to build.

Class Differences. In addition to the inherent biases of therapeutic approaches due to values, perceptions, and culture (Ullmann & Krasner, 1975), there can also be class differences. Unfortunately, the lower classes have a disproportionately larger number of minorities. Researchers and writers have long pointed out the bias and inadequacies of our conventional approaches and techniques when dealing with the lower classes; for example, McNeil (1970) stated that

> The symbolic abstraction that is language and the world of ideas, concepts, and thoughts are most comfortable and useful for the undisturbed members of our middle socioeconomic classes and may not be for the undisturbed members of the more heavily populated lower socioeconomic classes. The capacity of many members of our society to respond profitably to a talking relationship with a therapist may be quite limited by the nature of their early experiences and training. (pp. 157–158)

Lief, Lief, Warren, and Heath (1961) wrote,

> It is a wasteful procedure to include the lower classes of patients in clinics where the main emphasis is on teaching insight therapy. At the same time we cannot effectively perform our jobs . . . in terms of the mental health of the community unless we can discover methods of treatment appropriate to those in the lower classes, or more effectively use those in existence. (pp. 200–211)

Maher (1966) adds,

> The lower class patient is more numerous in fact and more likely in terms of probabilities to develop pathological problems, it seems to this writer a striking waste of time to continue to train clinicians to perform a service even the practitioners of which report is of no value to the bulk of the population of the mentally ill. (p. 469)

Poverty. In addition to those in the lower classes, there are those in poverty. The economic status of minorities has improved in recent years, with many more entering the middle class. However, there is increasing disparity between the haves and the have-nots (Global Policy Forum, 2001; Social Audit Gallup News Service, 2001), and many non-White minority groups can be characterized, when compared to the White population, as having a disproportionate number of people living in poverty (U.S. Census, 2000, Table 5). Levels of poverty among ethnic groups can be a measure of which ethnic group controls power and has access to resources. Poverty can be an effect of discrimination, and being poor can result in discrimination. Almost by definition, service providers live above poverty levels. Their economic life experiences may differ from those of many minorities. About 32.3 million American live below poverty levels. This is about 11.8% of the total U.S. population. Females who are heads of households, with no husbands present, make up 30.4% of those in poverty. If they have children, their poverty level is increased to 37.4%. About 9.8% of Whites live in poverty, and 24.7% of White females who are heads of households, with no husbands present, live in poverty; if they have children, this number increases to 31.6%. About 23.6% of Blacks live in poverty; 33.1% of those under 18 years old live in poverty. About 41.0% of Black females who are heads of households, with no husbands present, live in poverty, and if they have children, this number increases to 47.2%. About 65% of Black females 65 years old or older live in poverty. Approximately 22.8% of Hispanics live in poverty; 30% of those under the age of 18 years live in poverty. About 40.1% of Hispanic females who are heads of households, with no husbands present, live in poverty, and if they have children, this number increases to 46.4%. In addition, 46.8% of Hispanic females over the age of 65 live in poverty. Asian statistics in terms of poverty on these measures are comparable to statistics for Whites. About 7.7% of non-Hispanic Whites live in poverty. If the female is the head of household, with no husband present, 19.8% live in poverty; if non-Hispanic White females have children under the age of 18 years old, the number is increased to 26.1%. About 31.6% of American Indians and Alaska Natives live in poverty; 43.1% of those under 5 years old, 41.6% of 5-year-olds, 37.7% of 6- to 11-year-olds, and 33.1% of 12- to 17-year-olds live in poverty. If one is a minority in the inner cities or in rural areas, the chances of living in poverty are also increased.

Drugs. The Surgeon General's Report on Mental Health (1999) states that there is a growing awareness of ethnic and cultural variations in responses to drugs—ethnopsychopharmacology is a specialty that concentrates on this area of study. Responses to drug metabolism can be affected by genetic variation; diet; placebo effect; effects of traditional, cultural, endogenous drugs; and cultural practices and attitudes. These mediate not only the effects of a particular drug but also its side effects. There are genetic variations in drug-metabolizing enzymes (Brody, 1994). These differences can affect absorption rates, effects of the drugs, and the type, amount, and activities of the enzymes and medication. Lin, Anderson, and Poland (1997) report that 33% of African Americans and 37% of Asians are slow metabolizers of several antipsychotic medications and antidepressants (such as tricyclic antidepressants and selective serotonin reuptake inhibitors). The physician administering psychotropic medications to these two ethnic groups may use the same amount of medication as would be administered to a White person. This is understandable because the resources the physician relies on for norms and reports of results of the medication are usually based on White populations. Therefore, using the same amount of drugs on African American and Asian individuals may result in overmedication (Segal, Bola, & Watson, 1996) and very undesirable side effects (e.g., extrapyramidal effects, dystonia, akathisia, or parkinsonism; Lin et al., 1997). These experiences may contribute to a distrust of mental health services (Sussman, Robins, & Earls, 1987).

Diagnoses. European Americans are diagnosed differently from non–European Americans and have different rates of pathology; for example, non–European Americans are more likely to be diagnosed as schizophrenic and as having psychotic disorders (National Institute of Mental Health, 1980, 1981); they are likely to spend less time in the hospital for their problems; and they are more likely to spend more days on medication and spend more time in seclusion and in restraints (Gary, 1991). African Americans are less likely to be depressed (compared to European Americans), they are less likely to be diagnosed with depression and other mood disorders, and they are less likely to report substance-abuse problems (Kessler, 1994). Non–European Americans are more likely to receive unequal and poor mental health services (Sue, 1977). In relation to their proportions in the population, non–European American clients are less likely to be provided with traditional psychotherapy and are underserved by quality mental health services (Wu & Windle, 1980). Non–European Americans experience higher levels of poverty and social stressors that contribute to psychological disorders (Mays & Albee, 1992; Wu & Windle, 1980). Russell, Fujino, Sue, Cheung, and Snowden (1996) studied the diagnostic practices of European American, African American, Asian American, and Mexican American therapists. They found that ethnically matched therapists judged clients of their own ethnic group to have a higher level of mental health functioning, compared to therapists who saw clients who were not of their own ethnic group. Whaley (1998) reported that even where clinicians self-reported low levels of racial bias, their interactions with African Americans could result in differences by race in treatment and outcomes. Another study conducted by Whaley (1997) provided evidence that the differences of European Americans' diagnoses of African Americans might not be due to clinician bias. Instead, it may be due to European Americans and African Americans having different modes of expressing psychopathology and the diagnostician being unaware of or insensitive to such cultural differences. Westermeyer (1987) found that misdiagnosis, overestimation, underestimation, or neglect of psychopathology are frequent problems when clinicians and patients come from different cultures (p. 471).

In a diagnosis, the focus is on internal factors (biochemistry, genetics, personality flaws, etc.). There is direct or indirect reference to dysfunctions and disorders within the individual. The focus is on Axis I and II, and not on Axis IV of the *DSM-IV*. Diagnostically, we consider environmental factors and pathologies as secondary or tertiary to the problem. One could argue that the pathologies in the environment of non–European American populations are not the purview of psychotherapists and counselors. Mental health counselors deal with verbal, intrapsychic, and affective skills; therefore, working with social and economic forces is an activity that therapists are not skilled at doing and is not defined as therapy. One could also argue that these environmental pathologies are not the responsibility of the health field, educators, lawyers, social workers, the government, the clergy, and so forth. However, this would then call to question the relevance of psychological treatment to non–European Americans' mental health: Therapy would not be dealing with some of the most important factors that impact non–European Americans' mental health. It would be synonymous to stating that mental health therapists should not be involved in community prevention and education programs in alcohol, drug, partner, physical, and sexual abuse because these pathologies occur outside the office and deal more with environmental factors.

In discussing post-traumatic stress disorder (PTSD), Comas-Diaz (2000) wrote:

> Using individualistic, ethnocentric, and ahistorical approaches to psychopathology, the PTSD diagnosis tends to depoliticalicize systemic oppression, colonization, and racial terrorism. As such, it neglects society's accountability and responsibility, thus allowing it to act with impunity. The ethnocentricity of the PTSD diagnosis can overlook strengths and atypical disturbances and does not differentiate among defiant, adaptive, and maladaptive responses. (p. 1320)

She refers to a number of writers who warn us not to medicalize pathology without examining the ethnic and political aspects of the problem. Diagnosing problems as diseases places the solution to the problem in curing the person—when the problem could be the system and the solution is to change the system (not the individual). She provides examples of mental health professionals placing the blame on the individual, whereas the problem could be in the system: In the Soviet Union, dissenters were diagnosed with psychotic disorders (justifying their incarceration and the use of traumatizing medications), and in the United States, slaves who wanted to escape were labeled with a mental disorder ("drapetomania").

D'Andrea (1999) is one of many people who have pointed out the inadequacies of the *Diagnostic and Statistical Manual of Mental Disorders* (*DSM-IV*; American Psychiatric Association, 1994) in diagnosing cross-cultural and multicultural groups and individuals. He states that definitions of psychological problems are relative to the cultural group that defines them. The definitions of mental health and psychological wellness are dependent on cultural definitions. He advocates the development of alternative diagnostic frameworks to the *DSM-IV*. He (D'Andrea, 1999) wrote, "the monocultural, Eurocentric orientation that has dominated the profession during the 20th century [is] thought to be 'culturally-encapsulated' and guilty of unethical practice when counseling persons from other populations"

(p. 44). He wrote that counselors should take a relativistic, multiple, and multicultural perspective when working with cross-cultural populations.

Other Factors. Hui and Triandis (1986) found that peoples from Western cultures enter and leave relationships easily, whereas peoples from other cultures have relationships that are more intimate and longer lasting. Numerous authors (e.g., Atkinson, Ponterotto, & Sanchez, 1984; Root, 1985) report that honor is not as valued in Western culture as in Eastern cultures. Hui and Triandis (1986) reported that there are differences in emotional scripts, social bonding practices, and psychological defense mechanisms. Whaley (2000) reported cultural differences in the reasons for and consequences of physical punishment. He analyzed research on spanking behaviors of European American and African American families. He found European American families spanked their children for parent-oriented reasons (e.g., defiance of parental authority), whereas African American families spanked their children for child-oriented reasons—to prevent children from developing behaviors that would get them into trouble later. Spanking appears to induce disruptive and aggressive behaviors in European American children, whereas it appears either to have no relationship to African American children's subsequent behavior or to decrease disruptive behaviors. Vontress and Epp (1997) found that when the European American counselor interacts with the non–European American client, the counseling relationship may be superficial, meaningful therapeutic issues may not be explored, and issues that are cultural may be attributed to the individual's personal inadequacies. These factors may contribute to premature termination (Vontress, 1969).

The Surgeon General's Report (1999d) on the mental health of racial and ethnic minority populations states that when ethnic minorities were compared with "Whites" and with those providing services, there were differences found in the definition of types of problems; tolerance of problems; trust of service of providers; level of service; appropriateness of treatment; class orientation; cultural values and beliefs; biases; misconceptions; stereotypes; language; country of origin; acculturation; economic, social, and political status; stressors; experience of frequent, threatening, and uncontrollable life events; cultural identity; patterns of beliefs and practices; ability to respond to mental health services; coping styles; ties to family and community; expression of feelings; response to stress; avoidance of troubling internal events; willingness to disrupt social harmony; source of guidance; use of community and religion; experience of the discomfort associated with mental illness; normative group; characteristic modes of expressing suffering; "idioms of distress"; somatization; culture-bound syndromes; adherence to cultural practices; rates of divorce; placement of elders in nursing homes; use of the extended family; voluntary organizations

and clubs that often have political, economic, and social functions and affiliation with religious organizations; fluidity of household boundaries (e.g.,
the incorporation of relatives into the family and different definitions of
who family members are—they may or may not be related genetically); system of mutual aid; levels of relapse; amount of time for therapy; fear of
hospitalization and fear of treatment; stigma of mental illness; denial of
problem and self-reliance as a response to problems; clinician bias; utilization of treatment; help-seeking behavior; appropriate diagnosis; compliance
with treatment; premature termination of treatment; response to medications (pharmacotherapies); drug metabolism; diet; medication adherence;
placebo effect; simultaneous use of traditional and alternative healing
methods; effects of the amount of drug; and other psychosocial factors.

The preceding are examples of differences between the European and
the non-European that can impact the relationship between the European
American–trained therapist and the non–European American client. For
further differences among groups (e.g., Native American and Latin Americans), refer to the U.S. Department of Health and Human Services' (Orlandi,
Weston, & Epstein, 1992) *Cultural Competence for Evaluators.*

In terms of the relevance and impact of culture on counseling and
therapy, the counseling session lasts for only an hour, yet a person is in his
or her cultural environment constantly when outside the session. That
person's culture has been around and in him or her since birth. It would
take an enormous act of faith, surrender, or naiveté to conform to the
therapist's directions—both in and out of the therapeutic session.

In focusing on the differences between European Americans and non–
European Americans, I do not intend to induce dissonance between people.
By focusing on these differences, I am trying to point out that a lot of work
and learning still need to be done in the field of counseling and therapy.
The intention is to point to non–European Americans and say that there is a
place for them to contribute their knowledge to the mental health field. In
focusing on the differences among European American and non–European
Americans, I intend to point out that by not including non–European
Americans in at least the same proportions as they are in the general population, the counseling and therapeutic professions are limiting their knowledge, approaches, and techniques. These limitations inhibit the development
of a wider range of approaches and techniques that can be of value in treating
European Americans and non–European Americans alike—for example,
Karen Horney (1939) wrote, "acquaintance with a culture which in many
ways is different from the European has taught me to realize that many
neurotic conflicts are ultimately determined by cultural conditions" (pp.
12–13). It is my purpose to encourage people to understand and learn from
each other. With increased understanding, it is hoped that barriers will be
breached.

SOLUTIONS TO CONSIDER

Explore Alternatives—Be Creative

It has been a cliché among cultural anthropologists, ethnologists, cross-cultural psychologists, and a host of people in other fields that we should be aware of cultural differences—and that we need to modify and change interactions and communications in order to be more effective. But we still persist in adhering to our Eurocentric training. It is difficult to quantify the need to change in order to meet the needs of ethnic minorities and in order to improve our services. However, the field of business can provide proof that approaches need to be changed in order to be relevant to minorities. It is easier to institute new approaches in business because one can more readily measure success and failure—if more clients are attracted to the business, if sales go up, then these could be measures of the success of an approach. Mental health services and business are similar, in that one of their main goals is to communicate to people and to change their behaviors. The therapist wants the client to change dysfunctional behaviors and incorporate better ways of dealing with the problem. The businessperson wants the potential customer to change previous buying behaviors and use certain products or services. Traditional arguments for the mental health field to change to meet the needs of minorities have been based on altruistic, intellectual, moral, ethical, and humanistic reasons—for example, we need to change because we can learn from others or because it improves our ability to help people. I would like to add another dimension to this argument—from the pragmatic, functional, utilitarian perspective of business. The field of business more clearly demonstrates the need to change. The field of business provides clearer indices of what works and what does not. The entrepreneurial community has found that it is necessary to alter its approaches and techniques to convince ethnic groups to change their behaviors and buy the businesses' products. An extraordinarily huge number of businesses, including major corporations selling a wide array of products, have generated numerous methods (e.g., newsletters, websites, audio tapes, books, etc.) to educate their members and members of the business community on how to cater to foreign markets and to ethnic group members in the United States (e.g., Andreoli, 1994; Cebrzynski, 1998; Cui, 1997; Harrison, 2000; Haselow, 1997; Internet Business Video Network, 2001; Lewis, 1998; Miller, 1993; Noonan, 1999; Perkins, Thomas, & Taylor, 2000; Reese, 1997; Small Business Administration, 2000, 2001; Specialty Equipment Market Association, 2000; Sandlund, 1999; Tuckett, 1999; United States Dept. of Agriculture, 1991; Van Hoof, 1994). The following are some examples.

Haselow (1997) reports that there is enormous diversity in the world and that businesses have to adapt to this in order to sell their products. Among his guidelines are to gather local intelligence (know your clientele); beware of misunderstandings and missed communications caused by such factors as cultural miscues and local irreverence for deadlines; research the culture and the languages; research the best way to communicate (different groups react differently to the mode of interaction; any particular group may be more or less effectively communicated with by direct mailing, TV, radio, e-mail, newspapers, print media, posters, etc.); modify your core message for the various markets; translate carefully—there are not only primary languages but also dialects that might confound the message; research the political aspects of the message and the community; and use focus groups and cultural mediators, such as cultural anthropologists, to get your message across and to improve interactions.

Sandlund (1999) wrote that in order to be successful with minority groups, broad-based techniques are not as effective as marketing approaches that are tailored to each specific ethnic group. Marketing to minorities should include analyzing how the product fits the needs of the ethnic group, crafting the message appropriately, ensuring that the client has access to the product, communicating in the preferred language of the client, and demonstrating support for the ethnic group through hiring practices and community involvement.

Van Hoof (1994) found that marketing techniques for Whites differ from those for minority groups. Minorities differ from each other and from Whites in regard to responses to the media used (e.g., TV, radio, newspaper) and techniques used (e.g., portrayals in ads).

Miller (1993) wrote, "According to a new report by Market Segment Research, marketers can no longer count on minorities adopting the social and economic habits of mainstream America" (p. 6).

Tuckett (1999) wrote that the melting pot paradigm is gone and is replaced by a huge patchwork quilt, with each ethnic group contributing its own culture and identity. Therefore, new strategies have to be developed to interact with this diversity. "One mistake some advertisers make is trying to transform a general marketing campaign into a targeted one by simply changing the face from white to black or Latino. This simply does not work. Minorities have a heightened sensitivity to companies that seem patronizing"(p. 1).

The Small Business Administration (SBA) (2000) reported that not only are each of the major ethnic markets vastly different from one another, but there is also a great deal of diversity within a specific ethnic segment, based on country of origin and linguistic and sociocultural adaptation to the United States. In addition, there are many other differences such as generational differences. "Consequently, it is virtually impossible to create generic advertising or promotional tools that appeal to all segments of this diverse ethnic market. The solution is to pick a very specific target—a particular ethnic group in a particular location—and tailor your message to that target. If you are trying to attract more than one ethnic group, you may have to create more than one message" (p. 2). The SBA suggests that the company learn as much possible about the customer's traditions and beliefs and consult with those familiar with the culture. It recommends that ethnic stereotypes and clichés should not be catered to, and one should be sensitive to cultural slurs or taboos. In addition, it suggests that the business get involved with the minority community and be aware that courtesy behaviors can differ among various ethnic groups, as can business etiquette and the dynamics of business meetings. For example, there are ethnic differences in the way conflict is managed and power is accorded to the person in charge. In the next section of the report, the Small Business Administration (2001) mentioned that instead of looking to assimilate, certain ethnic groups such as African Americans, Asians, and Hispanics have fought to maintain their own cultural integrity. The writers of the Small Business Administration (2001) stated that expecting ethnic groups in America to assimilate into the mainstream over time has proved to be faulty reasoning—mainstream groups have to change to meet the needs of ethnic minorities.

Questioning Basic Assumptions

Among the suggestions to improve dynamics between the Euro-trained therapist and the minority member is to overcome cultural bias and differences between the European American counselor and the non–European American client. A common approach is to encourage European American counselors/therapists to engage in self-assessment and self-exploration and to learn about other cultures (D'Andrea & Daniels, 1991; D'Andrea, Daniels, & Heck, 1991; Ottavi, Pope-Davis, & Dings, 1994). These are commendable activities. However, there are some questions to consider in regard to these frequent recommendations to help counselors/therapists improve their cross-cultural competency skills. For example, how does the mental health professional know when effective levels of competency, self-knowledge, and sensitivity have been attained? This could be an open-ended process. Also, those counselors/therapists with high self-esteem and with low criteria for competence, or who are ignorant of how much there is to be learned, will quickly feel that they have reached levels of sufficient competence.

It does not necessarily follow that knowledge of another's culture leads to better counselors and more appropriate and effective therapy (Sue & Zane, 1987). Steward, Morales, Bartell, Miller, and Weeks (1998) found that learning about other people's culture through coursework or literature does not necessarily induce acceptance of multiculturalism or diversity. In addition, they found that whether or not trainees embraced the concept of multiculturalism, they viewed each other as being competent in the delivery of counseling services to minorities. Other problems entailed in teaching about other cultures are the enormous subgroup, generational, regional, religious, individual, gender, life-experience, and developmental differences within each culture. This makes learning about a person's culture extremely complex and full of nuances. Although it is very desirable to know as much as possible about other peoples' cultures, this is a process and only one of a number of factors to consider.

In terms of treatment, when the non–European American person fails to respond to the mental health professional, a frequent reaction is to attribute the unsatisfactory response to the non–European American member's culture or to the client's noncompiance—much like blaming men for their emotive inadequacies in counseling when they do not talk about their feelings to the satisfaction of the mental health professional (Nairfeh & Smith, 1985). Perhaps it is the therapist and the approach that are inadequate, not the client.

One frequently mentioned solution to non–European American mental health problems is to call for more mental health resources in order to provide better and more services. Although this is a desirable part of the solution, the results of such research as the Fort Bragg Demonstration Project study should be considered (Bickman, 1996; Bickman et al., 1995). The Fort Bragg experiment was a 5-year, $80-million project designed to test whether comprehensive mental health and substance-abuse services for children and adolescents had better therapeutic effects than traditional, limited services. The Fort Bragg research suggests that the mental health of communities is not necessarily improved with more and better mental health services. Another explanation for the lack of improvement with "unlimited" services is that there is an optimal level beyond which more and better services do not improve the community's mental health. Of course, such iconoclastic findings raised a plethora of controversy (Behar, 1997; DeLeon & Williams, 1997; Feldman, 1997; Hoagwood, 1997; Saxe & Cross, 1997; Sechrest & Walsh, 1997). For the non–European American, the Fort Bragg studies imply that the solution to problems does not strictly lie in the allocation of greater resources to mental health professionals and their delivery systems. Other changes need to be made as well.

Contributions of Other Cultures

Mental health professionals need to know what other cultures can contribute to counseling. Ethnocentrism limits learning from other cultures. For example, African and Asian cultures can contribute to the knowledge of human relationships: Many African and Asian cultures have developed relationship patterns that have lasted for centuries—if not millennia. The Chinese culture has existed for thousands of years and has been able to develop relationship patterns that have endured. This is in contrast to the comparatively short-lived European political, economic, social, and cultural systems. It may be of benefit for counselors to learn what are the ingredients that constitute enduring—or detrimental—human relationship patterns. The expansion of Europeans to all the lands of the earth has been, in great part, due to the inability of Europeans to resolve problems in their country of origin: The solution to their problems has been to remove, or force the removal of, dissenters to other lands—or to otherwise kill or neutralize them. For example, the Pilgrims and Mennonites came to the United States because either they or their native countries could not resolve their problems. This resulted in the dissenters leaving their countries. This is in contrast to the inhabitants of Asian and African countries that have, for the most part, remained in their countries of origin. It is interesting to consider the effects of the European's dichotomous, linear thinking in this process. Many authors (e.g., Feldman, 1997; Saxe & Cross, 1997; Smith, 1986) wrote that European thinking is characterized by exclusive thinking—that is, thinking in all or nothing, dichotomous, right or wrong, linear terms, whereas Asian cultures have been characterized by inclusive thinking—that is, thinking that recognizes that there are different paths to the truth, that there can be more than one answer to the truth. In the area of religion, this is manifested in the European thinking that adhering to one religion prohibits one from adhering to another religion at the same time. This is in contrast to such religions as Buddhism and Hinduism, where one can be a follower of a particular religion and still adhere to the gods and beliefs of other religions. Does the dichotomous, linear thinking that is characteristic of European thinking lead to fractious relationships? Can human relations be improved with inclusive thinking?

Broman (1996) cited literature pointing out that although African Americans are exposed to more stress (e.g., poverty, crime, unemployment) than are European Americans, their psychiatric morbidity rate is about the same as that of European Americans. One might expect higher levels of psychiatric morbidity for African Americans. The reason why there may not be higher pathology might be attributed to the coping strategies that African Americans have developed to deal with their problems. Many researchers (e.g., Murray & Peacock, 1996) found that responses to stress vary with the type of problem and personal characteristics. Broman lists strategies that are a response to stress. These strategies vary with problem type, social status, age, gender, education, and income. Ramseur (1991) examined factors central to African American psychological health. He cites the following factors:

1. Maintaining a positive self-image.
2. Maintaining a positive identification with the African American community.
3. Maintaining an accurate perception of what is happening in the environment.
4. Effectively adapting to African American and European American cultures.
5. Having emotional intimacy with others.
6. Maintaining a sense of competence and productivity.

Hayles (1991) reported that the strengths of the African American family included

1. Kinship and extended family networks.
2. Values of harmony, cooperation, interdependence, acceptance of differences, internal development, work and achievement orientation, and adherence to tradition.
3. Strong bonds between males and females.
4. Adaptability and flexibility of roles.
5. Supports against racism—for example, via emotional support from others or appreciation of one's roots.
6. Respect and utilization of skills and wisdom of senior family members.
7. Emphasis on children.

Develop Valid and Reliable Assessment Tools

It is understood that the area of assessment is a controversial one, especially when it comes to the assessment of non–European Americans. This is understandable because of the historical misuse of assessment when applied to non–European Americans—and to European Americans. However, the proper use of assessment can have a role in helping non–European Americans. Assessment can provide information about a person's interests, values, needs, and so on. Assessment provides mental health professionals and clients with information about themselves and how they compare to others. Of course, one of the criticisms of the use of assessment is that its development and validity do not accurately measure non–European Americans and therefore do not provide an accurate assessment—making comparisons spurious. The answer to this is not to abandon assessments. The answer is to develop valid materials. The capability of assessment to measure us provides a means to let us know how we are doing. This enables us to correct ourselves and develop a database from which we can determine what works or does not, and for whom. Without assessment, we would be in a state of perpetual uncertainty as to the validity and reliability of our behaviors and assessment materials. Non–European Americans should have the same opportunities to use assessment tools as do European Americans. We should not avoid assessment. Instead, we should develop better assessment instruments and exercise the appropriate use of them. The traditional use of assessment has been for placement and diagnostic purposes. Such uses can raise criticism and suspicion in the assessment of non–European American populations. A more constructive use of assessment can be to help the client identify strengths and weaknesses, as well as help the client obtain more information about himself or herself.

The advent of computer programs and user-friendly statistical programs has made the gathering and analysis of assessment data more expedient than ever in the past. Many computer-administered programs have the option not only of keeping data on clients, but also of accumulating the data and doing statistical analyses. These tools are readily available. Those who train counselors and therapists should be training non–European Americans to use these tools for the development of specific norms, assessment materials, approaches, and techniques for non–European American communities.

Empowerment

In therapy, individuals need to be empowered. They need to know their resources. They need to know who controls the resources and how to change and have access to these resources. They need to know strategies on how to change systems—strategies such as forming advocate groups, voting, petitioning, and confronting politicians and administrators. They need to know how to empower each other. Just as individuals need to be empowered, communities also need to be empowered. For communities to depend on outside forces (e.g., the state and federal governments) for their economic survival leaves the ethnic community very vulnerable to fluctuations in the power structure. For example, there may be years when politicians and political parties may support non–European American communities, and other years when they may not want to provide support. For non–European American communities to depend on fluctuations such as these leave them vulnerable and prevents the development of stable systems. Obviously, one could argue that no community can live in isolation, and therefore the development of endogenous systems would be counterproductive. But those communities that do not have their own pool of skilled workers, professionals, resources, and services are even more dependent and vulnerable to exogenous forces.

We need to train more professionals who are endogenous to their own non–European American communities. We need to facilitate the process of non–European Americans entering counseling and therapy educational programs. We need to train them to develop more viable approaches for dealing with non–European American members and communities. If there is a brain drain or a skills drain from minority communities, we need to develop systems to handle this frequent phenomena so that endogenous systems can be developed and maintained for the training, maintenance, and improvement of community entrepreneurs, service providers, and so on.

Most counseling occurs as a one-to-one interaction between the mental health professional and the client. What are the ramifications of this mode of providing services to a person from another culture? What are the ramifications of this mode of providing services to people removed from the context of their sociological, historical, political, developmental, community, educational, familial, and cultural milieu (e.g., Moll, 1990; Rogoff & Chavajay, 1995; Vygotsky, 1978)? In the office, it is the therapist's world. The effects of the therapist are maximized. The client is out of his or her element. The therapist has the power. The therapist allocates whatever power the client gets. Is this the best way to empower a member of an ethnic minority in counseling? Perhaps one solution would be to develop endogenous service providers or peer group–counseling programs to help empower minorities and their communities. The purpose of mental health services in the ethnic community should be to develop endogenous systems that enable the community to sustain itself and grow. Any system that promotes dependence on the therapist or on mental health services is detrimental to the minority community. Community service providers (e.g., "volunteers," "peer counselors," "paraprofessionals") should not be allocated a lower status than those with master's degrees; they should be allocated responsibilities commensurate with those of professionals.

Approaches and Techniques

The person providing services to minorities should investigate effective methods of doing so. I will later describe some other possible viable models and approaches in my chapters on technology and evolutionary psychology. Other authors have offered different approaches. For example, Alexander and Sussman (2000) state that traditional approaches engender barriers when dealing with minority groups. They propose being actively involved in the client's life and maybe moving out of the office and into the client's milieu. They present research to buttress their proposal to use music, food, art play, and folk tales in counseling clients from other cultures.

Numerous authors have offered models, solutions, steps, and observations of cross-cultural training, including Berry, Kim, Power, Young, and

Bujaki, 1992; Coleman, 1995a, 1995b; LaFromboise, Coleman, and Gerton, 1993; and Tyler, Brome, and Williams, 1991. Orlandi, Weston, and Epstein (1992) wrote an excellent monograph that provides cultural information on various ethnic groups. In the summary by Orlandi, the following general guidelines are provided for evaluating and implementing viable treatment programs in ethnic communities:

1. Demystify the role of culture in treatment programs by rigorous problem-solving analysis.
2. Develop a consensus on terms used in cultural studies.
3. Information should be shared and a common ground found for those with differing views.
4. The scientific measures used in evaluating treatment should be valued by those in the ethnic group who are being assessed.
5. The values of the agency a counselor works for, and that the agency is perceived to be loyal to, can have an impact on the treatment program.
6. Ethnic groups should be involved in the planning, implementation, analysis, training, and evaluation of treatment.
7. Distinction should be made between the person's culture and the culture of poverty.
8. Ethnic groups have subgroups. It is important to recognize that there can be major differences between subgroups.
9. Ethnic groups should be knowledgeable about what constitutes relevant evaluation and should not rely on outside expertise.
10. A culturally competent therapist has more than knowledge of a cultural group; the culturally competent therapist is on a continuum of developing knowledge, attitudes, and skills.

Another consideration is to train mental health professionals to develop effective methods to help the victims of racism deal with racism. Moritsugu and Sue (1983) analyzed those who have effectively developed psychological strategies to deal with racism. He found four methods:

1. Compassion. Although the targets of racism may react with extreme anger, they may attribute the offensive remarks or behaviors to shortcomings in the perpetrator.
2. Perspective. This means taking into consideration the context of the racist behavior and deciding what would be accomplished if one were to try to educate or change the offender.
3. Consideration of the end goals. This means not necessarily reacting emotionally, but instead considering the payoffs of whether or not to confront the perpetrator.
4. Flexibility. Evaluating the situation and taking action appropriate to the

situation—at times, forceful action might be warranted, and at other times it is better to remain silent.

D'Andrea and Arredondo (2000) present the following strategies for culturally competent counselors to deal with cultural oppression and institutional racism:

1. Continually educate oneself on manifestations of cultural oppression and institutional racism.
2. Despite others' efforts to prevent this, raise racist issues to administrators, colleagues, and students.
3. Offer to provide consultation and training to increase awareness of these issues.
4. Build alliances with those interested in social injustices.
5. Because many administrations and other power brokers will not make meaningful changes, the culturally competent counselor may need to organize students and the community to counter the various forms of cultural oppression and institutional racism.

In terms of the curriculum of cross-cultural counseling/therapy programs, I would include the following:

1. Teach cross-cultural nonthreatening gestures and behaviors, and know what the aggressive and rude gestures are.
2. Teach the mental health professional to accept that the client's needs come before the mental health professional's.
3. Learn cultural approaches and techniques to induce behavior changes (e.g., some cultures depend upon tradition, others depend on religious values—Whites depend more on logic).
4. Develop culturally meaningful methods of reassurance and caring.
5. Promote the use of the mental health professional as a resource.
6. Educate clients aboutwhat counselors/therapists do.
7. Learn how to determine the culturally relevant conditions that are conducive for effective counseling. These may include learning culturally relevant conditions that promote belief in the therapeutic effectiveness of the mental health professional (Frank, 1991). If nothing else, this may elicit the placebo effect as a therapeutic ingredient.
8. Learn how to provide therapy as a problem-solving service. Many of the present models and approaches entail many sessions, as well as the exploration of feelings and origins of thoughts and behaviors. These are intrusive, time-consuming approaches of questionable validity. A more meaningful approach might be to deal directly with the non–European American's problems. Such an approach would be less intrusive and

would decrease the client's sense of vulnerability. Such an approach would also make it clearer that counseling is more of a problem-solving endeavor and has less to do with having to surrender intimate thoughts and feelings to the counselor. Of course, behavioral, rational emotive behavior therapy (REBT), and cognitive-behavioral approaches are less intrusive and are more in the direct problem-solving mode suggested—but they need to be more culturally syntonic. If the exploration of thoughts and feelings is relevant to therapeutic change, then the person should be taught how to do it—and not to rely on the therapists to continually facilitate the process.

Another approach could be to determine the client's hierarchical needs and then provide therapy appropriate to that level of need. For example, if one were to use Erickson's hierarchy of needs (Corsini, 1977; Hall, Lindzey, & Campbell, 1998), different therapeutic approaches might be used to meet the needs at the different levels of the hierarchy. That is, people whose basic physical needs have not been met (e.g., the poor) may need coping skills and approaches that are more direct and geared toward problem-solving to meet their needs. Their needs are more urgent and should be resolved quicker. On the other hand, people whose basic physical needs have been met (e.g., the middle class) might be more amenable to affective, verbal, intrapsychic therapeutic techniques. Their needs are not as pressing, and they can afford the time to explore and delve into their psyches and feelings.

The listening, the commiserating, the warmth and kindness that are the hallmarks of our profession are very important. Nevertheless, many counselors may confuse these qualities as necessary and sufficient for therapy to occur. In order for the profession to develop, it needs to have a body of knowledge that can be tested. We need to be able to determine what works and what does not work, with whom, and when. Science allows us to do this.

SELECTION OF MENTAL HEALTH PROFESSIONALS, TRAINING, POWER, AND POLITICS

Counselor Selection and Education

D'Andrea and Daniels (1995) wrote that most counseling professionals will admit that racism exists in the United States and that it adversely affects this country. However, they also wrote that "it is interesting to note that almost no one has come forward to discuss the ways in which psychosocial pathology adversely affects the counseling profession" (p. 23). D'Andrea

(1992) provides some examples of the institutional racism that infects the mental health professions:

- Fewer than 1% of graduate counseling-training program chairpersons in the United States are non-Whites (whereas non-Whites constitute over 30% of the population and will soon comprise over 50%).
- There are few Latino Americans, Asian Americans, or Native Americans in high leadership positions in ACA or APA.
- Only one African American has been president of APA, despite the long existence of the organization.
- The five most commonly used textbooks in counselor-training programs in the United States do not list "racism" in their tables of content or indexes.
- A literature search done on the three leading professional counseling journals (*The Counseling Psychologist, Journal of Counseling and Development,* and the *Journal of Counseling Psychology*) over a 12-year period (1980–1992) found that only 6 of the 308 articles examined the impact of racism on mental health.
- With the exception of one African American editor, all ACA and APA journal editors are White.
- After more than 15 years of efforts, ACA and APA have yet to adopt a comprehensive set of multicultural counseling competencies and standards to formally serve as guidelines for professional training and development.

One of D'Andrea's (1992, 1993) conclusions is that non-Whites' opinions are "seriously restricted" in APA and ACA, in terms of developing organizational policies and in the dissemination of information.

Counselor education programs are basically the realm of European American counselor educators, working from positions of White privilege (Ivey, Ivey, D'Andrea, & Daniels, 1997) and fostering a monocultural ethnocentric perspective in their work (Daniels & D'Andrea, 1996). The U.S. Surgeon General reported,

> Research documents that many members of minority groups fear, or feel ill at ease with, the mental health system (Lin et al., 1982; Scheffler & Miller, 1991; Sussman et al., 1987). These groups experience it as the product of white, European culture, shaped by research primarily on white, European populations. They may find only clinicians who represent a white middle-class orientation, with its cultural values and beliefs, as well as its biases, misconceptions, and stereotypes of other cultures. (Surgeon General's Report on Mental Health, 1999, p. 1)

Counselor education programs are by and for the White, middle-class population. As of May 1, 2000, according to the U.S. Census Bureau (2000a), about 29.4% of U.S. Americans are classified as minorities. The percentage breakdown is as follows: 12.8%, Blacks; 11.7%, Hispanics (any race); 0.9%, American Indian, Eskimo, Aleut; 4.0%, Asians and Pacific Islanders.

Responses to a survey conducted by the American Counseling Association, in which 29,431 of 51,960 members responded, consisted of the following: Males, 30%; Females, 70%; African American, 5%; Asian, 1%; Native American, 1%; Hispanic/Latino, 2%; Caucasian, 90%; Other, 1% (information provided by ACA librarian, in a phone conversation on November 29, 1997).

The gender and ethnic demographics of counseling center directors are as follows: Males, 58.3%; Females, 41.7%; African American, 3.4%; Asian, 0.6%; Native American, 0.0%; Hispanic, 2.8%; Caucasian, 92.5% (Gallagher, 1995).

As the members of the American Psychological Association and the American Counseling Association are not required to list their ethnicity, the data on ethnic membership are incomplete. The data we have show meager representation of minorities in these professional mental health organizations. In regard to ethnic membership in APA, consider the data of two sources. One source is the "Handbook for Increasing Ethnic Minority Membership Participation in State Psychological Association and APA Division," published by the American Psychological Association Office of Ethnic Minority Affairs (2000), which states that 2,800 of its members list themselves as members of ethnic groups. The other source is the APA Directory Survey from the APA Research Office, which provides the following gender and ethnic demographics of the American Psychological Association membership (for comparison, I have placed in parentheses the national percentage of ethnic groups—from Richie, 1997; the national percentages are based on a U.S. population of 264.4 million, as reported by the U.S. Department of Commerce, Bureau of Census): Males, 52.7%; Females, 47.3%; African American, 2%; Asian, 1%; Native American, .02%; Hispanic/Latino, 2%; Caucasian, .71%; Other, 2%; multiple, 3% [*from APA Directory Survey, 1997 (APA Research Office, 2000), Table 1: Demographic Characteristics of APA Members by Race/Ethnicity: 1997*]. [*There were 20,051 members who do not specify their race/ethnicity included in the total; percentages of ethnic members were obtained by dividing the number of members in the ethnic group by 83,970 (the 83,970 is obtained by subtracting total membership of 84,426 from Multiple (294) and Other (162) categories.)*]. Though the latter data are fragmented and partial, there seems to be enough information to confirm the impression of ethnic minorities in APA that their membership is low and to warrant the present attempts of APA to try to increase their ethnic membership.

The Office of Ethnic Minorities of the American Psychological Association (personal communications, July 10, 2000) reported that minorities constituted 5% of its membership. The American Counseling Association reported (ACA librarian, personal communications, July 10, 2000) that approximately 10% of the ACA members are minorities.

These data suggest that non–European American membership is limited in the counseling and therapy professions. It might also be assumed that the number of members in each group reflects the power distribution and perspectives in these professions. The prevalence of European Americans is a measure of the main perspectives of these organizations. Such perspectives may hinder the ability of these organizations to critically analyze and objectively apprise cross-cultural issues. Ivey et al. (1997) state that counseling programs should follow Cheatham's (1990) and Pedersen's (Pedersen & Ivey, 1993) suggestions to engage in a paradigm shift from the traditional Eurocentric perspective and consider the contribution and perspectives of other cultures.

How does one explain the previously mentioned phenomena? Why is it that White therapists and counselors are represented in disproportionately high numbers in the mental health professions? Why is it that Whites behave the way that they do? Why is it that the data usually place minorities at the short end of receiving power and resources? There are many possible explanations. From the popular parlance, these phenomena may be viewed as aspects of racism. From political science, these behaviors can be explained as a desire for those in power to perpetuate themselves with those similar to themselves. From sociology, we find that people prefer to congregate with people similar to themselves. From biology, we find that people want to propagate themselves with people who have features they share in common. From social psychology, we find that people feel more comfortable with people like themselves. They evaluate those similar to themselves in more positive terms. They evaluate those different from themselves in more negative terms. Dovidio, Gaertner, Kawakami, and Hodson (2002) reviewed research on Black and White interactions. They found that when Whites interacted with Blacks there was a subtle, often unintentional, and unconscious damaging bias. When Whites interacted with Blacks they often denied racial bias and negative feelings toward Blacks. Whites maintain a nonprejudicial self-image and do not attribute their discrimination and negative feelings to racial bias. Instead they attribute their behaviors to other factors (for example, they may attribute a Black person not being hired to that person's lack of "necessary qualifications," instead of racism on the part of the person doing the hiring). Such interactions fostered miscommunication and distrust between Whites and Blacks. From a capitalistic perspective, we find that people want economic security, and they want to increase their resources and powers and exploit others to do so. It is obvious that the counseling and psychological professions have not escaped these forces. What is disheartening is that so little attention is paid to these phenomena within ourselves. It is hoped that increased awareness of factors such as these may overcome natural tendencies and induce changes that will help those we serve, as well as improve our profession.

The shift from the present Eurocentric power structure to the sharing of power with those of other cultures will be a difficult process for the following reasons: Institutions have a tendency to perpetuate themselves with people who share the values and characteristics of the power holders (Luttwak, 1969; Olsen, 1970). Ample research demonstrates that people are most likely to favorably value those they are familiar with and negatively evaluate those they are not as familiar with (Moreland & Zajonc, 1979; Saegert, Swap, & Zajonc, 1973; Zajonc, 1968). We also have more positive feelings for those we are more accustomed to (Jorgensen & Cervone, 1978). Recent research (Fiske, 1998) has found that people are more comfortable with those who are similar to themselves and evaluate their own group as both likable and competent, whereas groups that are not similar to theirs are evaluated as either likable or competent, but not both. DeAngelis (2001b) reports a series of studies by various authors; among their findings were that although people tend to view members of their own groups as having individual characteristics, they tend to view those of other groups in a homogeneous (e.g., stereotypical) manner. The less one knows of the other group, the stronger the effect; even if Whites consciously do not harbor negative feelings about Blacks, many Whites automatically react more negatively to Blacks than to Whites, and the closer Blacks come to invading the cultural values and behaviors of Whites, the more Whites view this as an invasion of their cultural integrity, and the more extreme the reaction. These factors are among the many that will perpetuate European American dominance of the counseling profession unless drastic force is applied to administrators and to those who train counselors and therapists in this country.

In terms of counseling programs (as compared to psychology programs), it is obvious that counseling programs have more discretion in the selection of who enters their program. Many counseling programs affiliate themselves with colleges of education. Programs in colleges of education typically do not rely on intellectual rigor, math, or science skills (which are easier to measure) for admittance into their programs or for the practice of their various professions. Similarly, counseling programs do not rely on intellectual rigor, math, or science skills and, typically, counseling programs do not rely as much on grades and national normed tests for admissions. They depend on other criteria for admissions—such as interviews and reasons for applying to the counseling program. This allows for an enormous amount of subjectiveness in the selection of students into counseling programs and into the practice of counseling. Unlike the sciences, where knowledge is the basis for entering and practicing in a profession, the counseling arts use qualitative methods to determine who enters and practices in the counseling profession. Such subjective, qualitative discretion may result in bias in the selection and evaluation process. People who are selected are likely to be the ones who are similar to those doing the selecting. These similarities can include similarities in values, speech, background, and so on. There is evidence to suggest that the more minority professionals are acculturated to "Western" values, the less preference they have for serving minorities, and they believe themselves to be less effective in providing services to minorities (Gurung & Mehta, 2001).

When we examine the skills that are desirable for counseling, we find that counseling calls for good verbal skills (Career Information System, 1998; Mayall, 1994). In regard to what kind of verbal skills are needed, we find that the standard measure of verbal skills is that of the European American middle class. This makes counseling a very expedient employment avenue for European American, middle-class people to pursue. But for those who are not European American and middle class, this can result in barriers. Other criteria might be considered for admission into counseling programs—for example, the needs of the people to be served and the needs of society. Does society need more middle-class service providers to deliver services to middle-class, White populations; or do we need people from all classes and ethnic groups to serve all peoples? We need counselors from all cultures. We need counselors to help the poor. We need counselors to help the disenfranchised. Middle-class verbal skills and behaviors may be good for middle-class populations, but how viable are they for serving all populations? To illustrate the logic of the previous point, consider the following. Imagine that Winnebago Native Americans controlled the United States. As a result of Winnebago's domination, therapists are trained in Winnebago schools, by Siouan-speaking teachers. Almost all of the teachers are disproportionately of Winnebago background, as are the students. Students have to speak in Siouan. They have to exhibit Winnebago behaviors and use techniques and approaches derived by, from, and for Winnebago populations. They have to wear Winnebago attire and assume Winnebago values and perceptions. Their training inculcates in them the universality of the Winnebago language, behavior, values, and perceptions, and they assume that their approaches and techniques are panaceas for problems in all cultures. Although Winnebago culture may be wonderful, and though Winnebago domination may be wise and just, it is highly unlikely that the Winnebago definition of counseling will meet the needs of all cultures. It is highly unlikely that European American counselors and the European American population will not have problems with this kind of training, perception, and dominance of the field. Yet minority groups are expected to accept the present European American domination and perceptions of the mental health field. Possible solutions to the preceding could include allowing greater variability in who is admitted into training programs, allowing great variability in verbal and behavioral skills, and expanding the opportunity to learn other approaches for different populations.

ETHICS

Much has been written on the ethics involving the mental health professionals' interactions with clients. The ethical standards of the American Psychological Association (1992) and the American Counseling Association (1995) often cloak such interactions in altruistic language—for example, the ethical standards are to protect the client or the "public's interest." Such issues as confidentiality, dual relationships, and sexual activities with clients (as well as standards of care of animals and appropriate behaviors with students and research participants) are important. However, there are aspects to these ethical values in regard to clients that appear to be serving the interests of the mental health professional. These ethical values can be construed as attempts to keep clients coming to therapy and counseling (thus keeping the psychologist and counselor in business). I subscribe to these values completely. However, there are other ethical values that may be more in keeping with the minority and poor client's needs, for example, ethical values that require the mental health professional to speak out against discrimination and fight against institutional racism. The implementation of such ethical values would be of great value to ethnic minorities and the poor. It is true that there are statements in the "Ethical Principles of Psychologists and Code of Conduct" (1992) to respect other people's rights and dignity (Principle D), to be concerned for others' welfare (Principle E), to have social responsibility (Principle F), and to take such action as speaking out when the mental health therapist's professional values are in disagreement with the institution's. But these are platitudes that appear to have never been operationalized—for example, I know of no mental health therapist who has had sanctions brought against him or her for not taking action against racism. It seems to me that the implementation of sanctions for contributing to racism is as relevant to helping minorities and the poor as the present focus on such activities as having dual relationships and breaking confidentiality.

Another ethical aspect of professional relationships is that revolving around issues of teachers and supervisors and those they teach and supervise. Wester and Vogel (2002) cite authors who criticize teachers and supervisors for their failure to fulfill their responsibilities and for engaging in unethical behaviors when they do not encourage and support those they teach and supervise to explore and have their own views; do not provide those they teach and supervise with a diversity of views; knowingly or unknowingly coerce those they teach and supervise to assume the views of the teacher and supervisor; and provide a limited view of psychology and counseling. Such behaviors on the part of teachers and supervisors limit the potentials of both White and minority people they teach and supervise. They impede learning, inhibit exploration, hinder potential solutions, promote bias, and limit the expansion of psychology's knowledge and approaches.

These are just two limited and superficial examples of ethical behaviors that if implemented would be more relevant to minorities. The ethical aspects of mental health professionals and minorities and the poor are voluminous, and there needs to be much more focus on this area of ethics—liberations theology and liberation psychology provide germane insights into ethical behaviors and responsibilities in interactions with disenfranchised groups.

INSIGHTS FROM ASSESSMENT

It is interesting to look at the assessment arena to see what insight we might garner in terms of the characteristics of those who are providing services to minorities. When the Personality Research Form (Jackson, 1989), which measures needs, was correlated with the Strong Vocational Interest Blank (Siess & Jackson, 1967, 1970), results indicated that counselors had higher correlations in their interests and need to dominate and control. Because many counselors work in bureaucratic settings, is the need to dominate and control a characteristic of those who work in bureaucratic settings? Other questions might include: Are counselors who work in bureaucratic settings more willing to delay gratification for the security of distant goals—for example, retirement? Are they more concerned about security, and therefore, are they more willing to sacrifice their views and values and follow those of institutions that will provide them with security?

When one looks at national-based test scores, would test results offer any insight into the characteristics of people who are serving minorities? Many therapists are trained in colleges of education. Those who enter colleges of education typically have some of the lowest scores on such national tests as the American College Testing (ACT) exam and Graduate Record Examination (GRE). Depending on the test, these tests measure such skills as math, verbal, or analytic skills, or some combination of these. Van Laar (Waters, 1999) analyzed data from 5,000 university students and found that "In most cases, students who had a high level of racial tolerance earned higher grades, but students whose racial attitudes differed from others within their major got lower grades" (p. 6). Are there certain characteristics of people who have lower scores? For example, are they less knowledgeable about other people—and do they assume societal stereotypes? Are they more insecure in the employment arena and thus have greater fear of competition from minorities? Do they have less of a need for understanding others, and if so, what ramification does this have for minorities? Correlations between the Personality Research Form's need for "Understanding" scale with the Strong Vocational Interest Blank suggest that guidance counselors have a low need for understanding (Jackson, 1989). There are also correlations among the Personality Research Form's need for "Understanding" scale with the Jackson Personality Inventory's "Tolerance" scale and the California Psychological Inventory "Tolerance" scale (Jackson, 1989) The greater the need for understanding, the greater the tolerance. There is also the matter of the effects of intelligence. Because colleges of education historically attract the lowest performers on nationally normed tests, if there is correlation between these tests and intelligence, what might be the implications of this? For example, if there is such a correlation, does the correlation between the Personality Research Form's need for "Understanding" scale and the inverse scores on the Bentler Interactive Psychological Inventory's "Intelligence" scale (Jackson, 1989) have any significance for therapists trained in colleges of education and their receptivity to people who are different from them?

If we look further into colleges of education and examine people who graduate from these programs, questions can be raised as to the caliber of these persons. These are the personnel who run our schools and institutions of higher learning. These people admit minorities into colleges and exercise power over them during their sojourn in higher education. Colleges of education produce personnel who work in college admissions, counseling, residential programs, and so on. We need to examine the role they play for minorities. Hernandez (1997) is one of the very few people who have provided insight and a critical account of some of those who work in such settings. Her book provides an account of admissions counselors. Hernandez reported on her experiences with Ivy League colleges. Her characterization of the admissions counselors at Ivy League colleges is probably not different from those of many other colleges. If anything, it is probably the case that people who work at Ivy League universities are of a calibre better because the prestige of these schools might attract more candidates to choose from. Little has been written on the characteristics of counselors and therapists who work in bureaucratic settings; however, what Hernandez has written of admissions officers working in bureaucracies may be applicable to counselors working in bureaucracies. Admissions officers frequently have similar backgrounds to those of counselors. They are often graduates of colleges of education. They are often trained in the same departments and are similar in academic performance. Hernandez divides the admissions officers into two groups. The first group is interested in education. Its members are high-level performers, with intellectual proclivities, and they tend to be risk-takers. The second group consists of "lifers." Members of this latter group are often products of colleges of education. They are mediocre academic performers, who graduated from mediocre colleges, and who are concerned about the security of their positions. They are not intellectuals or scholars. They often have limited life experience and have a propensity to make decisions with limited input from people with greater intellect and broader life experience. They have little understanding of people with outstanding talent and resort to applying formulas in their decision-making when interacting with talented individuals. And they tend to make a career of their positions. On the other hand, members of the former group often have talent and move on to other jobs. Hernandez offers the caveat that there are exceptions to her characterizations of these two groups.

If her characterization of these people as mediocre is valid, what are the consequences of this? Are mediocre people more likely to stick to the norm? Are mediocre people more likely to be concerned about job security? What are the implications of this on their problem-solving and interacting with non–European Americans? Are academically mediocre Whites less willing to accept people who are different—such as minorities? Are academically mediocre Whites able to analyze and go beyond the usual prescribed criteria—which is geared toward members of their own ethnic group? If mediocrity is a valid characterization of European American personnel in higher education, we cannot accept this situation for non–European Americans working with college minority students. We need non–European American personnel and counselors who are better trained than the present generation of European American college administrators and personnel. We need new people who can problem-solve, who can explore new and different ways of doing things. We need people who can deviate from the norm and develop mechanisms to attract, process, teach, and provide therapy to a more diverse population.

MENTAL HEALTH TRAINING AND THE POOR

Although there may be differences between the counselor educator and non–European American students, the differences between the European American mental health professional and non–European American clients are even more pronounced: The clients have not been through the same educational acculturation process as the European American and non–

European American counselors. Often, when the European American counselor interacts with the European American client, there is compatibility of ethnicity, values, socioeconomic class, and so on. There can almost be a friendship quality between the European American mental health professional and the European American client. Both participants in the therapeutic interaction know their roles and functions—for example, the client is to talk about feelings and the therapist is supposed to facilitate this process. When the European American mental health professional interacts with the non–European American client, there can be multiple differences; for example, the minority client may view the exploration of feelings as intrusive, and the exhibiting of these feelings in the context of the client's ethnic cohort may be dysfunctional and may leave the client vulnerable to ridicule and insults. These differences, along with the history of one group's behavior toward the other, can inhibit interactions and effective therapy. If we do not close the gap between the two groups, the division will increase.

NECESSARY AND SUFFICIENT SKILLS

The purpose of counselor and psychology education programs is to teach and train counselors and therapists. It is logical for counseling and therapy educators to impart the skills and knowledge that they have. However, for those interested in providing services to non–European American populations, this should only be the beginning of the process. The next step is for students to develop their own models and approaches and to increase their understanding of providing effective services for non-European American populations. For those training students to work with non–European populations, the measure of a mental health professional educator's success could be the degree to which that teacher graduates students who are interested in helping, who are creative, and who are willing to explore. In addition to their regular curriculum, mental health professional educators could train those who provide services to non-European populations to develop alternative ideas, techniques, problems, and solutions.

One could raise the argument that there is little room for incorporating into counseling programs non–European American issues, ideas, or alternative approaches and techniques. A counterpoint to this argument is to question the value and validity of what is presently being taught in our curriculum (Hagen, 1997; Procidano, Busch-Rossnagel, Reznikoff, & Geisinger, 1995; Stern, 1984.) Instead of using ad hominem appeals, if one uses quantifiable, scientific measures, psychotherapy has a long history of critics as to its effectiveness (e.g., Eysenck, 1952; Szasz, 1974, 1978). With the exception of behavioral approaches, there is very little good research to substantiate that the present approaches and techniques are of better therapeutic value than no treatment or treatment with alternative approaches and techniques (e.g., pet and plant therapy). However, what is clear is that these approaches and techniques are ones that fit the characteristics already endemic to the White middle class—the ability to use words and talk about their feelings. A study by Illovsky (1993) raises questions as to the effectiveness of counselor knowledge. In this study, the mental and physical health of master's- and doctoral-level mental health professionals were compared to those not in the mental health field. The results failed to reject the hypothesis that there was no difference in measures of the physical and mental health of people trained in mental health techniques (therapists) and those not trained in mental health techniques. This calls to question the value of what is taught to help us deal with our problems. It is suspected that the divorce rate of counselors (even among marital counselors) and laypeople will be the same. If the counseling skills that are taught and exercised by counselors do not necessarily help those counselors then questions can be raised as to the efficacy of the skills that they are taught and that they use on their clients; therefore, why not encourage European Americans to explore other approaches and techniques?

Bergin and Garfield (1994) report studies that found that there is not much difference in therapeutic effectiveness between experienced and inexperienced therapists. In terms of diagnosing, Walter Mischel (1968) wrote that

> In general, studies show no clear advantage for trained judges; psychologists are not consistently better or worse than nonpsychologists (e.g., secretaries, college students, nurses), and clinical training and experience usually [do] not improve the accuracy of global judgments (e.g., Danet, 1965; Goldberg, 1959; Kremers, 1960; Luft, 1951; Soskin, 1959). If anything, clinical training and experience may be somewhat detrimental and reduce judgmental accuracy, or at least introduce systematic biases such as a greater emphasis on pathology and less favorable prognoses (e.g., Soskin, 1954; 1959; Taft, 1955). Sarbin, Taft, and Bailey (1960), in their review of studies comparing trained and untrained judges, reach a similarly negative conclusions. (p. 116)

There has been a lot of attention justifying therapeutic services based on client satisfaction ("Mental health . . . ," 1995). If mental health professionals were to justify the effectiveness of their services through the client's satisfaction with counseling and therapeutic services, then they would be on spurious grounds. The justification of counseling based on people's perceptions that therapy has helped needs to also consider if similar results would be obtained with other approaches and techniques that are not usually taught in counseling programs. For example, can the same effects be obtained through prayer, plants, pets, crystals, bibliotherapy, belief in the therapist, and a multitude of other approaches and techniques? These and a host of other interventions have been found to be helpful in alleviating problems and obtaining satisfaction from those treated (American Psychosomatic Society, 1995; Castelnuovo-Tedesco, 1991; Fisher & Greenberg, 1989; Frank, 1991; International Journal of Psychosomatics, 1984; Jerome, 1989; Jospe, 1978; Simmons, 2001; Turner, Gallimore, & Fox-Henning, 1980; White, Tursky, & Schwartz, 1985).

There are also the effects and functions of education, inservice, and professional development programs that are directed at training European Americans to deal with non–European Americans. These programs do not deal with the crux of many of the mental health problems of non–European Americans—lack of power, unemployment, underemployment, and racism. The function of educational, inservice, and professional development programs is to train mental health professionals in the maintenance of the status quo. This provides the illusion that something is being done. It does not address the issue that the mental health professionals are themselves a great part of the problem. It is very much like the training and education of overseers of slaves and of colonial civil servants. They can be trained to have a benevolent attitude. They can be trained to follow professional standards. They could have good intentions. Within the framework of their perceptions and ethos, they may even do good work. However, they have adjusted themselves to inequities and racism. Their efforts neglect the essence of the problems of people they control and are supposed to serve: lack of power, lack of meaningful employment opportunities, and racism.

In his book *Power and Illness*, Krause (1977) wrote that health care is the product of political, economic, and social factors. These are controlled by forces outside the community. His analyses focus on the medical system. However, what he wrote is equally apropos to the mental health system. He wrote that "Power is presently being used by those who possess it against the interests of the majority of citizens, and yet most people are only dimly aware of what is going on" (p. xi). In his chapter on "The American System: Have and Have-Nots," he wrote that within the health care system there are tiers among the service providers. These tiers serve as barriers to those without power and of lower status and hinder them from obtaining the training and credentials to move up into controlling positions. In terms of the provision of services, he wrote that there is a two-class system: one is for the poor and the other is for the rest of society. This results in segregated services—with poor communities having poorer facilities, as well as overworked staff who are also underpaid and who frequently have negative perceptions of their clientele. This may engender the poor staying away from service providers and resorting to them only under dire circumstance. The poor may have different definitions of what constitutes good and bad care. They may find the geographic location where the service provider is located to be inconvenient (e.g., they may not have the means to go to the facility). They may encounter intrusive questions and bureaucratic labyrinths that act more as barriers than as expeditious access to services.

Sue (1995b) wrote that in order for the counseling profession to meet the needs of racial, ethnic, and cultural groups, the profession needs to broaden its definition of counseling. He wrote that the present definitions of counseling are too narrow and should include understanding and interacting with the organizational and social barriers to minority mental health. He goes on to describe the reasons for the reluctance of counselors to expand their horizons to meet the needs of minorities. The reasons include

- Counselor roles are defined; if counselors assume other roles and functions, then these are not defined as counseling.
- There is a common belief that the key to therapy is to understand internal processes. The assumption is that there is some deficit in the person; this is the preferred mode of providing treatment, rather than by dealing with organizational and social factors that induced the problems.
- Counselors believe that the therapeutic elements of counseling occur in their office. They believe that dealing with organizational systems is not relevant to their work. They do not realize that they are dealing with organizational systems whenever they do counseling: their roles and functions are dictated by organizational rules, regulations, and policies—who they can see as clients, the length of treatment, and the definition of what counseling consists of, which services will be reimbursable, and so on, are controlled. Sue wrote that for counselors to do effective counseling, to maintain the integrity of counseling, and to protect the client when institutions place their own needs before those of the client, counselors need organizational knowledge and skills to work with organizational systems that impact them and their clients.
- Counselors are trained to use remedial and clinical approaches. They are trained to deal with the aftermath of problems. "Would it not make more sense to take a proactive and preventative approach by attacking the cultural and institutional bases of the problem?" (Sue, 1995b, p. 476).
- Sue challenges the view that dealing with organizational changes belongs to the realm of industrial/organizational psychologists. He wrote that we should learn from industrial/organizational psychologists in order to be more effective in protecting the interests of the counseling profession and the client. In addition, we should learn from industrial/organizational psychologists because such knowledge can help impact the curriculum and operations of the monocultural models and approaches of education and psychology programs—and of our professional organizations.

Fostering awareness of relevant impinging systems and showing clients how to control and use them can also be of therapeutic value for the client. Axelson (1993) wrote, "Supporting clients and showing them how they might advantageously confront the imperfections and complexities of the system will help counteract impressions of powerlessness" (p. 255).

Therapeutic Approaches

If counselors and therapists had been at work during the pre–Revolutionary War period, they would have counseled their clients to look within themselves and learn ways to manage their anger and their frustration at having troops quartered in their homes and at their second-class status. If counselors and therapists had been at work during the pre–Civil War period, they would have counseled slaves to look within themselves and learn ways to deal with oppression and the yearning for freedom as a solution to their being beaten and having their families being torn from them (slaves who wanted to escape slavery purportedly had a psychiatric disease that was diagnosed as "drapetomania"). If counselors and therapists had been at work with Native Americans before the turn of the last century, they would have counseled Native Americans to examine themselves when they had problems with depression, alcohol abuse, sexual diseases, and social anomy as a result of Whites introducing genocidal practices, diseases, alcohol, and so on. If counselors and therapists had been at work at the turn of the century, they would have counseled Chinese males who were lonely and depressed to look within themselves and adjust and develop coping skills as solutions to immigration laws that prevented the immigration of Chinese females and prevented Chinese males from marrying. From these examples, it may become obvious to some readers that social, economic, and political conditions can have an impact on people's mental health and that intrapsychic counseling may not be the most relevant approach to alleviating the problems encountered by these groups of people.

Recently, those involved in cross-cultural therapy have developed models and approaches that challenge the manner in which we are providing therapy to cross-cultural clients. Ivey (1995) wrote, "Counseling is in the midst of a revolution, but many counselors and therapists remain unaware that it is even happening. Specifically, we are learning that our present theories and techniques are bound up with a particular and necessarily limited cultural framework" (p. 53). He discussed one of the central focuses of therapy—individualism: "The individualism usually associated with traditional psychology is not eliminated, but is recognized for what it is—a cultural variant, most likely appropriate for those from a European American background (p. 70). It is increasingly being recognized that the traditional counseling and therapeutic models, approaches, and techniques are the expressions of European values and perceptions and that these are just one set of a host of other ways of treating mental health problems. Multicultural counseling and therapy (MCT) is increasingly being recognized as another approach that can be used.

In comparing traditional approaches with MCT, one can find the following:

- Traditional approaches focus on the individual. Psychoanalytic, humanistic, and cognitive-behavioral approaches have been criticized for emphasizing social adjustment and focus on the self. Therapy is primarily concerned with maintaining the status quo. There is only perfunctory acknowledgment, as well as interventions, in regard to recognizing and changing the context of the individual's problems. There is little recognition that social, political, and economic factors can have an impact on psychological and physical health. Conversely, MCT approaches look at the client in relationship to others and in relationship to the context and culture the person is in.
- The traditional approaches were developed from the works of a single person or from small groups of individuals, whereas MCT developed, and is developing, from a collage of multiple sources and experiences.
- Western and present American therapies entail hierarchical interactions in which the therapist is in charge and in control. The therapist is considered the expert. Distinctions between the therapist and client are clear. With therapy as it is presently practiced, the therapist is the expert and defines reality (e.g., what is normal and healthy behavior). In MCT, however, the therapist and client are partners in exploration; there is generous giving to each other. Problems are posed and the therapist and client—or group—work together, in an egalitarian activity to find answers. Answers can include looking at the context of the problems. Therapy can consist of making not only personal changes but also changes in the systems that impact the client and the community. Problems (including internal ones, such as self-identity) are viewed in the context of others. Cheatham, Ivey, Ivey, and Simek-Morgan (1993) and Ivey (1993) provide more specific skills and strategies for helping clients using this framework.

Perhaps we can apply ideas and approaches from liberation psychology to help minorities and the poor. Liberation psychology gets many of its ideas from liberation theology. Liberation theology has proponents in South America, where religious workers think that a moral and ethical person has an obligation to correct injustices toward those who are exploited and who are poor. Ignacio Martín Baro in *Towards a Psychology of Liberation* (Aron & Corne, 1994) wrote that when we serve the poor, we need to de-

velop assumptions in psychology that relate to the poor—rather than believe that the assumptions developed by mainstream psychology are apropos for everyone. Needs are identified, rather than problems. Individuals,
families, and communities are not necessarily viewed as dysfunctional; instead, problems could be defined in terms of the inequitable distribution
and use of power. The client is viewed as a partner in activities, not as a
patient or client. Oppression is viewed as part of the problem, and social
change is viewed as part of the cure. Liberation psychology aims at long-
term processes of empowerment and the promotion of dignity. Martín Baro
wrote of our blindness to institutional violence toward the poor, the uses
and misuses of the media and religion, and the essential connection between mental health, human rights, and the struggle against injustice.

Alsup (2000), drawing from Ignacio Martín Baro's works, wrote that
liberation psychology uses psychological services to promote self-
determination. Alsup wrote about the practice of psychological genocide
toward Native Americans by mainstream psychologists. Creative social action is advocated. He wrote that we need to free ourselves from elitist at-
tachments and the power structures that we serve. We need to be creative
and not dogmatic. We need to develop healthy individuals and communities. We need to confront the political and economic injustices that are
responsible for the debits of basic needs in our communities and that create despair and drain motivation. Direct action is needed to create nonvio-
lent, democratic communities. We need to develop systems that stymie the
diseases of poverty, sexism, racism, and violence. "An authentic liberation
psychologist embodied in his social creativity models the virtues of kindness, selflessness, civility, firmness, courage, lawfulness, self-mastery, love,
and Truth." Alsup (2000) wrote that liberation psychology outlines 10 categories of qualities for a good life: physical requirements; trust and hope;
safety, security, and competence; uniqueness, gender, and culture; respect,
love, and nonviolence; courage, creativity, and exploration; belonging, affiliation, and attachment; power and justice; liberation, freedom, and self-
determination; and spirituality, prayer, and service.

Power Dynamics

Power has its own dynamics in this country, whereby those with power
develop systems and mechanisms to maintain and perpetuate themselves
(DiNitto & Dye, 1987; Domhoff, 1971, 1978, 1980, 1990, 1996; Domhoff &
Dye, 1987; Dye, 1971, 1976, 1998, 1999, 2000, 2001; Dye, Gibson, &
Robinson, 1999; Dye, Greene, & Parthemos, 1980; Dye & Zeigler, 2000;
Mills, 1995; Zweigenhaft & Domhoff, 1982, 1998). This process excludes
minorities from obtaining, exercising, and developing meaningful power
and making relevant changes. The perception is fostered that there are

positive qualities in those with power, and those without power are lacking some of these positive qualities. However, this may be inaccurate—those with power may have attained their positions because of their affiliations with the power holders (e.g., they share similar ethnicity and social-economic backgrounds) and not necessarily because they have such qualities as being smarter, harder working, and so forth.

European Americans control this country through power—economic, political, social, and military power. Because the effects of power on minorities are so profound, this section of the chapter examines the dynamics of power. Such an examination provides insight into aspects of the mental health profession that are not usually examined. It provides some insight into what might occur during a therapy session. It provides awareness of forces that impact minority communities. And it serves as an example that the relevant factors that impact minority mental health are not necessarily treated in the typical therapeutic session.

There has been an enormous amount of material written on the sociology and psychology of power. Many authors draw on Max Weber, Marx, C. Wright Mills, capitalistic theorists, and so on. More recently, much of the literature on power is coming from women writers. They view power dynamics as being relevant to our daily lives and permeating our society. Their analyses are usually from the perspective of White males interacting with females. But their analyses might provide insight into those who control the systems in this society that affect minorities—and how we react to them.

The dynamics of power in organizational settings is highly relevant to counselors and therapists. Counselors and therapists are trained in organizational settings, by professors who work under organizational parameters. Almost by definition, counselors and therapists who interact with non–European Americans are agents of institutions: They work for state, municipal, and other bureaucracies. They work in such organizational settings as schools, colleges, universities, mental health agencies, hospitals, social services, human services, the military, and so on. However, there has not been much scientific investigation into the characteristics of those who work in bureaucratic settings. What draws them to work in these settings? What is the impact of bureaucracies on those who work in them? Is there a selection process in regard to who works for organizations? Are these people who want to be taken care of by others? Do people who are independent, creative, or risk-takers avoid working in institutions and in the counseling professions? Are people who are attracted to working in institutions those who are willing to sacrifice their values and cater to organizational values? This may have tremendous ramifications in regard to their perceptions of reality and in terms of what they bring into the counseling session. For example, does the mental health professional's dependence on institutions project onto his or her clients? Do counselors induce client dependence on institutions and counselors? Are the counselors' and therapists' activities directed toward organizational needs rather than toward therapeutic needs? For example, Cripe (2002) wrote that the original main function of clinical records was to help communications between clinicians and as aids to the clinician's memory. Nowadays, their function is to appease administrators, reviewers, and other third parties and to avoid litigation and the displeasure of quality control members. The assumption is that the better the records, the better the care. Cripe reviewed the present purposes of record keeping and wrote that nowadays records do not necessarily provide the accurate and valid information that is sought (to avoid litigation, for quality assurance, etc.), and, "The more obsessive writer is not necessarily the more accurate observer or the better clinician" (Cripe, 2002, p. 8). Thus, catering to institutional demands does not necessarily improve client care.

Do bureaucracies attract those with greater tendencies to respond to authority and power? If so, what are some of the dynamics that might be operating? The following are some of the views of authors in regard to power dynamics. A number of authors have noted that power permeates our lives (Masserman, 1972). Schimel (1972) wrote that power relations exist in the family, in therapy, in our schools, on the job, in professional organizations, in the government, and in international affairs. Eric Fromm (1969) wrote that many of us have the tendency to relinquish our freedoms. He wrote that some people have an innate desire to control and dominate others; for most of us, along with the desire for freedom, there is also the innate desire to submit, to cater to overt power and to internalized authorities. Fromm's book explores the dynamics of why humans try to escape the freedoms we can have and why we choose to be controlled and submit to those who want to control us. The power I am referring to here is not the healthy individual power we may try to inculcate in our clients, that is, the power that comes from good ego strength and a firm self-esteem. This provides us with the basis to enjoy other people and to endure ambivalence and uncertaintly. The power I am referring to is the power one person or group has over others. This kind of power is often accompanied by anxiety, apprehension, impaired intimacy, and ongoing obsessional struggles over self and others (Schimel, 1972). Chancer (1992), along with others (e.g., Bierber, 1972), views the dynamics of power as a sadomasochistic phenomenon. Chancer applies existentialism and psychoanalysis to examining why and how we submit to power and incur powerlessness in our personal lives, in our workplaces, and, on a larger scale, in our political lives. She wrote that "Rather than sadomasochism being merely the property of individuals, our culture itself is deeply oriented in a sadomasochism direction. We are living in a society sadomasochistic in that it bombards us with experiences of domination and subordination far more regularly than it exposes us to sensations and inklings of freedom and reciprocity" (p. 2). She described how bureaucracies promulgate hierarchies, dependencies, and superior versus inferior roles. She, along with many others who analyze hierarchies and group behaviors, draws heavily on the works of Max Weber. Her analysis of bureaucratic behavior is interesting; for example, she describes the paradoxes and ironies of the position of bosses. Bosses want to control others. They want such control not only to have power over others, but they also want control because they feel that power will put less limitations and restriction on them and will make them less vulnerable. However, when they assume power and have control over their peers, they will be limited and restricted because their control is mitigated by their attempts to seek the approval of their superiors, by their attempts to ingratiate themselves to those they supervise, and by their vulnerability to their superior's whims. Thus, the lose control over their own lives. Chancer wrote that hierarchical divisions provide attributions of superiority to those who are in charge and inferiority to those who are controlled. Those in charge will want occasional resistance, so that they can exert their power. Those in charge will try to initiate changes so there will be resistance and then will want compliance so that there will be demonstrations of loyalty from subordinates. Chancer and others who study power have provided interesting dimensions to human and bureaucratic behavior.

Many of the problems endemic to minority mental health are related to power—lack of power to control their lives, having to deal with those who control their lives, and so on. It would behoove minorities to examine the dynamics of power in their lives and determine better ways of responding.

Politics and Economics

Although counselors and therapists may not see the relevance of power and politics in ethnic minorities' lives, it is interesting to note how they see the relevance in their own lives. Mental health professionals' political activities are usually directed toward self-aggrandizement—for example, licensure, third party reimbursement, grants, and so forth. As with all professions in this country, the function of professional organizations is to increase their clout and benefits. This is usually ritualistically done, with the excuse that the profession's activities are for the purpose of protecting or helping the public. The mental health professions are no exception. For example, the American Counseling Association (2000) stated that in addition to its activities of obtaining more positions and funding for counselors, "too often we focus on the services, communications and discounts of membership" and "membership offers a number of very substantial and tangible benefits, from financial savings to better communications" (pp. 22, 29).

Van den Berghe (1972) wrote, "It is much safer to study the psychody-namics of racism rather than its economics, or to study the culture of pov-erty as distinguished from the politics of oppression" (p. 235). The provision of mental health services in minority communities is considered by many to be a benign, altruistic, benevolent activity. Certainly, this is the image that the profession seeks to impart. However, other aspects to this relation-ship are not mentioned—that is, the economic effects of counseling. What are the economic repercussions of European American mental health pro-fessionals working in non–European American communities and with non–European American clients? One can make a case that counselors and therapists perpetuate the economic, political, and social effects that Ameri-can society, in general, has on minority communities. That is, the relation-ship is an exploitive, mercantile, and imperialistic one. It is more concerned with maintaining the status quo than it is with dealing with the real issues that pertain to the mental health of ethnic minorities.

Colonialism

Although there are different definitions of colonialism, the definitions could be divided into those offered from three perspectives: the European, that the former colonies and underdeveloped countries, and a third perspec-tive (Colony, 1973). The European definition is more restrictive and con-sists of defining a colony as a dependency without full government, with administrative functions being held by a mother country; the colony is pre-vented from developing its own laws and from making its own decisions in regard to social, economic, and political matters; in addition, laws are made by the mother country and enforced by agents outside the community. Another definition, often offered by former colonies and underdeveloped countries in Asia, Africa, and Latin America, is broader. Under this broader definition, a colony is any territory whose economic and political systems are controlled by outside entities. This does not mean that the colony does not have its own economic and political structures, but it does mean that those outside the community control these structures and functions and ultimate decision-making. The third definition, offered by independent observers, defines a colony as a territory where social, economic, and po-litical conditions are greatly influenced by outside forces.

Mercantilism

Mercantilism (Encyclopaedia Brittanica, 1973) is an economic theory that stated that there is a fixed amount of wealth available; therefore, if a group wants to prosper, the net worth of exports must be greater than that of the imports, or the group has to conquer and keep the resources of others. It was an operating model in Europe from the 16th to the 18th century and accompanied European imperialism and colonialism. It promoted the interest of the state and major entrepreneur interests at the expense of rivals. The British replaced this system—at least, theoretically—with a commonwealth model, in which all participating counties (former colonies) worked in collaboration with each other, to promote the common interest of all the participants.

Blauner (1969) and Moore (1970) are among those who view the relationship between minority and majority communities with a colonial model. This relationship is similar to the one that the mother country had to its colonies during the European mercantile and imperialistic period. Non–European American communities are prevented from developing themselves because they are prevented from having access to the factors needed for their development. The mercantile system that developed under the imperialistic model entailed a mother country (country of greater technology and military might) going into countries of lesser technology. There, the mother country treated the country of lesser technology as a consumer of the products of the mother country. The country of lesser technology was prevented from developing personnel and systems necessary for its own development (these were monopolized by the mother country).

The net result of the economic and political interactions of the outside community with the minority and ethnic communities is similar to that of a "mother" country with a colony under the mercantile system. When one examines the economies of poor and minority communities, one finds analogs for the colonial and mercantile systems. Minority and poor communities are often treated as consumers of the goods and services of the group in power. Minority communities are consumers of cigarettes, alcohol, mental health and health care services, police and educational services, and so on. Minority communities provide a living (with the outside consumer exporting goods and services to them) to the outside groups. Endogenous systems are not developed. Systems that are developed are controlled by outside groups. Though outside groups employ some endogenous individuals, they are often employed for reasons that may not be in the best interest of the endogenous groups—for example, to help control members of their own group, to prevent rebellion, and to provide a façade that members of the endogenous ethnic cohort are being employed and have control over their own communities. Endogenous community members are also siphoned off from the community to serve the needs of systems outside the community.

Under mercantilism and imperialism, the businesses, banks, universities, and so forth that were needed to develop the economy and train the personnel were not developed—leaving the country of lesser technology perpetually poor and serving as a consumer of the outside force's products and services. Similarly, when one examines the higher rate of employment of European American counselors/therapists, and the lower rate of employment among non-European clients, questions are raised as to the reasons and ramifications of this. The lower rates of non–European Americans' admissions to counseling programs and the lower number of non–European American counselors/therapists in the field have the effect of European American mental health professionals taking the place of non–European Americans in the provision of counseling services. This adds to the lack of training and higher unemployment among non–European Americans. The non–European American community is in a situation of constantly being the consumer of services delivered by personnel (e.g., mental health professionals) who are trained by, for, and as European Americans. The non–European American community is serviced by mental health professionals trained by universities outside the community. The non–European American community is not being empowered to develop its own systems and train personnel to analyze and meet its own needs.

The exploitive and detrimental aspects of the mental health professionals interaction with minorities need to be examined. More beneficial and constructive approaches to minorities need to be developed.

3

—◄○►—

Minority Mental Health Research

Examination of minority mental health research is important for a number of reasons, including the following: Billions of dollars have been poured into minority mental health. Research in this area affects the lives of millions of people. It defines our problems. It directs where and how our resources are spent. It is the foundation upon which our information is based. It helps define our perceptions of the American population. It influences what is taught in our training problems and in the delivery of services. A great deal of the material in this book is based on research data. The past and present data on minorities are based on research; it is assumed that the future data will be as well. Therefore, it behooves us to examine the research upon which so much of our information is based and that helps direct the allocation of resources.

The research in this area is often conflicting and confusing; some of the factors that may impact the study of ethnic minority mental health data collection and research are examined in this chapter. The confounding factors that are examined include impediments in the accumulation of accurate national data, the effects of culture on psychopathology, the diagnostic and data-gathering process, the assessment instruments that are used, the methods of data gathering and classification, and the misuses of minority data in society by researchers, institutions, and administrators.

MINORITIES IN THE GENERAL MENTAL HEALTH LITERATURE

There is a need to have a more diverse representation in the selection, analysis, and publication of psychological information. Gary VandenBos, APA's executive director of publications and communications, stated (as cited in Carpenter, 2001) that in the last 5 years, only about 4.5% of ad-hoc

63

editorial reviewers were known members of ethnic minority groups. Linda Garcia-Shelton, the associate editor of *Professional Psychology: Research and Practice*, observes (as cited in Carpenter, 2001) that when participants of a study are predominately White, there is less of tendency to challenge the generalizability of the findings. However, if the participants in the study are predominately ethnic minorities, then there is a tendency to view the limitations of the generalizabilty of the study. APA editors have long called for more minority participants in the review of journals. This would help deal with the biases in the selection and review of journals and would broaden the perspectives of the journals (Carpenter, 2001).

Pope-Davis, Ligiero, Liang, and Codrington (2001) reported that reviews of other journals indicated that there has been an increase in the publication of ethnic minority articles. For example, Ponterotto's (1988) analysis of the *Journal of Counseling Psychology* between 1976 and 1986 indicated that 6% of the articles were on ethnic minorities. Perez, Constantine, and Gerard's (2000) review of this same journal between 1988 and 1997 found that 12% of the articles were on ethnic minorities.

Pope-Davis et al. (2001) reviewed the content of articles published between 1985 and 1999 in the *Journal of Multicultural Counseling and Development*. They found that the group most written about was African Americans. In terms of content, multicultural competence/counseling accounted for 21% of the published articles, psychosocial adjustment/development accounted for 14%, multicultural training/curriculum 10%, and worldview articles 9%; 8% were on women, and 6% on men. Older persons were written about the least (1%). And about 3% of the articles were on religion, disability, sexual orientation, and other forms of diversity. About 48% were expository or descriptive, 47% were quantitative, and 3% were original qualitative research. There were redundant calls to do periodic reviews and summaries of the literature. Although Atkinson and Thompson (1992) are cited as stating that there should be more focus on racioethnic identity, acculturation, and cultural mistrust, only 4% of the articles were on identity development, 2% on acculturation, and 2% on racism, discrimination, and prejudice. Little was written on the subgroups of the major ethnic groups, career development, academic achievement, indigenous models of healing/alternative treatment, assessment, systemic influences, professional issues, religion, sexual orientation, disabilities, or middle-aged and older persons.

MINORITY MENTAL HEALTH RESEARCH

Although the use of large-scale surveys to determine the prevalence of psychiatric disorders in noninstitutional populations began around the 1950s with the Midtown Manhattan Study (Vega & Rumbaut, 1991), accurate national data in terms of types and rates of minority mental health problems have yet to be obtained. These are some impediments to the accumulation of minority mental health data:

- Survey instruments are needed that can express and measure what is desired to be measured with cross-cultural populations.
- There can be confounding factors that limit accuracy and validity of the data that are gathered. For example, some minority members may be suspicious of inquiries by data gatherers, and therefore may not participate in information-gathering attempts, or they may provide incomplete or inaccurate information (e.g., some minorities may modify their responses based on the data gatherers' ethnicity or gender); they may underutilize the use of a site that provides the data—for example, Asian women may frequent a clinic at lower rates than European American women do because they are more reluctant to deal with sexual issues.
- Data are obtained only at selective sites, with specific problems, with specific populations—for example, a study might provide incidences of HIV/AIDS cases reported by Puerto Ricans in some New York hospitals.
- There could be differences in definitions and expressions of mental health problems among minority groups and between minority groups and European Americans; for example, in terms of the definition of problems, the use of peyote among some Native Americans may be viewed as a healthy, spiritually enhancing activity, whereas in the European American community, this is defined as an illegal, deviant activity that is indicative of an Adjustment Disorder, a Substance Abuse, or an Oppositional Defiant Disorder.
- The resources do not exist to coordinate and obtain minority mental health data on a national scale.

Plans are in place to obtain better data—surveys are being funded through grants provided by such federal agencies as the National Institute of Mental Health (1994, 1995b, 2000b, 2001) and the National Institute on Alcohol Abuse and Alcoholism (2000). According to Joan G. Abell (chief, Information Resources and Inquiries Branch Office of Communication, and public liaison, National Institute of Mental Health), "The Institute has several large ongoing epidemiological studies designed to answer many questions which will help us better understand mental outcomes in minority populations. However, data from these studies will not be available for several years" (May 1, 2001, personal e-mail communication). The federal government's attempts to accumulate national data will be valuable, but will inevitably raise more questions and controversy—just as the U.S. Census's attempts to gain an accurate count of the U.S. population have raised a ruckus (e.g., U.S. Department of Commerce . . . 1998). Ethnic minority mental health data collection and research have always been controversial (and in the political arena) because these data help define who we are, what the problems are, and where we should direct our resources.

CULTURE AND PSYCHOPATHOLOGY

Regeser-Lopez and Guarnaccia (2000) reviewed cultural psychopathology research from 1988 through 1998. They found that despite the fact that much has been learned in this area of study, very little of it is being communicated to mainstream investigators. Their review indicates that recidivism and relapse rates, symptoms, severity, definitions, and perceptions of psychopathology are influenced by values, beliefs, culture, and the environment. They also reviewed some of the problems in cross-cultural research—problems of interpretation, validity, reliability, approaches, instruments, survey techniques, item comparability, and so on. They drew on the research of many investigators. Although this chapter reports on some of their findings, the reader is encouraged to refer to their article for the sources from which they make their comments. Their article also contains references to other summaries.

Regeser-Lopez and Guarnaccia (2000) reported that in studies of distress and psychopathology, problems have been operationalized through the examination of specific values and beliefs. This has helped advance the course of examining the effects of culture on mental problems. For example, researchers have found that both internal factors, such as values and beliefs, and external factors, such as cultural expectations and harsh environment, can affect the expression of distress and psychopathology.

Regeser-Lopez and Guarnaccia also found that researchers in ethnic studies have made it clear that culture is a process and not a static entity. The process of culture is changing with the life histories and circumstances of the group. It changes and evolves with intracultural diversity and with social class, poverty, and gender. These processes affect different levels of mental health, both within and across cultural groups. They report that research is attempting to delineate general processes that occur across cultures, general processes that occur within a culture, and specific processes that are unique to certain groups and individuals (e.g., processes unique to females, lesbians and gay males, those with depression, etc.).

They wrote that researchers have pointed out the importance of the revised *DSM-IV* and the *World Mental Health Report* (Desjarlais, Eisenberg, Good, & Kleinman, 1995). Three important contributions of the *DSM-IV* are presented; (a) it points out the importance of cultural factors in the expression, assessment, and prevalence mental health problems; (b) there is an outline of clinical diagnosis to complement the multiaxial format; and (c) there is a glossary that contains some culture-bound syndromes. The group that was responsible for investigating the cultural aspects of the *DSM-IV* was the *DSM-IV* Culture and Diagnosis Task Force. Desjarlais et al. (1995) reported that more complete results of the *DSM-IV* Culture and Diagnosis Task Force's findings are available in the *DSM-IV Sourcebook* (Mezzich, Kleinman, Fabrega, Parron, & Good, 1997) and in such publications as a special issue of *Psychiatric Clinics of North America* (Alarcon, 1995), a special issue of *Transcultural Psychiatry* (Kirmayer, 1998), and a compilation of relevant papers (Mezzich, Kleinman, Fabrega, & Patron, 1996).

There have been a number of criticisms of the *DSM-IV*'s approach to cultural issues. Among the criticisms are the following: The *DSM-IV* has not included many definitions and syndromes seen in other cultures; disorders such as anorexia nervosa and chronic fatigue—considered by some to be phenomena shaped by North American culture—have been excluded from the "Glossary of Culture Bound Syndromes"; and the *DSM-IV* conveys the impression that it is an objective, universal clinical diagnostic document, when it is actually an expression of a particular culture. The cultural aspects of it are not simply the syndromes in the "Glossary of Culture Bound Syndromes"—the entire manual is a heavily loaded glossary of culture-bound values, perceptions, definitions, and syndromes.

The *World Mental Health Report* (Desjarlais et al., 1995) is another important contribution to the mental health field and to the study of ethnic mental health. It is important because it is an attempt to define, catalog, provide incidence rates, and make comparisons across cultures. It demonstrates clearly the role the environment plays in the range of mental health and behavioral problems—for example, that lack of employment and social support can lead to substance abuse. There is strong evidence that hunger, work, and education can play a role in determining whether a person adapts or fails to adapt to stressors and problems presented by the environment. As with the *DSM-IV*, there are also critics of the *World Mental Health Report*. Among the criticisms are that the data are inaccurate because of reporting problems and differences in definitions. For example, different countries have different numbers of medical and mental health professionals. This may result in higher rates of reporting for those countries with more service providers. And despite the fact that the World Mental Health project tries to standardize diagnostic categories and criteria, there is still enough flexibility for service providers to vary in their definitions.

Though there are many differences between the *DSM-IV* and the *World Mental Health Report*, both clearly show that mental disorders and the investigation of cultures should not be the sole concern of a group of cross-cultural specialists—all users of the *DSM-IV*, policy makers, mental health researchers, and practitioners should be aware of the role that culture plays in mental health. Accordingly, they should change their approaches and techniques when conceptualizing problems and interacting with those with mental problems.

In Regeser-Lopez and Guarnaccia's (2000) examination of the literature on culture and psychopathology, they focused on anxiety, schizophrenia, and childhood psychopathology. Their review indicated that culture shapes, modifies, and defines almost all aspects of mental health. For example, they report the research on *ataque de nervios*. This is a feature prominent among Latinos from the Caribbean and often follows a stressful event related to family or significant others (e.g., death, divorce). A general feature of *ataque de nervios* is a feeling of loss of control, sometimes followed by amnesia, and then usually followed by a quick return to previous levels of functioning. The numerous studies done with Puerto Ricans living in the United States found that those who experienced these attacks frequently had problems with significant others in their lives. These attacks were also often associated with a wide range of mental disorders—frequently, anxiety and mood disorders. The group that most often experienced this disorder was women, older than 45 years, from lower socioeconomic backgrounds, with little power, and with disrupted social relations (e.g., jeopardized marriages). There was a clear relationship between those who experienced this disorder and the conditions they encountered in their environments.

In their review of the cross-cultural literature on psychoses and schizophrenia, Regeser-Lopez and Guarnaccia (2000) reported that researchers repeatedly found connections with cultural environments. They reviewed studies in which it was found that schizophrenia affected individuals and communities differently. The differences were attributed to whether the culture perceived the person with schizophrenia as being autonomous or connected to the community. They reported lines of research conducted by the World Health Organization (WHO), in which it was found that there was a connection between the course of schizophrenia and family climate. Interestingly, there were studies indicating that schizophrenia in developing countries had a more favorable course than in developed countries. There were no cogent explanations as to why this was the case. They reported on studies of Mexican Americans who had psychotic problems. They found that those who returned to families with warmth and support were less likely to relapse. This was in contrast to those who returned to families that were not warm and supportive—that is, families high on criticism, hostility, and emotional involvement. Persons who returned to such families were more likely to relapse. Studies conducted in Italy and Yugoslavia also found that warmth was related to the course of the schizophrenia. However, there was no such relationship in the studies done of Anglo-Americans in the United States. Family warmth was not predictive of relapse for the Anglo-American person with schizophrenia who returned to the Anglo-American family. In such a family, whether the person returned to a family high on criticism was more predictive of relapse; in other words, an individual who returned to an Anglo-American family that was highly critical of him or her was more likely to relapse.

Other studies have also shown that psychological clinical syndromes are not entirely the purview of intrapsychic, internal, individual phenomena. In studies with Thai children, it was found that children with mental problems were more likely to internalize their problems (e.g., anxiety and depression), whereas U.S. children were more likely to externalize their problems (e.g., with acting-out behaviors). One interpretation of these differences attributes the internalization of problems to Thai cultural norms of not externalizing their problems—as compared to U.S. children, who may tend to externalize their problems. In another series of studies on immigrants, it was found that Mexican-born Americans had lower rates of mental disorders than Mexican Americans born in the United States. Studies done in Great Britain found the reverse of these patterns—Afro-Caribbean immigrants had higher rates of schizophrenia than did other ethnic groups. Studies conducted in the United States found that compared to White patients, African Americans with panic disorder and agoraphobia were more likely to have been separated from their parents as children and were more likely to have come from divorced families. Researchers have found that a concept discarded in the United States, neurasthenia, can still be used to describe conditions experienced in some Asian populations (e.g., Chinese-Vietnamese). The concept is still being used in China and parts of Asia. Neurasthenia is often characterized as a condition in which a person experiences fatigue or weakness and has a variety of psychological (e.g., poor concentration) and physical (e.g., diffuse aches and pains) symptoms. Cultural factors and immigration may influence the expression of these symptoms. In studies with Latino adolescents in Miami and Houston, researchers found relationships between immigration, acculturation stressors, and behavioral problems.

Regeser-Lopez and Guarnaccia (2000) wrote that cultural psychopathology should integrate ethnographic, observational, clinical, and epidemiological research approaches. They wrote,

> Culture is important in all aspects of psychopathology research—from the design and translation of instruments, to the conceptual models that guide the research, to the interpersonal interaction between researcher and research participants, to the definition and interpretation of symptom and syndromes, to the structure of the social world that surrounds a person's mental health problem. . . . It is important that cultural research not obscure the importance of other social forces such as class, poverty, and marginality that work in conjunction with culture to shape people's everyday lives . . .

The ultimate goal of cultural psychopathology research is to alleviate suffering and improve people's lives. This requires attention to the multiple levels of individual, family, community, and the broader social system. Our enhanced notion of culture leads to analysis of the expression and sources of psychopathology at all of these levels. Our commitment to making a difference in people's everyday lives argues for the development of treatment and prevention interventions at these multiple levels as well. The increasing cultural diversity of the United States and the massive movements of people around the globe provide both an opportunity and imperative for cultural psychopathology research. (pp. 19–20)

It should be pointed out that there are excellent books written on the cultural aspects of clinical psychopathology. If readers are interested in this area of study, they can refer to such materials as those by Mezzich and others—for example, Guimón, Berrios, & Mezzich, 1989; Mezzich & Berganza, 1984; Mezzich & Cranach, 1988; Mezzich, Honda, & Kastrup, 1994; Mezzich, Jorge, & Salloum, 1994; Mezzich et al., 1999.

ANALYSES OF MINORITY MENTAL HEALTH RESEARCH

Various authors have examined mental health publications on minorities. Smith and Wang (1997) did an analysis of the statistical methods used in minority health research and recommended that researchers use more sophisticated statistical analyses. Wiese (1992) studied the principal journals in school psychology and found that African Americans were studied most frequently, followed by Mexican Americans. Sedlacek and Kim's (1995) article on multicultural assessment offers caveats in regard to the instruments that researchers use to measure minorities:

1. Just because we allot a label to a minority group and to the topic we are investigating does not mean that we are really measuring the group or topic.
2. Measures are often developed and normed on White populations. Using these measures to assess non-White people raises questions as to the validity of what is being measured; for example, if different people have different cultural and racial experiences and present their abilities and perceptions differently, it is unlikely that a single measure accurately assesses every group equally well.
3. Cultural assumptions are endemic in the creation of assessment devices. There may be an unknown Eurocentric perspective in the instrument used. Therefore, comparisons between different cultural groups may be spurious.

4. We do not have enough valid information to determine which measures are appropriate to use with particular clients or groups.

The Educational Research Policy and Priorities Board convened a panel to discuss "Creating a New Research Agenda on Race, Gender, and Class Impacts on Educational Achievement and Underachievement" (Bhattacharyya, 1998). Their findings, analyses, problems, and solutions are applicable to the field of psychological research. The following are among their recommendations:

- Race should be considered a process and not a category.
- Racial interactions between individuals and institutions should consider racial histories, traditions, practices, values, norms, and stratified hierarchies.
- Racial categories change over time. And these categories are used differently for different purposes by those within the categories.
- Experiences are felt differently by members in different settings.
- Nuances of categories and subcultures should be considered.
- Responses to oppression can take different forms—these should be considered when examining minority group members.
- Analyses should consider the isolated and interactional effects of race, class, and gender.
- Identify the problems that have not been addressed for political reasons.
- Facilitate the development of peer networks.
- Identify communities at risk of becoming destabilized and identify what is needed to stabilize them.
- Consider the causal model that prompts people to draw a relationship between a particular reform or intervention and its likely outcome.
- There should be recognition of the rapid pluralization of society and the need to increase categories to keep up with the number of groups that are emerging.
- The development of interdisciplinary efforts is needed. These efforts should incorporate community participation and make use of local and transnational connections (there is a need to find places for such research in universities).
- Focus on the intersection of macro- and microlevels is needed . . . looking at the interactions at the institutional, structural, interpersonal, and daily experience levels.
- Efforts should be directed to identify the types and cycles of oppression and discrimination, as well as ways in which oppression in communities occurs.
- There should be more extensive use of ethnographic approaches, and attention should be directed to the quality of ethnographic training.

- Race should be treated as an equal, not an inferior, topic in research.
- The resources of different racial groups need to be studied.
- More studies need to examine how education, racism, and the subtleties of racism are experienced in different racialized settings. Answers are needed in regard to how these factors translate into marginalization of different groups and how these combinations result in simultaneous advantages and disadvantages for some groups. . . . Also, how do communities come to understand how they are situated in racial structures of opportunity?
- Race and the categorization of race may be viewed differently by individuals, compared to the views of institutions and researchers.
- Determine how to stabilize families facing harsh economic conditions, find a setting or two to stabilize, determine what scale of investment is needed, and invest and study.
- Determine how one might help build coalitions between marginalized groups who have access to limited resources.
- Study how individual students navigate or how different models come to dominate particular schools in terms of process; study decisions made on the part of young people to utilize opportunities.

Panel members state that researchers need to be aware of the politics of research. Why is some research funded and other research is not? Why does some research fail and other research does not? What political goals is a researcher advancing? Is the researcher's "neutrality" serving a purpose for institutions? Is the researcher really "neutral"? Members reported,

> Future research must talk about the political economy and the power structures; education and anything else is also economic. Power affects a lot that happens on an individual level because of economic structures, constructs and institutional racism. Include these areas and these perceptions in research methodology and conscious; incorporate structural dimension and more complex modeling; look at process as not being "economic, political and social" but being quite synchronic processes. Researchers are more comfortable examining individual perceptions and experiences as opposed to the institutional side and also as opposed to process. Though researchers need to focus on individuals, on who people are and where people are, researchers must fix attention on the structural dimensions of inequality. (Bhattacharyya, 1998, pp. 28–29)

In addition, panel members said that future research must examine the definitions of community. These definitions may not be in sync with the researchers'—people may live in one community, work in another, do business in another, and associate socially in another. The development of a paradigm that can operate on different levels would be methodologically useful. This paradigm should be able to analyze behavior on an individual, family, classroom, and peer group level. It should also be able to take into account interactional effects. Future research should gather data differently. Future research should broaden the contexts examined, increase the depth and detail, add new measures for background characteristics, and aim for consistency across data-gathering efforts.

Under the rubric of the American Psychological Association, five ethnic-minority psychological associations provided "Guidelines for Research in Ethnic Minority Communities" (Office of Ethnic Minority Affairs, 2000). They do not claim that the guidelines are comprehensive and encourage researchers to take a less superficial look at minorities. They state that psychologists should consider their Western/Eurocentric biases in their collection and interpretation of ethnic minorities data. They caution us to be aware that there are big differences within ethnic groups, and we should be careful about making generalizations. They found that socioeconomic factors can play an important role in the interpretation of minority data, and, to obtain more valid information, the researcher may consider whether a cultural informant or expert in the area is warranted.

Ponterotto (1988) did a content analysis and methodological critique of racial/ethnic minority research in the *Journal of Counseling Psychology*. The following are among his findings: Like Smith and Wang (1997), he found limited use of sophisticated statistical techniques in the research on minorities; there was disregard for intracultural or within-group differences in the minority samples; there was a tendency to sample easy-to-obtain participants—these may not be representative of the larger group; there were often failures to provide relevant demographics of the sample; there was a tendency to rely on psychometric instruments that are limited in their generalizability; and there were failures to delineate how generalizable the results are. In his "Recommendations and Conclusions" section, he stated that much of the research was not driven by a conceptual or theoretic model; instead, the research was done out of curiosity or because of convenience. He wrote that we have relied too much on an atomic approach in our endeavors to isolate and identify causal factors. He stated that it is time to broaden our research vision to embrace methodologies that have proved their effectiveness in ethology, ethnology, cultural anthropology, sociology, cross-cultural psychology, ethnopsychiatry, and political science (p. 415). He goes on to say that we should be careful in making intercultural comparisons because of possible differences in participants' conceptualization of the questions; the questions being investigated may not have the same meaning across cultures; different valences could be attributed to problems and questions; and we may be defining "normality" from a Eurocentric perspective. He wrote that investigators have a tendency to use constructs that are different from those used by the ethnic group being investigated—for example, the investigator's definition of depression could be different from that of a Chinese person who is being investigated. He also wrote that research needs to concentrate on the strengths of minority cultures—for example, researchers need to examine the positive coping strategies that are used by minority group members. He goes on to report that minority mental health researchers often place an overemphasis on client–counselor processes and have a disregard for factors outside of counseling that impact the client. There is also too much reliance on experimental analogues, which does not reflect factors that are really impacting the client (factors such as discrimination and poverty). Another criticism he found in the literature is that there is failure to be responsible to the minority subjects. He stated that the effects of culture are too complex to be examined within the traditional counseling context. He said that we need to investigate those factors that transcend culture and that are common to all people—factors such as economic deprivation, reactions to uncertainty and loss, and ways of reacting to change. He concludes by saying that criticisms have been levied against minority mental health research in that it has had little impact on minority lives.

ETHNIC GROUP CLASSIFICATION

The classification of minority group members is an ongoing problem in research. I have written an article (Illovsky, 1994b) on the problems of ethnic classifications, problems in sampling and research, ethnicity measures, and models and approaches, and I have provided a sample of how ethnic research could be improved. In the article I have written on the inadequacies of biological, cultural, legal, and social definitions in conducting non–European American research. Biologically, there is greater genetic variability within ethnic groups than there is between groups (Morrison Institute for Population and Resource Studies, 1999). Garn (1981), Tuller (1977), Rothwell (1977), and Vogel and Motulsky (1979) are among the many who have pointed out the inadequacies of biological ethnic differentiations. Cultural definitions change with time and are permeable to the constant influx of other cultures. Legal and social definitions of race and ethnicity vary among the states ("What Makes . . . ," 1982), cultures, and particular periods (Banton, 1980; Oboler, 1995) and the time the study is done (Clarkson, 1981). Non–European Americans are studied under such terms as *race, Asian American, ethnic, Black, Latino, Native American, minority, Chinese,* and so on. Terms like these encompass such diverse populations that little is learned or described from studies using these descriptors. In studies of these populations, we use limited samples and generalize inappropriately. As a variable, ethnicity is not an all-or-nothing construct (Cohen, 1974). There can be different degrees of manifestation (Barham & Helms, 1981; Cross, 1971, 1978, 1995; Tokar & Fischer, 1998). De Vos and Romanucci-Ross (1975) state that ethnic identity might change with a changing environment and affect a person differently during a life span. Many people in this country have multiple genetic and cultural backgrounds (Kerwin & Ponterotto, 1995)—raising the problem of classifying them. Ethnicity may differ based on the purpose of the study (Amante, VanHouten, Grieve, Bader, & Mangules, 1977). Numerous authors have offered ethnic measures, including Cross (1971), Gordon and Grantham (1979), Grieger and Ponterotto (1995), Jackson and Kirschner (1973), and Vontress (1971). One approach to measuring ethnicity is to obtain the perceptions (worldview) of the person. Instruments that measure worldview include those of Berg-Cross and Chinen (1995); Ibrahim and Kahn (1987); Ibrahim, Ohnishi, and Wilson (1994); Ibrahim and Owens (1992); Jacobsen (1988); and Washington (1994). In trying to measure ethnicity, we encounter the problems engendered by acculturation—that is, the psychological and social changes that an individual makes as a result of encounters with another culture. Instruments that measure acculturation can be found in Dana (1993), Grieger and Ponterotto (1995), Paniagua (1994), Ponterotto and Casas (1991), and Sabnani and Ponterrotto (1992). Numerous writers have presented approaches to defining ethnicity (Dashefsky, 1975; De Vos & Romanucci-Ross, 1975; Gynter, Lachar, & Dahlstrom, 1978; Henry, 1976; Holloman & Arutiunov, 1978; Howell, 1977; Isajiw, 1974; Jenkins & Morrison, 1978; Keyes, 1976; Marrett & Leggon, 1980; McCready, 1983; Obidinski, 1978; Padilla, 1980; Peng, Nisbett, & Wong, 1997; Phinney, 1992; Pope-Davis, 2001; Reminick, 1983; Smith, 1980; Triandis, 1980).

Many other factors can complicate the measuring of ethnicity. Longitudinal factors need to be considered: over time, there may be changes in the individual's self-perception (Brigham & Weissbach, 1968) or definition by others (Brigham & Weissbach, 1972a; Karlins, Coffman, & Walters, 1969). There are regional differences, or different factors are used to define ethnicity (Pettigrew, 1959). There may be self-misidentification (Greenwald & Oppenheim, 1968) and changes that are the result of reaction to others (Brigham & Weissbach, 1972b), or definitions of ethnicity may be modified by contextual factors—for example, the presence or absence of ethnic cohorts (Brigham & Weissbach, 1972b). One of the suggestions I make in how to conduct ethnic research is to apply a criteria to define ethnicity—for example, an ethnicity scale—when selecting participants in the research. I also suggest we do periodic meta-analysis of minority data.

The issue of ethnic categorization needs to be addressed at the national, professional, and scientific level. It is commonly recognized that this is a problem. Now, we need to do something about it in order to advance the state of knowledge in the study of ethnic groups.

MISUSE OF MINORITY DATA REPORTING

This next section deals with abuses in minority research. First, there are examples of abuses in society, in general. Then, there are examples of abuses in minority research in the social and behavioral sciences.

In Society

In general, the abuse of minority data collection and the abuse of programs to help minorities are well documented. For example, Enchautegui, Fix, Loprest, von der Lippe, and Wissoker (1997) found that barriers and misrepresentations occurred in the awarding of grant money to allegedly minority-owned businesses. They found abuses that took the form of minorities not having access to political, social, and economic power brokers that award grants and control resources; Whites using minorities as "fronts"; the extensive use of waivers to allow White contracts to circumvent government regulations to facilitate minority business development; limited notices to minority businesses of competitive contracts; the notification of White contractors of minority contractor bids to enable the White contractor to underbid the minority bid; the defining of women as minorities so that people of color are excluded; defining women as only White women so that minority women are excluded; and the list of circumventing techniques goes on and on.

The *Hartford Courant* (D'Arcy, 1999) found no accountability in the state monitoring of diversity laws. It found that there were inherent problems in the law, whose intent could be circumvented in terms of whether minorities were being served and in terms of reports of expenditures. The vague documentation involved and the lack of timelines or requirements negated the intent of the law to diversify. Misleading reports were filed to present the illusion of compliance to diversification. Though policies in schools were written and a law was passed by the state, little was actually done in terms of diversification. The state and school systems have false data, and it took the newspaper to disclose the inaccuracies.

Velez (1999), a mathematics academician, found differences between what was officially reported and the number of minority mathematicians who actually graduated. He wrote that inflated figures were reported on the number of minority mathematicians who graduated from his department. The inflated figures were obtained from the National Opinion Research Center—a contractor to the National Science Foundation.

Forbes (1990) wrote that politics may be involved in the categorization of minority groups—that is, millions of Native Americans have been placed into the "Hispanic/Spanish" category for political reasons, and this method of categorization does not reflect a true count of either group.

Fretwell (1990) wrote that colleges might misrepresent themselves in their efforts to recruit minorities. In their efforts to attract minorities, colleges may give the impression that their campuses have features that they really do not have.

The U.S. Department of Education's Educational Research Policy and Priorities Board convened a panel to discuss "Creating a New Research Agenda on Race, Gender, and Class Impacts on Educational Achievement and Underachievement" (Bhattacharyya, 1998). Panel members said,

> Since politics is involved, researchers need to worry about being too power neutral when recommending supplementary education strategies. Unless scholars understand what the politics is, they cannot strategize about how to change the situation technically, but also need to strategize how to do the politics necessary to get these changes implemented and so there has got to be both sides of these situations. . . . There is a political economy, and scholars must remember it's not just that research failed to do it, there are reasons why research has not been able to do it. Also, some topics are always left out of research, why are these things not addressed? (Bhattacharyya, 1998, p. 24)

Members of the panel just cited stated that people involved in education research do not identify those problems that have not been addressed for political reasons (Bhattacharyya, 1998, p. iv); "they need to engage in the identification of types and cycles of oppression and discrimination, and ways in which oppression of communities occurs" (p. v).

It is highly unlikely that the social and behavioral sciences have escaped some of the problems encountered in areas outside their fields. It is highly unlikely that they are removed from the possible corrupting impact of institutions, individuals, and social, economic, and political factors.

In Minority Mental Health Research

Copious amounts of material have been written on problems in doing minority research. This material has included problems in obtaining and analyzing accurate data in census-taking, affirmative action, numbers in schools, recruitment, and hiring practices; criminal, health, and education statistics; profiling in search and seizures; and so on. Among the more prevalent articles that deal with minority research problems are those that present views on: how to increase minority participation in surveys (Jackson & Ivanoff, 1999); the problems revolving around classifying those with multiple ethnicity (Matier & Larson, 1995; Orlans, 1989); and the problems in the classification of ethnic groups (U.S. Census Bureau, 2000b). Some of these problems have gained the attention of the popular press (Forbes, 1990; "When the category . . . ," 1991; Goldner & Smith, 2000). Books, articles, and conferences provide expositions that deal with methodology, validity, and reliability problems. Researchers in the social and behavioral sciences have discussed the misuse of statistical techniques and analysis (e.g., Helberg, 2000). They have examined the inadequacies of approaches and data gathering techniques when dealing with minority groups. But very little attention has been paid to problems in data collecting that are outside the realm of regular standard statistical methodology and approaches.

Little attention has been paid to erroneous data being obtained and fallaciously analyzed because of institutional, social, economic, and political factors that might corrupt the data. In one of the few mentions of this, the American Psychological Association's (1996) *Monitor* published an article on "When Policy-Makers Misuse Psychological Data." In the article there are statements of how some policy-makers, politicians, and "experts" present inaccurate psychological data to buttress their own political agendas and values. It would not be surprising if this is also occurring in the arena of minority data and research—especially in the context of minorities being a controversial and political topic in our society. Yet we treat this area of study as if it existed in isolation of forces that might compromise the validity and reliability of our studies. Researchers studying minorities often depend on institutions to provide valid data on minorities in a community or site. They depend on institutional data to present accurate figures on the expenditures of resources for minorities. They depend on institutions to determine which data are obtainable and which data are not. They depend on institutions to provide accurate data on recidivism and which programs work and do not work. They may depend on institutional reports to help determine what research would be useful, and so on. But we do not question the accuracy of these figures that are provided by institutions. The administrators in institutions who provide these data, and who provide the interpretations of the data, may have their own personal agendas to pursue, and they may be putting the institution's interests before those of minorities and the truth. Thus, the accuracy of the information that they provide may be mitigated. We need to examine factors that might compromise our data and that might perpetuate the abuse of minorities. Because the abuse of data is a process that can be obscured and manipulated by institutional administrators, valid figures are not reported and are difficult to obtain. Therefore, we need to have a greater reliance on qualitative approaches. The following is based on experience and on anecdotal information provided by minority administrators and colleagues working with White administrators. I hope this information helps those gathering and interpreting minority data from White institutions.

1. To demonstrate to the federal government that they are catering to guidelines to increase minorities, some institutions inflate figures in order to give the illusion that the institution has more minorities than it actually has. For example, in reporting the number of African Americans at an institution, the institution might include in the counts African Americans who have left the institution, Blacks from Africa, and Black South Americans. Another method would be to count persons of multiple ethnic heritages into more than one category (Orlans, 1989). If the researcher depends on data provided by the institution, the researcher might obtain inflated figures on the number of minorities in the institution; thus analysis of the subsequent data might be incorrect.
2. Institutions provide fallacious reports on the use of funds for minority positions and resources. Positions and funds are solicited in the name of helping minorities and are then used for other purposes. But when figures are reported, it is reported that these resources have been directed to help minorities. The researcher might look at the institutional figures on the amount of resources directed to minorities and not be aware that the resources are really being directed to Whites—or for the administrator's own purposes.
3. Institutions hire White women instead of minorities to reflect the number of minorities hired. The researcher might look at the data and, without further investigation, might not be aware that the figures obtained refer to women and not ethnic members.
4. To decrease the appearance that large numbers of Whites are being served, institutions might use mixed ethnicity classifications to lower their figures. For example, an institution may have 95% White, but when it uses the "mixed" category, the figure can be lowered to 73%—making it appear that the Whites are not being served to the degree that they are. Although it appears that the institution is making these changes as a means to use a better classification system, the "mixed" category can also be used as a mechanism to decrease the apparent large number of Whites served by the institution. The researcher investigating this data may erroneously assume that a smaller number of Whites are being served and a larger number of minorities are being served.
5. Institutions may present one set of statistics that favorably reflects on the institution and may obfuscate other statistics that do not present the institution in a favorable light. For example, the number of minori-

ties who enter a school is publicized, but not the number who fail to return after the first year; or the focus of the data is on the number of African American students at a university, but no mention is made of the low number of minority faculty and staff. In another example, the institution might provide select figures to demonstrate success, but the reality is otherwise. For instance, Asians might be used as a "model minority" group of economic success; however, this example of success is misleading—some groups of Asians (Japanese, Indian, Filipino, Chinese) have incomes above the general mean, whereas others (Koreans, Vietnamese, Cambodians, Laotians) are below the general mean—and the disparity between these haves and have-nots seems to be increasing. The overall poverty level of Asian Americans is 1½ times greater than Whites. The reports that Asian Americans have higher family incomes than Whites do not mention that the Asian family has more members working, for longer hours, and for less pay than the White family. The minority mental health researcher might look at the set of data presented by the institution and be convinced of the success of Asians and may not be aware that other data are as important, or may be even more important, to consider.

6. There could be an erroneous interpretation of data. For example, if an institution has problems retaining Black members, it can easily attribute this egress to "cultural differences" that dissuade Blacks from staying. However, the real reason could be subtle or institutional racism. Racism can take various forms; for example, minorities have fewer social credits, they are more closely watched, there is less tolerance of them for unacceptable behaviors, and there is more negative connotation attached to their behaviors. The mental health researcher investigating this situation will be told by the institution that the exodus of minorities from the institution is the result of cultural factors (the minorities are leaving because the institution does not have the cultural milieu that minorities want) or that other places have provided greater incentives to attract them. The researcher who accepts the institution's explanations may come to an erroneous conclusion as to why minorities are leaving the institution.

7. Institutions may lower and change their standards to put Whites in positions. Education, experience, credentials, and competence have been the traditional rationale for putting people in positions of power. But with the increase in education and experience of minorities, Whites can no longer adhere to these criteria. Therefore, they change the rules. Whites are promoted based on the hiring administrator's idiosyncratic criteria—under the auspices of using "qualitative" criteria. This allows for enormous room for bias in the selection process. The biases that may be in effect include the following: Whites want to perpetuate power

with those similar to themselves. They tend to interpret the behaviors of people similar to themselves more positively, and they tend to evaluate people different from themselves in a more negative fashion. The researcher investigating the institution's employment practices, and who depends on institutional records and statements, may accept spurious reasons as to why there is a lack of minorities in the institution—for example, not enough minorities apply, the educational system has not provided enough qualified individuals, minorities are not interested in these positions, and so forth. In reality, the problem is that the hiring agents are overlooking and ignoring qualified individuals.

8. Institutions are often given guidelines to monitor and improve the conditions of minorities. In compliance, institutions select individuals to implement these guidelines. They often select individuals who are controlled by administrators and who are responsible to the administrators. This results in the provision of token support for minorities and the serving of the aims of the institutions. With the selection of an affirmative action officer (or similar functionary with different titles—"compliance" officer, "equal" opportunities officer, etc.), and with the allocation of resources for the position, there is the illusion that the institution is attempting to increase diversity and provide services to minorities—but the data often demonstrate that the diversity goals and statements of the institution are not actualized. Researchers who examine the conditions of minorities in these settings and who rely on institutional statements as to what is being done obtain the impression (and perpetuate it to others) that the institution is supportive of minorities, when in fact it is not.

One method to circumvent reliance on administrators' figures is to obtain data and information from minority groups and individuals, both within the institution and outside the institution, who are familiar with the institution. This would include obtaining information from secretaries, janitors, ministers, maintenance workers, and so on—and not simply relying on the traditional sources of information. It is important to be aware that institutions may encourage researchers to view minority perceptions as being anecdotal (or the opinions of disgruntled employees) and induce the view that the institution's statements are authoritative and factual.

9. Those who accredit, certify, monitor, or endorse institutional standards and compliance are often Whites—or they are implementing White standards. Therefore, they are more ready to accept the explanations of their White institutional cohorts who are seeking accreditation as to why there are shortcomings in the institution's treatment of minorities. These Whites who accredit institutions are not as likely to be concerned about human rights violations. They are not as likely to be aware of the du-

plicitous techniques that can be used to give the impression of compliance. Or, they are more likely to dismiss and minimize the significance of data that shed light on the institution's poor treatment of minorities. They may also have different criteria as to what constitutes "poor" treatment. A simple, universal technique to use to obtain accreditation and bypass the need to improve treatment to minorities is for the institution to state that it has intentions and goals to increase minority presence in the institution. With such claims, the institutions are absolved from doing anything in fact. Claims of noble intentions to improve are often accompanied by statements that it is society's fault or the minorities' fault that changes are not implemented; for example, in terms of the hiring and promotion of minorities, the usual excuse provided by institutions is that minorities are simply not applying or there is a limited minority talent pool. For the researcher, the activities, definitions, and criteria of accrediting bodies cannot be depended on to redress the shortcomings of the institution. Accrediting bodies have their own measures of qualitative, ethical, and moral standards, which may conflict with those of society and minorities.

Grants

Before I conclude this chapter, I would like to briefly share some of my and my colleagues' observations in regard to grant funding and grant uses. Although there is no question that outside funding can be of value to communities, the possible negative aspects of soliciting grants should be considered.

No matter what the purpose of the grant, the net result is usually to provide support to the person administering the grant. The function of grants should be to develop endogenous, self-perpetuating, economic, entrepreneurial, and professional services and systems. The eventual goal of grants should be to have community members assume responsibility for all the roles and functions of service providers.

One has to also consider the effects on the community, and perceptions of outside groups, when funding for grants is being solicited (e.g., Dineen, 1996). In order to show need, grant applicants have to present a dire picture of those for whom they are trying to obtain services. This engenders a pathetic view of the community to those outside the community. This fosters clients seeing themselves in a pathological, abused, victimized manner. If clients do not share this view, then the rationale for obtaining the grant is threatened. These effects of grant solicitation may have consequences that need to be examined.

Frequently, funds are not being used for the populations they are supposed to be helping and for the purposes they were solicited for. When funds are obtained with the purpose of helping minorities, administrators often redirect the funds to meet their own needs—and not to meet the needs of minorities. One solution to this problem is to have grant recipients be accountable to minority groups for how funds are used. Minorities should have a full account of all resources and funding that are made in their name. The performance of those who administer the grant should be evaluated by the minority community—and not by White-controlled administrators. For years, the funding for minorities has been siphoned off by White administrators, giving the illusion that services and funds are being allocated for minorities.

These are not pedantic and esoteric issues. Disparities between minority groups and Whites can have important consequences. For minorities, the disparities can result in detrimental physical and mental health (Williams, Yu, Jackson, & Anderson, 1997); higher death rates from nearly all causes of death (National Center for Health Statistics, 1987); more exposure to violence, drugs, and diseases; poorer schools; men, women, parents, and children with shattered dreams; and the continued sowing of the seeds of discontent, distrust, and cynicism of minorities toward Whites—conditions conducive to social upheaval.

The researcher working with minority data cannot rely on traditional methods of gathering information. In addition to using the usual information-gathering techniques, the researcher has to consider other methods. Institutions may have their own agenda, which is often in conflict with the minorities'. The researcher cannot rely on the institution's data or on the institution's administrators and representatives. The competent, ethical researcher will need to compare figures, talk privately to ethnic minorities, and learn of the ways that institutions try to manipulate the data in terms of gathering, analysis, and reporting. This requires integrity and special skills.

4

─◄◦►─

Using Technology

The uses of technology and computers in psychology and counseling are amazing. Although the technology and applications presented in this chapter may seem avant-garde to therapists and counselors, they barely touch the technologies we have available and their many applications. Brain imaging, artificial intelligence, and so on may seem like science fiction to the mental health professional, but to those familiar with science and technology, these technologies are old stuff. Suler's (2002) wish list of the characteristics of a good therapy program—the Ultimate Computerized Psychotherapist program—can be easily catered to. He wants computer therapy programs that can be personalized, be humble, provide unconditional positive regard, reflect feelings, provide wisdom (universal truism), provide cognitive restructuring, allow for free associations, provide take-home tasks, rate for distress, determine when to terminate, and assess when human backup is warranted. Computers can easily fulfill this wish list for a good therapy program—and can do much, much more.

New technologies are being created at an incredible rate. Cutting-edge technology and ideas quickly become mundane. I hope, as the reader reads this chapter, that new applications and possibilities will come to mind. This is a very exciting field, with enormous room for creativity and with boundless applications.

One of the traditional criticisms against the use of computers in counseling is that computers do not allow for face-to-face interactions. It is a common belief among counselors that face-to-face interactions are necessary for effective counseling to be done. It is believed that face-to-face interactions are necessary because of the bodily, facial, and nonverbal signs that can provide grist for the counselor to use. However, face-to-face interactions are just one, and not necessarily the only, approach to use in therapy. For example, Freud did not sit face-to-face with his patients. He sat behind his patients because he was concerned that his bodily, facial, and nonverbal signs would interfere with the patients' free flow of information. Rogerians believed that empathy, rapport, warmth, and unconditional positive regard constitute the main ingredients in effective counseling. Some Rogerians could state that face-to-face encounters are not a necessary condition for therapy to occur; that they can provide therapy over the phone or on the Internet. They might also say they can provide group therapy despite not having face to face contact with everyone. A behaviorist might argue that the most effective element in therapy might not be the face-to-face encounter; instead, the most important element might be to obtain accurate information on what maintains a behavior and what is needed to change the behavior. Thus, some Freudians, Rogerians, and behaviorists might argue that face-to-face interactions may not be necessary or sufficient for effective therapy to occur. However, even if one were to believe that face-to-face interactions are necessary, it should be pointed out that there are various electronic forms of imaging and monitoring that allow the therapist and client to see each other as they interact (as well as observe and measure brain and body functions). Whatever the argument against the limitations of computers, it is possible to argue that these limitations can be overcome, that they can be compensated for, or that the limitations are not outweighed by mitigating impediments in human interactions.

HUMAN IMPEDIMENTS

In *Simulation and Gaming* (Illovsky, 1994), I wrote of the use of technology in counseling. I wrote of the human impediments (both the counselor's and the client's) and the role of computer science. The mental health professional can bring material into the counseling session that may impede counseling (Adebimpe, 1981; Bergin & Garfield, 1986; Beutler, Crago, & Arizmendi, 1986; Dyer & Vriend, 1977; Garfield & Bergin, 1986; Good & Good, 1986; Jones & Thorne, 1987; Lambert, Dejulio, & Christensen, 1983; Lee & Richardson, 1991; Lopez, 1989; Mukherjee, Shukla, Woodle, Rosen, & Olarte, 1983; Neighbors, Jackson, Campbell, & Williams, 1989; Orlinsky & Howard, 1986; Rogler, Malgady, & Rodriguez, 1989; Weinberger, 1993; Westermeyer, 1987). This material can include such factors as class background, education, personal experiences, gender, ethnic heritage, counseling model and approach, personal values, sexual orientation, religion and religiosity, regional differences, dialects, and a host of other factors. Destructive therapeutic problems that can occur would include racism, sexism, dual relationships, sexual abuse, and countertransference. The mental health professional can erroneously interpret behaviors and words. For example, Li-Repac (1980) reported that when European American therapists interacted with Chinese American clients, the European American therapists were more likely to rate the Chinese American clients as anxious, awkward, confused, and nervous. When Chinese American therapists' evaluations of Chinese American clients were compared with those of European American therapists, the European American therapists were more likely to rate Chinese American clients as being more depressed, more inhibited, less socially poised, and having less social skills. Chinese American therapists rated these same clients as alert, ambitious, adaptable, honest, and friendly. In addition, the client himself or herself may behave differently when interacting with the European American mental health professional. Research indicates that when there is a match to the client's ethnicity and language, there is a decrease in the dropout rate and an increase in the utilization of services (Takeuchi, Uehara, & Maramba, 1999).

Differences in the client's and counselor's ethnicity may play a role in attitudes toward counseling (e.g., Austin, Carter, & Vaux, 1990), trust (Biafora, Taylor, Warheit, Zimmerman, & Vega, 1993; Biafora, Warheit, Zimmerman, Gil, Apospori, & Taylor, 1993), and counselor preference (Parham and Helms, 1981). Phelps, Taylor, and Gerard (2001) found that cultural mistrust, ethnic identity, and racial identity accounted for 37% of the variance in self-esteem for African American university students. Thompson, Neville, Weathers, Poston, and Atkinson (1990) found that "paranoid" experiences reported in Blacks may be attributed to reactions to racism. Watkins and Terrell (1988) reported that highly mistrustful Blacks expected White counselors to be less accepting, trustworthy, and expert; they also expected less in terms of counseling outcome. Counseling approaches can have an effect on counseling effectiveness (Bergin & Garfield, 1986; Lambert, 1983; Lambert, Dejulio, & Christensen, 1983). However, a mental health professional might not use a more effective approach because of limitations in his or her training, background, ethnicity, and personality. For example, despite a client's needs, the mental health professional might use a Rogerian technique because that is what the therapist was trained in. Or, a mental health professional who is not well versed in science might ignore the findings of the scientific literature and continue using approaches of questionable effectiveness. Some mental health professionals might use only Western approaches to therapy because that is what they are familiar with. Some mental health professionals may work more on the affective level. Others may work more on the cognitive level. Some use reflective approaches and others use more directive ones. The preceding methods can hamper effective therapy when they are not in keeping with the client's needs.

Computer Science

Computer science can play a role in dealing with some of the problems in cross-cultural counseling. Artificial intelligence computer programs and expert systems (Bowerman & Glover, 1988; Davis, 1990; Kirsh, 1992; Lawyer & Yazdani, 1987; Polson & Richardson, 1988; Shirai & Tsujii 1984; Widman, Loparo, & Nielson, 1989; Yazdani & Narayanan, 1984; see Sharf's 1985 review covering Eliza, Parry, and Client 1; also Weizenbaum, 1966, Doctor; and California Scientific Software, 1993, Brainmaker) can provide services by mimicking the therapeutic approaches, techniques, and language of cross-cultural experts. These programs can communicate in a multimedia, multisensory fashion. In conjunction with cybernetic approaches, the programs can help determine what is the most effective treatment for a particular individual or group, and these programs can provide the best way to get a particular client or group to accept information. Cybernetics principles (Arbib, 1972; Caianiello & Musso, 1984; Cocking, 1979; Fuchs, 1971; George, 1977; Gold, 1965; Ozer, 1979; Powers, 1979; Smith & Smith, 1966; Encyclopaedia Brittanica, 1990) can be used to modify a program based on the client's needs and preferences.

What we have learned from cybernetics, artificial intelligence, and psychology can be readily applied to the development of computer programs that can overcome multicultural barriers. The programs can help deal with impediments between the mental health professional and the client. The program can cater to the needs of the client and modify interactions to more effectively provide treatment to the client. Wright, Salmon, Wright, and Beck (1998) created an interactive computer-assisted psychotherapy program to help patients cope better with emotional problems. It is a multimedia self-help program. Presently, it is designed to provide help to fight depression and anxiety. It can also provide customized homework assignments for each patient. They plan to develop computer programs to help treat anxiety disorders, substance abuse, and a variety of other conditions. Facilities such as the Massachusetts Institute of Technology Media Lab (Weil, 1999) are planning to design computers with emotional and affective intelligence. These computers will be able to measure and react to feelings. For example, the program will be able to gauge and react to blood pressure, heart rate, and other measures of inner turmoil—indices of such conditions as stress. Though not mentioned in the article, there are other possibilities. Computer programs can store an incredible amount of therapeutic information (a computer can keep a record of everything that transpires in therapy); therefore, therapeutic patterns can be detected. Computer programs have been developed that can scan faces and examine microexpressions to detect emotions and lying ("Liar, Liar, Face on Fire," 1999). A program can include other indices such as muscular responses, galvanic responses, eye pupil responses, changes in the voice, body language, and a host of other psychophysiological responses. If we add brain-imaging technology to this repertoire (which may include the ability to detect such phenomena as when a person is lying or guilty—Boyce, 2001), the capabilities are increased exponentially.

Though it may be true that face-to-face therapist and client interactions have the benefit of enabling both persons to watch facial expressions and body languages, for non-European clients this may engender problems: Because cultures have different ways of expression, the mental health professional may have faulty interpretations and faulty impressions of the minority person's expressions and behaviors. Computer programs have such advantages as not being as likely as mental health professionals to erroneously interpret behaviors. For example, a behavior could be mistakenly interpreted by the therapist as resistance. But the behavior may actually be a function of clients' ethnicity or emotional and experiential styles. Countertransference problems are less likely to occur with computer programs. When problems are found in computer programs (e.g., the program has racist or sexist statements), one can simply change the words. When a mental health professional needs to be corrected, one may need to deal with egos, defensiveness, passive-aggressive behaviors, resistance, sulkiness, and so on. Computer programs can also be changed to incorporate the latest therapeutic information, whereas human therapists are more likely to continue using the approaches and techniques they usually use.

In a study published in the *Journal of the American Medical Association* (Kobak et al., 1997), researchers found that respondents were more willing to admit their psychiatric disorders to a computer than to the primary care provider. They found that respondents were twice as likely to admit alcohol abuse on the computer than they were on other tests. The computer was able to detect obsessive-compulsive disorders at three times the rate of the primary care physicians. However, the computer was not as able to detect panic disorders. Research such as this suggests that computers can serve a valuable role in obtaining information from those seeking services from care providers.

Newsweek magazine published an article (Kalb, 2001) on online counseling. Its report was based on interviews with clients and professional therapists. They reported that the advantages to online counseling included these benefits: Online counseling is more accessible. People can call from their home or office. Travel time is cut. There is more anonymity, and people are less inhibited (because it does not require face-to-face interactions). People are less self-conscious. Although they revealed to a computer as much as they revealed to a human professional about nonembarrassing medical problems (nosebleeds, chest pains), they revealed a lot more to a computer about sensitive issues (sexual problems or substance abuse). With online interactions, people may be more focused and may come to quicker resolution to their problems. They don't need to get dressed (it's informal). And, it is cheaper.

The article (Kalb, 2001) also contained respondents' feelings about the drawbacks of online counseling. The drawbacks included lack of meaningful visual and other sensory cues, such as smell (e.g., the smell of alcohol on an alcoholic's breath). It is easy to lie on a computer, whereas it might be more difficult to lie to a human. Unqualified people might be providing the online counseling. There are legal and ethical problems of counseling across state lines. A suicidal client might not be able to reach a counselor online. Confidentiality is not assured. Computers can crash at critical periods of counseling.

Computer programs can be developed to more effectively meet the needs of specific populations. For example, some computer programs can translate languages in real time (Wallich, 1999). Such programs can allow the therapist and client to converse even though they may not share the same language—programs can also listen and talk without the presence of a therapist (Rist, 2000). In addition, computer programs can be developed to determine the best way to communicate with the client. The programs can use the language, symbols, and specialized norms of particular populations.

MINORITY EDUCATION, TRAINING, AND COMMUNITY DEVELOPMENT

It is critical that technological advances not be in the hands of those who use it as an avenue to exploit minority communities and who use it to the detriment of the community (Gladieux, 2000). As one goes through minority communities, quite often the proliferation of alcohol, tobacco, and other products and messages provides examples of exploitive and detrimental uses of technology and the media. Computers, the Internet, and numerous other technologies can be used to educate, inform, empower, and increase development, or they can be used to cater to baser behaviors.

This book advocates the continued efforts of minority communities to meet their own needs. For example, peer-helping programs can be established. TeenCentral.Net (Hayes, 2001) is one such Internet website that provides teenagers with the opportunity to interact with each other, discuss their problems, share resources, and provide solutions. With the advent of computers, the Internet, electronic mail, and the myriad of technological advances, many possibilities are available.

Mental health therapists can increase a client's self-locus of control, improve self-efficacy, enhance coping skills, promote optimism, and decrease stress by empowering those without power. Increasing the client's knowledge and resources can do this. Through electronic technology, mental health professionals can be trained in their own communities. Community members can learn more about mental health through computers, technology, and distance learning. The present applications of technology to help minorities are limited only by the creativity and efforts of people. Further developments in the field of technology augur amazing promises. Ingress into homes and sites is now possible through such technologies as cable, fiber-optics, TV, VCRs, CDs, phone lines, and satellite dishes. With the rapid turnover of technology, secondhand computers and electronic accoutrements should be readily available to the poor. By interacting with other communities in this country and throughout the world, minorities can circumvent White mediators who might filter and modify the communiqués, and exchange information directly. For example, minority communities might benefit from using models that explain the underdevelopment of low-income countries:

> The underdeveloped countries are underdeveloped because, in some way or another, they have not yet succeeded in making full use of their potential for economic growth. This potential may arise from the underdevelopment of their natural resources, or their human potential, or from the "technological gap." More generally, it may arise from the underdevelopment of economic organization and institutions, including the network of the market system and administrative machinery of government. The general presumption is that the development of this organizational framework would enable an underdeveloped country to make fuller use not only of its domestic resources but also its external economic opportunities, in the form of international trade, foreign investments, and ethnological and organizational innovations. ("Economic Growth and Planning," 1997, p. 885)

Distance Learning

Mental health professionals have numerous models to copy from in terms of training, education, and the delivery of services to minority communities. Distance learning is just one of a number of ways of reaching into communities. The use of distance learning is an area of education that mental health providers and educators can garner from. However, "although distance learning as formal instruction has grown at an explosive pace since 1987, few applications have been designed focusing on specific ethnic or cultural goals" (Barrera, 1993, p. 6).

Distance learning provides skills. It provides opportunities for minorities to interact with people outside their communities. It can inform those outside the community of the minority member's life and community. And it can meet the intellectual needs of those within the community who are interested in learning. Numerous problems can be overcome with the use of distance learning and technology to impart and obtain information from minority communities. The following are some examples.

- One dismal attitude of some youth is that education is viewed as a "White" activity. With the advent of technology, one can learn in one's own home and not have to deal with the impeding attitudes of others.
- Staying in the community may ameliorate some of the child-care problems that may be entailed if one were removed from friends and relatives.
- One might not have to deal with the problems of transit and transportation if one were to remain in one's own community.
- One could continue to remain in the milieu of one's own community instead of entering the cultural milieu of the college environment.

Many governments with limited resources are looking at distance learning as a means of providing an education (Dhanarajan, 1997). Lajos (1997) reported the use of distance-learning technologies to meet the needs of foreign students. Students who used to go to a host country for education could now remain in their own country to obtain an education (many of those going to other countries for an education were ethnic members facing discrimination in their own countries; therefore, they had to leave their home countries to obtain an education). It is interesting that many of the dynamics, problems, and fears of the host country, and the country from which the foreign student originates, are similar to those encountered by our universities in their dealings with minorities and their communities. These include the following.

- There is fear that the foreign students/minorities will bring in crime.
- The country/community from which the student originates may lose the student if he or she does not return to the native country/community—causing a dearth of needed skills in the country/community of origin.
- Distance learning allows the student flexibility and independence.
- It provides a means for faculty and students at their universities to learn more about those in the participating ethnic communities.
- It teaches students the use of technology.
- It breaches the barriers between university and community, the haves and the have-nots.
- It increases the options a university has to provide services to its students.
- It allows students to maintain relationships in their communities.
- It allows students to continue working in their communities.
- Students can apply what they have learned to their own communities and make their education more relevant to their own communities. Presently, with traditional on-campus learning, what the student learns may suit the needs of the college environment or the needs of those who control the political/economic/social systems of society.
- Students might be able to provide tutoring services to members of their

own communities—or learn from knowledgeable persons in their own communities.

- Students can develop methodologies and technologies relevant to their own communities.
- Distance learning may decrease the cost of education to students' families or countries.
- Distance-learning providers may be able to teach in the language of those receiving their services.

It is interesting to note that fewer students may be leaving their countries to receive an education from countries with more educational resources. This may be due to their own countries developing educational systems to meet their needs (Lajos, 1997). The question arises as to whether the same phenomena would occur if minority communities developed their own educational systems and credentialing processes.

Chale and Michaud's (1997) proposal for using distance learning in African countries can provide valuable guidelines for applications to ethnic communities with limited social and economic power. Their proposal is for educational services. But what they wrote can also have applications to the delivery of mental health services and to the education of mental health deliverers. They suggest

- Investigating alternate teaching and learning approaches and strategies.
- Examining the communities' infrastructure and available personnel.
- Examining the needs in long distance learning, in regard to such factors as the need for formal and informal courses, short- and long-term courses, structured or unstructured learning, and, of course, topics to be taught.
- Examining the relevant issues in the community and determining the courses' relationship to these issues—for example, language used, health needs, business needs, and environmental needs.
- Determining the language and style of learning needs.

Once again, in the case of what is learned with minorities, the approaches and techniques used can be applied to the general population. The National Center for Education Statistics (2001) show that only about 3 out of 14 students are less than 22 years old and attend full-time in residence. It is predicted (Dubois, 1996) that the demographics of the U.S. population will change and that the majority of the students will expect and demand more convenient modes of learning, greater access to education, and asynchronous communications. They will demand more time- and place-independence, and they will want more technologically based learning opportunities. Students will need to be trained, retrained, certified, and credentialed. The delivery of services to minorities can serve as a prototype to delivering services to larger populations.

Resources

There are an amazing number of resources on the Internet. These resources and websites come and go; therefore, it is hoped that the sites in this chapter are still functional by the time of this book is published. However, if these sites are not available, it is hoped that the reader will not be discouraged—the point of my presenting these sites is not that they are the definitive ones that I recommend; rather, these sites serve to illustrate that plenty of sites are available for the reader to obtain information from.

One program to help minorities through technology is the Star Schools Program. The Office of Educational Research and Improvement (U.S. Department of Education) has the Star Schools Program to help provide instruction in such subjects as mathematics, science, foreign languages, literacy skills, and vocational education. The purpose is to use technology to serve: underserved populations, people who are disadvantaged or illiterate, those with limited English proficiency, and individuals with disabilities. The Star Schools Program was first authorized in 1988 and was reauthorized most recently under Title III of the Improving America's Schools Act (PL103-382). Through this program, technology-learning services have been brought to over 200,000 students, 30,000 teachers, and 5,000 schools. These services have been provided in all the states, in the District of Columbia, and to several territories. The Star program attempts to begin the process of providing students with access to and equity in education in particular areas. "It remains for future projects to address the holistic needs of linguistically and culturally diverse students" (Barrera, 1993, p. 6).

Grambling University, a historically Black university in the rural Deep South, has written good "how to" materials on how to develop a distance-learning program. These deal with technical and support staff, policies and procedures, instruction, program identification procedures and marketing processes, instructional design, and development systems. Providers of telecommunications have included the Public Broadcasting Service (PBS), the Central Education Telecommunications Consortium (CETCO) of the Black College Satellite Network, the Instructional Television Fixed Service (ITFS), and Mind Extension University.

Diversity University is a project of DUETS, Inc. It is a 501(c)(3) non-profit educational organization dedicated to meeting the online distance-education learning needs of individuals and institutions. Diversity University is a real-time, Internet-accessible, virtual reality educational environment. Students, teachers, and administrators worldwide use DU classes, literature, and consulting services. DUETS, Inc., gets its financial support, as do other nonprofit organizations, via grants, technical assistance fees, and philanthropic donations.

There are many useful sources pertaining to the use of technology. Crawford (1997) reported that studies have documented the benefits of educational technologies. He cites that researchers offer numerous ways in which such computer-based technologies as multimedia, e-mail, and the World Wide Web can help enhance achievement for language-minority children (Soska, 1994). Any improvements in learning may not be due to the technologies themselves, but rather may be due to improved teaching strategies. Cummins and Sayers (1995) found that global learning networks have helped students confront their own prejudices and better appreciate their own culture. Interactive electronic learning environments can foster second-language acquisition and higher-order thinking skills (Dolson & Mayer, 1992; Ramírez et al., 1991). Hypermedia can also provide meaningful contexts and whole-language environments for those with limited English proficiency (Bermúdez & Palumbo, 1994). The advent of computers and electronic interactions might also produce new means of assessing problem-solving abilities and linguistic and academic competencies (Zehler, 1995).

It is gratifying that some libraries are already transforming themselves so that their resources will be available via electronic access (Association of Research Libraries, 1998). Such services will be a boon for those trying to receive an education from a distance.

It is extremely distressing that there is such a big a technological gap between the haves and the have-nots in this country (Alter, 1999; Foxhall, 2000; National Telecommunications and Information Administration, 1995; Rozner, 1998; Wresch, 1996). The Benton Foundation has provided an excellent analysis of the growing technology disparity between the poor and those who have better access to technology. The analysis (Goslee, 1998) is of the trends in the technology gaps in low-income communities. It examines the barriers to closing the gaps. And it examines the policies that are needed to close the gaps. The report stated that the new technologies may be increasing the disparity between the "haves" and the "have-nots": People are leaving the inner cities and rural areas to seek opportunities in areas that have greater technology—suburban areas—because of greater educational and employment opportunities. Technological developments in poor neighborhoods are hindered by a lack of the infrastructure that is available in affluent areas; phone and cable companies are not as likely to upgrade poorer communities; and the lack of adequate telecommunications facilities in poorer neighborhoods makes them less attractive to businesses. With telecommunications, it is possible to leave poor city centers and to provide services from more attractive suburban facilities. Poor neighborhoods are likely to have less access to information because the Internet—to which poor communities have limited access—is replacing the traditional sources of obtaining information. With limited access to communications, there is less access to engage in civil activities that can lead to improving conditions, and there is less opportunity to exchange information and solve the communities' problems. With limited telecommunications access, poor communities are handicapped in obtaining updates on pending legislation and funding opportunities. The barriers to closing the technology gaps include the low priority society places on providing technological advances to poor communities and the skepticism the poor have that technology can benefit them.

The report (Goslee, 1998) suggests that one of the key factors to providing telecommunications to poor communities is to have universal access—everyone should be provided with the same access to the Internet. One step in the direction of universal access is through the 1996 Telecommunications law, by which primary and secondary schools and libraries can obtain 20–90% discount rates for basic and advanced services. The National Urban League would like to extend this to include educational and developmental nonprofit organizations.

The Telecommunications Development Fund can make loans to small businesses to promote telecommunication competition and stimulate new technological development. Corporations can help by providing the infrastructure to support technology in schools. The Telecommunications and Information Assistance Program (part of the Commerce Department's National Telecommunications and Information Administration) has awarded grants to nonprofit hospitals, tribal and local governments, libraries, schools, and community centers to promote information technologies. We need strong state regulatory commissions to make sure that the grants are being used appropriately. The commissions need to be vigilant to avoid technological exploitation of poor communities. They can look for ways to promote the provision of services to the poor. All parties should be vigilant when major telecommunication providers merge; these can be opportunities for the poor to be included in obtaining benefits.

The Benton report stated that technology will not eliminate the problems of the poor—broader underlying problems of inner cities and disadvantaged rural areas need to be addressed. Some of these problems can be addressed by providing technological equity in schools and by providing job training in technological areas. The role of transportation should also be examined—the benefits of transporting workers to sites outside the community should be weighed against the benefits of providing jobs within the communities.

The report further stated that community-based initiatives are needed. Communities should define their own goals. Individuals and organizations should be given support in their endeavors. Community leaders should be identified and supported in their attempts to bring technology into the community.

Economic Development

The U.S. Department of Commerce's mission can be of value to minorities in providing opportunities to obtain distance learning, technological infrastructure, and entrepreneur skills and avenues. Its goals and objectives for commerce, economic infrastructure, science/technology/information, and resource and asset management and stewardship activities (U.S. Department of Commerce, 1999) are stated in the *Department of Commerce Strategic Plan for 1997–2002* (U.S. Department of Commerce, 1999a). Of particular relevance are the sections on the Economic Development Administration [EDA] (U.S. Department of Commerce, 1999b) and the Minority Business Development Administration [MBDA] (U.S. Department of Commerce, 1999c).

Internet Sites

For those interested in using the Internet for information about minority issues, there are numerous websites—new ones are popping up every day. One simply has to type in an area of interest—for example, multiculturalism, diversity, minorities, Asian mental health, or Latino/Hispanic psychology—and often there will be literally hundreds or thousands of hits. The following is a sample of websites that provide information about minorities.

The U.S. Library of Congress has information on minorities that can be obtained through its webpages. At its website, information can be obtained by typing in terms such as *ethnic press, ethnic relations, ethnology, minorities, Arab Americans, Indians, Puerto Ricans,* and so on. In addition, it has a website (U.S. Library of Congress, 1999) with information on the following groups: Asian American ethnic groups, Chinese Americans, Filipino Americans, Japanese Americans, European American ethnic groups, German Americans, Greek Americans, Irish Americans, Italian Americans, Polish Americans, Scandinavian Americans, and Slavic Americans.

The National Association for Ethnic Studies (http://www.ksu.edu/ameth/naes/) provides an interdisciplinary forum for those interested in the national and international aspects of ethnicity. It provides links to ethnic studies programs and ethnic websites.

MedWebPlus (http://www.medwebplus.com/subject/Ethnic_Groups.html) provides medical information on minorities.

Ethnic News95 (http://www.oclc.org/oclc/man/6928fsdb/ethnicnews95.htm) is a subset of Ethnic NewsWatch. It provides a comprehensive full-text database of newspapers, magazines, and journals of the American ethnic, minority, and native press. About 8,000 to 8,500 new articles are added each month. It also covers international culture and history.

The American Psychological Association's Public Interest Directorate has a website with a section titled "Section II: Racism in Psychology" (http://www.apa.org/pi/oema/racebib/racismin.html). It provides a bibliography and reviews of many books, authors, theorists, journal articles, and chapters in books that deal with racism, minorities, and ethnicity.

The Benton Foundation has an excellent site (http://www.benton.org/Library/Low-Income/resources2.html) that contains information and links to organizations and projects that provide technology to low-income communities.

Santa Clara University (California) has excellent websites and links on diversity. Its "Electronic Resources on Diversity" (http://www.scu.edu/SCU/ Programs/ Diversity/esources.html) has sections on African Americans, Asian Americans, Middle Eastern Americans, and Native Americans. Its "General Information" section has good links to other information and resources.

Oakland Community College, in California, has a website (http://www.occ.cc.mi.us/library/multicu1.htm) that offers a Diversity Bibliography. This includes "A Selected List of Multicultural and Diversity Resources" at its libraries and information on Diversity in the Workplace; Minorities—United States; Multicultural Education/Multiculturalism; Selected Multicultural & Diversity Websites.

Fisher College, Ohio State University, provides information on diversity in the workplace (http://www.cob.ohio-state.edu/~diversity/). The site has information on Teaching, Diversity, Bibliography, Tips on Mentoring, Age, Disabilities, Gender, Religion, Sexual Orientation, Social Class, Asian American, African American, European American, Hispanic/Latino, Middle Eastern, and Native American.

Rob Kabacoff, PhD, of Nova Southeastern University has a website: Resources for Diversity (http://alabanza.com/kabacoff/Inter-Links/diversity.html). This site has information on Intercultural Classroom Connections, JustCause Diversity Activism, Minority Studies Page, Multicultural Pavilion, UM Diversity Database, Ethnicity & Culture (Specific), African Studies Web, Chicano-LatinoNet, Latin World, Latin American Network Information Center, NativeNet, NativeWeb, Disability, American Sign Language, Cornucopia of Disability Information, Gender, Feminism Resources, Women's Studies Database, Women's Studies on the Web, Sexuality, Gay/Lesbian Resources, Lesbigay Resources, Religion, Minority Experts Database, MOLIS—Minority Online Service, Standards—A Multicultural Ezine. See also, The Human-Languages Page.

University of Maryland's Diversity Database (http://www.inform.umd. edu/EdRes/Topic/Diversity/) has a comprehensive index of multicultural and diversity resources. It has resources pertaining to cultural diversity and multiculturalism; diversity plans, statements, and initiatives of institutions in the country; and definitions of words, phrases, and policy relating to multicultural and diversity issues. UM has established the first campus news bureau devoted entirely to diversity-related news; it has directories on Age, Class, Disability, Gender, National Origin, Race and Ethnicity, Religion, and Sexual Orientation.

Cornell University's School of Industrial and Labor Relations has a website (http://www.ilr.cornell.edu/library/e_archive/GlassCeiling/ about.html) that contains information on barriers that prevent qualified women and minorities from advancing within their organizations. These barriers result from institutional and psychological practices.

Minority Online Information Service (MOLIS) (http://web.fie.com/ web/mol/) has information about government research and education opportunities for minorities. It deals with Historically Black Colleges and Universities and Hispanic Serving Institutions. These sources have information about faculty at these institutions, scholarships and fellowships for minorities, and important current events (including faculty appointments, job openings, etc.).

The National Clearinghouse for Bilingual Education (NCBE) (http:// www.ncbe.gwu.edu/about.htm) is funded by the U.S. Department of Education's Office of Bilingual Education and Minority Languages Affairs (OBEMLA). It collects, analyzes, and disseminates information relating to the education of linguistically and culturally diverse learners in the United States. NCBE provides information through its World Wide Web site, produces a bi-weekly news bulletin, and manages an electronic discussion group. It works with other service providers (foreign language programs, English as a Second Language programs, Head Start, Title I, Migrant Education, or Adult Education programs) to help states and local school districts develop programs and implement strategies for helping linguistically and culturally diverse students in the United States.

DIScovering Multicultural America (http://www.galegroup.com/) is part of a subscription service to libraries offered by the Gale Group. Contact your librarian for more information about accessing this source. DIScovering Multicultural America is a multimedia reference source that offers information on America's largest ethnic groups: African Americans, Asian Americans, Latino Americans, and Native North Americans.

In conclusion, I would like to reiterate that cross-cultural models and approaches that are used for non–European American populations can be applied to meet the needs of all individuals and groups. Cross-cultural mental health professionals can play a major role in this new area of study and application. We can either wait for the mainstream mental health profession to provide models and approaches—and then criticize them—or we can be at the forefront of the formation of new models and approaches that would be relevant to the wide populations of peoples that we serve.

5

—◀○▶—

Evolutionary Psychology– with Cross-Cultural Applications

The reason for this chapter on evolutionary psychology, as with the previous chapter on technology, is to provide an example of how new models and techniques can be explored. Such explorations are needed to determine which approaches and techniques are viable for which populations. Among the questions to which we seek answers are: Which models, approaches, and techniques can be applied universally across cultures, and which should be applied only to specific groups? In pursuit of the possible answers to these questions, I offer the following postulates:

- The delineation of universal behaviors can be ranked into a sequential arrangement—the biologically based ones being more fundamental than the higher ones that involve cognition and culture. The biologically based ones are more universal, and those that are mediated through signs and symbols (language) are usually more local and specific to a culture. This parallels phylogenic, ontological, and brain development from more primitive to more complex—and Freud's progression from the id to the superego. Thus, the functions of eating and living are more basic, to be followed by culturally based methods of expressing language, child-raising, communication, organization, problem-solving, and so on. Ample studies have demonstrated that there are universal behaviors and patterns across species, mammals, primates, and humans (e.g., Badcock, 1991; Barkow, Cosmides, & Tooby, 1992; Bolles & Beecher, 1988; Buss, 1988; Chapple, 1970; Cherry, 1994; Gould, 1982; Plotkin, 1988; Reynolds, 1981; Rushton, 1995; Scott, 1989; Trivers, 1985; Wiggins, 1996). This adds to the credence that there are universal behaviors not only across cultures but also

across many species. It should be noted that the preceding sequence does
not imply that there is a hierarchy of better or worse.

• Those psychological models and approaches that are more biologically
  based are more applicable across cultures.
• The psychological approaches and techniques that are more language-
  based are more closely related to the cultures from which they derived.
  The language-based therapies would include those that are insight-based
  and those that depend on the exploration of feelings—for example, psychoanalysis, Gestalt, and Rogerian therapy. Such approaches use language
  as the principle form of therapy. On the other hand, I would define behavior modification (and medicine, chemistry, and mathematics) as being less language-based and therefore more directly applicable across
  cultures.

    In addition to the reasons just mentioned, the evolutionary model is
being explored here because

1. It is a model that has been successful in explaining phenomena.
2. It appears to be a model that can be applied more readily across cultures.
3. It appears to be a unifying model that can explain phenomena across
   species and time.
4. Instead of just applying a set of approaches, techniques, and labels, the
   mental health professional can have some possible explanations for
   behavior.
5. This model provides a more universal means of communicating to members of the mental health profession in other cultures (e.g., through such
   common concepts and terms as *adaptation, mutation,* and *natural selection*). Indeed, it uses concepts familiar to people in other sciences—such
   as those in biology and zoology.
6. It provides explanations for psychopathology; for example, the psychopathic behaviors could be viewed as having a function at one time, but
   they are now inappropriate to modern life. Or the behaviors may be
   considered exaggerated responses of natural behaviors. They may be
   faulty responses. Or they may be responses based on genetic aberra-
   tions. Such a perception can help provide a more objective and scientific explanation for the behavior and mitigate some of the present stigma
   associated with mental illness—for example, sometimes a person with
   mental illness is perceived as being responsible for it in some way, has a
   lack of will power, or has some kind of weakness. Although these latter
   social and psychological explanations might still be cogent mechanisms
   involved in the behavior, the underlying reactions could be biologically
   based (e.g., although an adult might have learned as a child to be anx-

ious when exposed to open spaces, the anxiety response could be considered a biologically based one and could be a natural one that served as a survival function at one time).

Because evolutionary psychology is relatively new to most mental health workers, the following sections will familiarize the reader with this subject. Let's start by providing information on the foundation upon which evolutionary psychology is based: biological evolution. The reader should be aware that what is presented in this chapter are superficial summaries of concepts that are the result of a plethora of research. Evolutionary biology and evolutionary psychology (and the related fields of ethology, anthropology, social psychology, comparative animal studies, sociobiology, etc.) have made major strides and produced an incredible amount of material in recent years. The reader is encouraged to read the references that are cited here and explore other sources for a better understanding of what is presented in this chapter and in this book.

EVOLUTION (BIOLOGICAL)

Evolution can be defined as changes in a gene pool over time. A *gene pool* is the common set of genes shared by a species or a population. In order for evolution to occur, there has to be changes in the genes. These changes can occur through mutation, natural selection, recombination, genetic drift, and gene flow. *Mutations* are changes in the nucleotide DNA sequence that may lead to the synthesis of an altered protein or the loss of the ability to produce the protein. If a mutation occurs in a germ cell, it can be transmitted from generation to generation. Mutations may also be in somatic cells and are not heritable in the traditional sense. *Natural selection* is the process by which traits that are not adapted for an environment are decreased and traits that fit the environment are passed on to the next generation. *Genetic recombination* may be defined as the breakage and reunion of homologous DNA sequences to generate new linkage arrangements. *Genetic drift* is the process in which genetic diversity is rapidly changed (e.g., lost in small populations) because not all genes are passed from one generation to the next. This theory posits that some mutations (5–10%) are neutral and can show up in certain populations and do not seem to have any survival value (for example, Native Americans have very little blood group B; the relative absence of this blood type and the higher frequencies of it in other populations do not seem to have any evolutionary function). *Gene flow* is the movement of genes among populations through reproduction. *Genetic variation* (traits) consists of differences in the genes carried by members of a population (like color of eye and hair). These are the biological mechanisms that form the basis for the maintenance and changes in behaviors.

Another interesting aspect of an evolutionary approach is *mosaic evolution*—this theory posits that there are different rates of changes in body structure and functions. Therefore, not everything changes at the same rate, and changes are not necessarily coordinated with each other. For example, when humans started walking on two legs (bipedal location), this was not accompanied by changes in skull and brain size—these occurred later. From an evolutionary perspective, for human development, it may be that standing upright was more important than greater brain size. Another example can come from technology and other developments—just because we have technological developments does not necessarily mean we have the accompanying emotional and ethical developments to parallel these technological developments.

Another interesting area of evolutionary approaches comes from the field of sociobiology. An area of sociobiology suggests that culture and behavior can effect evolutionary changes. Traditional evolutionary theory focuses more on the survival value of a behavior for an individual—each organism behaves in ways to maximize its chances to pass its genes on to the next generation. However, this does not seem to explain certain behaviors of groups of organisms within a species; for example, some ants and humans may sacrifice their lives for the common good (the individual organism dies and therefore cannot reproduce). However, this "cultural value" (e.g., altruism) or behavior seems to have an evolutionary function and is passed on to successive generations.

The main message of sociobiology is that whereas biology can influence behavior and culture, behavior and culture can also influence biology. Though the ultimate mechanism at work in evolution is DNA, "The relationship between organic evolution and cultural evolution is complicated, since each form appears to have differing mechanisms. Culture as a uniquely human attribute seems bound to affect the totality of humanity and through this totality the patterns and results of human reproductive behaviour; this, in turn, must affect the human gene pool and the selective processes that act upon it, which is the essence of human evolution" (Encyclopaedia Brittanica, 2002, p. 808).

EVOLUTIONARY PSYCHOLOGY

"Evolutionary psychology is an approach to psychology, in which knowledge and principles from evolutionary biology are put to use in research on the structure of the human mind" (Cosmides & Tooby, 1997, p. 1). Evolutionary psychology tries to delineate the evolutionary algorithms of information processing and behavior by studying evolutionary biology and psychology (McGuire & Troisi, 1998, p. 38). Evolutionary psychology seeks the universal mechanisms that underlie human behavior. It examines the environment that man developed in. It examines the behavioral mechanisms that were developed to enable man to survive through the millenniums in various environments. Evolutionary psychologists assume that there is a genetic basis for these behaviors. It examines modern behaviors of man across cultures and seeks the universal origins of these behaviors.

Spriggs (1998) wrote,

> At the core of evolutionary psychology is the belief that all humans on the planet have innate areas in their brains which have specific knowledge that help them adapt to local environments. These areas are highly specialized, and only activate when the information is needed. These areas, when activated, give the brain specific algorithmic (step by step) instructions that have evolved from our ancestral pasts to adapt to all situations that we now face as humans. Some scientists speculate that these areas are attachments to long-term memory areas, and assist in problem-solving. These areas of the brain have a number of names: special learning mechanisms; psychological mechanism devices; mental mechanism devices; evolved cognitive structures; functionally specialized computational devices; and Darwinian algorithmic mechanisms.
>
> The ability to find the precise locations of these algorithmic modules is still years away, but the general location of these areas has been culled from brain scans which locate neural activity, and from the study of behavioral dysfunctions resulting from brain damage or other malfunctions.
>
> Knowing how these areas work in relation to the environment and the culture in which the human organism finds itself are the other areas of research in which evolutionary psychology shows the greatest promise. These spheres of research aim at configuring behavior models based on primate studies, hunter-gatherer research, and anthropological evidence into the best possible problem-solving probabilities of our ancestral behavior patterns. It is from these studies that evolutionary psychologists build behavior probabilities into our modern cultures and show us why we do the things we do—based on biology. (p. 1)

McGuire and Fairbanks (1977) contributed the ethological perspective to studying cross-cultural behaviors. Ethology is the study of the origins and nature of behavior patterns. McGuire and Fairbanks apply their perspective to the study of psychopathology. Ethology works within the framework of the evolution. McGuire and Fairbanks's views of behavior are (a) variability exists among all species, (b) this variability may be transmitted to next generations, and (c) individuals differ in their survival and reproductive success. Based on animal and human studies, McGuire and Fairbanks (1977) present a hypothetical relationship between normal and abnormal behaviors: Abnormal behaviors are those that are in the hyporesponsive and hyperresponsive range, whereas normal behaviors are in the average range of responsiveness. Esser and Deutsch's (1977) work illustrates this point. They found that part of the symptoms of schizophrenia can be attributed to hypersensitivity of dopamine receptors in the brain—the receptors in the dopamine-sensitive R-complex drive our reptilian behavior (MacLean, 1975). McGuire and Fairbanks (1977) postulate that there are multivariate determinants of behaviors that facilitate or inhibit normal and abnormal behaviors. These are genetic predisposition, environment, learning, development, psychological makeup, and extraneous factors. They present three models for the study of evolutionary behaviors in animals: (a) Homology, which entails the detailed observation of closely related species; (b) Survey, which entails gathering data on ecological divergence and convergence patterns in relation to phylogeny of different species; and (c) Optimality, which usually entails focusing on maximizing individual fitness to the environment (it is primarily a mathematical or logico-deductive model). In developing an ethologically based psychotherapy, they stress the need for it to be research-based and free from theoretical language and perspectives—and, of course, within the evolutionary framework. They emphasize the following points in the use of ethological approaches:

1. There is a reliance on observation and description—instead of on assuming theoretical perspectives.
2. The gathering of empirical data that is precise and systematic is critical.
3. There is the supposition that the organism enters the world with predispositions. These predispositions can be modified by the environment, critical periods, preparedness, learning, and developmental processes.
4. Behavior is functional; that is, it has a purpose.
5. Behavior is related to multidimensional causes.
6. The study of similarities and differences across species can contribute to the knowledge of the principles of human behavior.

(For more information on this perspective of behavior, read the following sources: Barkow, 1989; Butterworth, Rutkowska, & Scaif, 1985; Martin, 1956; McGuire & Fairbanks, 1977; Nesse, 1991, 1993; Sciences, 1992; Steen, 1996; Wilson, 1975.)

Exaptations and spandrels have recently received a lot of attention in the literature (Buss, Haselton, Shackelford, Bleske, & Wakefield, 1998). These mechanisms offer possible explanations for many of the phenomena of interest to psychologists—for example, art, language, commerce, and war. Like biological evolution, psychological evolution theory accepts the critical role of adaptation and natural selection. However, the changes in evolutionary structures and functions (exaptations) and the secondary and tertiary aspects of evolutionary structures and functions (*spandrels*) can also be of importance. *Exaptation* can be defined as the new use of a previous adaptation—which parallels Darwin's preadaptation. A bat's wing and a dolphin's flipper can serve as examples of exaptation: Both the bat and the dolphin had anatomical structures that preceded their wings and flippers; however, through exaptation new structures and functions were derived.

The unintended effects of evolution structures and functions, called spandrels, may also account for some of what we see in human behavior. Blood can be used as an example of a *spandrel*. We need blood to survive. It is a primary, basic evolutionary mechanism. Among its functions are to transport (e.g., carry nutrients and chemicals), provide for the body's defense (e.g., provide white corpuscles and aid in clotting), and maintain biological functions (e.g., oxygenate and prevent dehydration). Blood is also red. Red is a color that readily attracts visual attention. This latter characteristic is very functional in alerting individuals that they have been wounded. However, the redness of blood (a *spandrel*) is not the main reason for its existence. The redness is the result of hemoglobin, which we need to live. Iron gives hemoglobin its red color. Another example of a *spandrel* is brain size. It may be the case that humans do not have a larger brain to facilitate the development of language capabilities. Instead, one of the side effects of having a larger brain is the development of language. Yet another example of a *spandrel* can be mental disorders. It seems that many of the mental problems we see in humans are not seen in other species. It may be that one of the side effects of having the characteristics of homo sapiens (e.g., having the capacities of a developed neocortex—to engage in such activities as complex thinking and problem-solving) is having mental disorders. Buss, Haselton, Shackelford, Bleske, and Wakefield (1998) wrote that through the examination of the mechanisms of *exaptations* and *spandrels*, we can increase our understanding of the development of present behaviors.

Among the many other mechanisms at work, that of natural selection is also important and needs to be examined to determine its role in behavior. Although most evolutionary psychologists recognize the crucial function of natural selection, some (e.g., Pinker & Bloom, 1990) also recognize that there are competing features of natural selection and behavior that may control behavior. For example, within the controls of White American values, should one deprive the body of food and lose weight to obtain more status or should one cater to this biological drive, eat, gain weight, and lose status? Another example: should a woman stay in the security of a familiar environment and put up with an abusing spouse, or leave and enter an unfamiliar environment for the protection of her physical safety? For the psychologist, there may not be simple cause-and-effect mechanisms to account for behaviors; instead, there could be many competing mechanisms.

MENTAL DISORDERS

Persistence of Mental Disorders

Why do mental disorders persist? If they are deleterious (decrease survivability), shouldn't they have been eliminated from the gene pool? As mentioned previously, in the section on exaptations and spandrels, one set of explanations suggests that mental disorders do not necessarily serve a function; instead, they are the byproduct of having human features. The following are other explanations as to why mental disorders may be persisting in the gene pool (McGuire, Marks, Nesse, & Troisi, 1992):

1. Although the deleterious gene may reduce the number of offspring, it does not do so at a significant enough rate to eliminate them from the gene pool.
2. The onset of some of these disorders (e.g., depression) often occurs after peak reproductive periods and the disorders are therefore transmitted to the next generation.
3. Although the full complement of genes responsible for a mental disorder may be deleterious (e.g., homozygous sickle cell anemia), having only some of them may be of value in some situations (e.g., heterozygous sickle cell anemia enhances resistance to malaria) and are therefore perpetuated.
4. The gene that causes a mental disorder occurs infrequently and is not deleterious enough to eliminate it from the gene pool.
5. The disorder may be acceptable and functional in one culture, but not acceptable in another culture—for example, the features we view as paranoid in the United States may have been viewed as appropriate behaviors in the Trobriands (Malinowski, 1961).

   Another reason can be added to the previous list:

6. The disorder may be advantageous at certain times—for example, during times of war, such features as psychopathic characteristics, anger, and paranoia may have survival value.

Psychoses

There are an amazing number of explanations of psychoses from an evolutionary framework (Crow, 1995a, 1995b). The psychoses are explained from such perspectives as brain dysfunctions, genes that had a selective advantage, physiological and intelligence factors, and personality and sociality variations. These involve such features as myelination, synaptic processes, hemispheric symmetry, intercortical connections, dorso-lateral prefrontal connections, cortico-limbic pathways, the superior temporal sulcus, the amygdala, the orbital frontal cortex, the subcalcarine visual cortex, the homo sapien sapien specific neocortex, hierarchy and territoriality, facial recognition, sex-related factors, phylogeny, ontogeny, neoteny, encephalopathology, and the bicameral mind. Among the more recent interesting theories is that offered by Feierman (1994). He presented findings that indicate that schizophrenia is the result of the nocturnally evolved mechanisms of the brain processing information in our wakeful (diurnal) state.

From an evolutionary perspective, there are no definitive or agreed-upon explanations for the various psychopathologies. The following is to give the reader some ideas of what is in the literature:

Crow contends (Crow, 1986, 1990, 1995) that the psychoses (schizophrenic and affective psychoses) are all related to a single gene. The diversity of disorders that we see is the result of selective pressure and extreme variation of this particular gene. He argues that this particular gene separates homo sapiens from other primates. According to Crow, this psychosis gene is a cerebral dominance gene; it is located within the pseudoautosomal region of the sex chromosomes; it developed later in evolution and is directly related to human speech and communication. In addition, the studies of Crow, Done, and Sacker (1995) indicate that the psychoses differ between the sexes (e.g., age of onset) and control the development of the cerebral hemispheres—with the arrested development of cerebral asymmetry (Crow & Harrington, 1994).

Helfrich (n.d.) wrote that normal and pathological behaviors are on a continuum and that what is normal or abnormal is defined by the adaptive function it serves in relationship to the environment—whether it is acceptable (in a social context) or beneficial (in a social or biological context). Helfrich reported that most evolutionary theories consider the basis of psychotic and mood disorders to be related to variations in the distributions of personality, social skills, and intelligence. Extremes in personality and social skills can be related to the various psychopathologies. In terms of the reasons for hallucinations that are often seen in psychopathology, there are various explanations; for example, it is a prelanguage and prelogic part of the brain manifesting itself (Matte-Blanco, 1971, 1972); it is the prereptilian brain that generates these psychiatric syndromes (MacLean, 1985; 1993).

Stevens and Price (1996) offer the following evolutionary functions of various pathologies. They suggest that the *affective disorders* are evolutionary mechanisms for adapting to the allocation of resources; for example, the *depressive symptoms* that follow the loss of a job or loved ones are mechanisms to help us stop from investing our energies into these situations. *Antisocial and histrionic personality disorders* are the result of individuals attempting to obtain a disproportion of the group's resources for themselves. *Type A* characteristics and *narcissistic personality disorders* have their roots in attempts to attain status: With increased status comes greater resources and greater access to sexual mates and the production of offspring. *Dependent personality* disorders have their roots in most species having to live in a hierarchy: Submissiveness to the leader and fear of the loss of the group are genetically embedded in us. *Obsessive-compulsive disorders* may have functioned as means to avoid dealing with anxiety provoking thoughts, to gain control over one's environment and thoughts, to do things correctly to avoid being criticized by others, or to check on resources to make sure they are secure. *Anxiety disorders* have their basis in arousing the organism to respond, via the limbic system, to deal with threats from the environment. The various *phobias* served to protect the organism from specific threats; for example, the freezing response of acrophobia could have originated to immobilize the organism and thus help prevent the person from falling. The fear of open spaces that is characteristic of agoraphobia could have its origins in an era when being in open areas exposed us to attacks. Similarly, the fear of strangers, snakes, and so on had life-saving functions at one time. *Post-traumatic stress disorder* could be a mechanism to remind us to avoid the traumatic event. The *eating disorders* could be biological mechanisms to deal with fluctuations in the food supply; they could be attempts to display social status and assume attributes of higher status, or they could be a method of altering the timing of reproduction. People with *borderline personality disorders* could be attempting to obtain secure, reliable figures that they did not have during early stages of development. When they believe they have found such figures, they find that the figures cannot give them the attention, love, and protection that they want. They may then feel anger, resentment, and so forth, and engage in self-damaging behaviors, despair, and so on. The *schizoid* genotype could have served the function of enabling people to separate from the values and thinking of the main group—the deviant borderline psychotic behavior of the leader helps the leader believe that he or she is special; likewise, it helps the followers believe that they and their leaders are special—with a mystical, metaphysical buttress for their values and behaviors.

Delusional and somatoform disorders. Hagen's (2002) studies indicate support for the hypothesis that delusional and somatoform disorders occur to lessen the effects of social exclusion and ostracism. That is, when we are under stress and face the hazards of social exclusion and ostracism, we exhibit delusional behaviors and somatoform disorders in order to get the group to help us.

Psychodynamic mechanisms. Nesse and Lloyd (1992) wrote that psychoanalytic concepts will match evolved functional aspects of the brain. They posit that psychoanalytic personality factors (psychological defenses, repression, intrapsychic conflict) derived from evolutionary functions. Such mechanisms as repression and ego defenses could function to help people avoid pain and unnecessary suffering, or these could delay pain and repress reality or enable us to deceive ourselves so that we could more convincingly deceive others.

Psychopathology and consciousness. Maynard Smith (1993) wrote of the relationship of organic evolution to the understanding of psychopathology, the relationship of consciousness to the evolution of the nervous system, and the underlying brain structure and triune brain. Smith reported that the ancient part of the brain and more primitive neural parts are involved in the psychiatric syndromes.

Drugs

Nesse and Berridge (1997) point out that the human brain was not developed to deal with the pure psychoactive drugs that we have today. Pure psychoactive drugs circumvent intervening adaptive information-processing systems and go directly to the ancient brain mechanisms that control emotion and behavior. The drugs that make us feel good convey false signals of the benefits of the drug and can induce the continued use of the drug even after it is no longer useful. Drugs that block uncomfortable emotions may be circumventing mechanisms that serve the purpose of warning us that something is wrong and to initiate action. Drugs unnaturally interfere with these mechanisms and interfere with adaptive responses and behaviors—for example, analgesic and anxiolitic drugs interfere with pain and the anxiety defense that evolved to provide information to the organism. It is suggested that when doing research and providing treatment, it would behoove us to consider the evolutionary function of the emotions and the responses we are trying to modify.

Emotions

Just as all human groups may have the same personality types—for example, introverts and extroverts (MacDonald, 1998; McCrae, Costa, Del Pilar, Rolland, & Parker, 1998; Trull & Geary, 1997), so too, they may also have the same emotions, such as sadness, happiness, and fear (Buss, 1988;

Chapple, 1970). Nesse (1990) wrote that the various emotions have evolved as specific responses to specific conditions. At one time, these physiological, psychological, and behavioral responses served important functions for our survival. For example, the subtypes of fear developed to deal with specific threats; that is, the fear of spiders helped us avoid being bitten by spiders, the fear of blood helped us avoid getting hurt, and so on. Happiness and sadness have evolved to help us deal with favorable and unfavorable situations, and social responses are evolved adaptive responses to help us deal with relationships. *Anger* (Nesse, 1990) is a message to others that a person may abandon a relationship. It is a message that we may attack, even irrationally, possibly at great costs to ourselves. It may serve to protect us against exploitation; it may also deter attack.

Anxiety disorders were examined by Marks and Nesse (1994) to determine their evolutionary functions. Marks and Nesse state that the emotional response of anxiety helps the organism defend against potential threats. Anxiety disorders contribute to our survival (Nesse, 1988) by altering our physiological mood to deal with the situation, providing motivation and behaviors to avoid the threatening situation, increasing our alertness to the threatening situation, and inducing us to think of plans to avoid the situation. There are different types and degrees of threats and hence different types and degrees of anxiety. The following are some of the subtypes of fears and the corresponding situations that elicit these fears (Nesse, 1990): *Panic* is a response to imminent threat; *agoraphobia* is a response to potential threats from our environment; *general anxiety* is a response to a generally unsafe environment; *conflictual anxiety* is a response to socially unacceptable impulses; *social anxiety* is a response to perceived possible lost of status; *hypochondriasis* is a response to the possibility of catching a disease; *separation anxiety* is a response to the possible loss of a protective figure; *personal inadequacy* is a response to possible rejection; *obsessive hoarding* is a preparatory response to the possible loss of resources. Anxiety problems may be attributed to defects in regulatory mechanisms; they may be a result of normal emotional responses that are inappropriate or ineffective for dealing with the situation; or the emotional response may be normal and useful, but painful.

Anorexia nervosa. Voland and Voland (1989) reviewed the literature and examined case histories to determine the evolutionary mechanisms (e.g., reproductive suppression, kin selection, and parental role) involved in the development of anorexia nervosa. Anorexia nervosa was viewed as an adaptive evolutionary strategy to obtain support from the social environment or to withdraw from ontogenetic problems.

Postpartum depression. Hagen (1999) reported that the loss of interest in the infant that is seen in postpartum depression is an evolutionary mechanism to allow the mother to determine whether to invest in the infant. It is also a mechanism either to determine if there is support for the care of the offspring or to elicit social support. If the infant is not viable (for organic, social, or other reasons), the depression and withdrawing of interest in the infant could be mechanisms to distance the mother from emotional, time, energy, and other investments in the child. These behaviors could have been functional and adaptive at one time, but that may not be the case at this present time.

EVOLUTIONARY APPROACHES
TO CROSS-CULTURAL THERAPY

It is critical that we understand the evolutionary function of a behavior. This will help us understand how the behavior contributes to the survival of the species and its adaptive value (McGuire & Fairbanks, 1977; Weisfeld, 1977). Such an understanding will enable us to more effectively develop treatment applications. Also, obtaining an accurate understanding of the elemental reasons why such emotions as prejudice, hate, and anger evolved will increase our ability to deal with these destructive elements in our society.

Diagnosing

In his book *Evolution of Sickness and Healing,* H. Fabrega (1997) offers parameters for diagnosing sickness and providing treatment (healing) across cultures. Though his parameters are for the field of medicine, they should also be relevant, with modifications, to psychological diagnosing and treatment.

Social Medical Properties. Obtain information about the epidemiological characteristics of the client's problems. Obtain such information as nutrition; type, rate, and severity of problems; group characteristics; sociomedical problems; strengths; and weaknesses.

Organismic Manifestations. Know the signs and symptoms of problems, keeping in mind that the separating of problems into mind and body problems is not shared by many diverse cultural communities.

Knowledge. Learn the indigenous knowledge that the cultural group has about the problem.

Meanings. Become familiar with what the problem means to the person and the group the person belongs to. For example, is the problem believed to be the result of breaking taboos or of faulty ritual and morals?

Responses. Know how the person is supposed to respond to the problem in his or her culture.

Expectations of and Attitudes Toward Healing. What is the person's attitude toward those who deal with the problem, and what does the person expect of a healer?

Access to Healers and Settings of Healing. Who are the healers in the person's community?

Sick Role Conventions. How is the sick person expected to behave and what is he or she expected to do?

Sick Role Exploitation. What are the cultural conventions in terms of what the persons can or cannot socially manipulate because they have the presented problem—what can they get away with?

Stigmatization of Sickness. What does having the problem mean to people in that society? What are the cultural meanings? What are the markers of social identity and worth? Does it mean that one is weak, has a chemical imbalance, is impure, or is cursed? Does it mean that the person should be ostracized or discredited?

Healing (Therapy)

Number and Types of Healers. Who are the formal and informal healers? What is their prestige? What are the problems they have influence over? It should be noted that family members can be considered potential healers.

Knowledge of Healing. What is the knowledge level of the healers in the community? Are they respected? Are they trustworthy?

Meanings Associated with Healing. What are the meanings assorted with healing? Is it a technical procedure, a religious one, a ritual?

Responsibility and Accountability. Who is responsible and held accountable for the cause, conduct, or outcome of treatment (or any combination of these)? Is it the specialist, the sick person, the sick person's family, or the purity or cleverness of the healer?

Healing Actions. What interventions are used—medicines, incantations, anatomical manipulations, group activities, and so on?

Uncertainly and Probability of Relief. What are the person's perceptions of the probability of being successfully treated?

Relationship with the Sick Person. What is the quality of the relationship between the sick person and the healer—is it one of trust, with expectations of future reciprocation? Is it egalitarian, impersonal, moralistic, condemnatory, exhortatory, or supportive?

Influence on Sick Role. Who are the people, or what are the factors that endorse, authenticate, or verify the person's illness?

Competition Among Healers. Who are the people competing to offer services to the sick person? Which of these service providers are credible to the client?

Remuneration. How is payment usually made—favors, money, and so forth?

Ethical Codes. What are the ethical codes that the ethnic service providers subscribe to?

If the reader is interested in learning what physicians need to know in order to apply evolutionary approaches to medicine, see Nesse and Williams (1997) for curriculum and learning objectives.

Applications to Psychotherapy

McGuire and Troisi (1998) offer the following principles for therapeutic treatment from an evolutionary psychiatric perspective. It is recommended that the reader read their book to obtain more and better information about what I am briefly describing here. They state that warmth and understanding are very important as a basis for therapy. They divide their treatment principles into three groups: Group 1: Information Collection; Group 2: Causal Analysis; Group 3: Intervention Strategies.

Group 1: Information Collection

Principle 1: Functional Evaluation. This entails obtaining information about the development of the problem—including the onset, duration, intensity, and consequences of the problems—as well as examining functions that are impaired and those that are not, examining compensatory strategies, and investigating factors (internal and external) that contribute to the problem.

Principle 2: Functional Capacity Evaluation. This entails an analysis of capacities before and after the onset of the problem. McGuire and Troisi (1998) provide a detailed listing of factors (45 of them) to check for, in the following categories: information processing; social understanding behavior; social maintenance behavior; social manipulation behavior; social exchange behavior; self-understanding behavior; self-maintenance behavior (from McGuire & Troisi, 1998; *Darwinian Psychiatry*, Table 4.2, pp. 72–73).

Principle 3: Evaluation of Biological Goals and their Current Priorities. Assessing goals and priorities of the dysfunctional behavior. This can change with different biological states and stages of the individual—and can determine the optimal intervention strategies.

Principle 4: Resource Allocations. This examines the biological, physical, and psychological resources being allocated to the behavior/problem. This can help determine the individual's priorities and therapeutic goals.

Principle 5: The Costs and Benefits of Achieving Biological Goals. What are the benefits and costs for the individual experiencing these problems?

Principle 6: Person–Environment Interactions. This consists of examining the social aspects of the behavior, the person's interpretation of options available, the options society provides, and the environments that support the person's behavior.

Principle 7: Condition-Contributing Traits and States. An evaluation of the factors contributing to the individual's traits and states provides information about possible causes and treatment options.

Principle 8: Strategies. This principle examines the strategies people use in the implementation of their dysfunctional behavior; examining the ineffective strategies can provide information on appropriate interventions.

Group 2: Causal Analysis

Principle 9: Ultimate Cause Contributions. This principle tries to answer the question: What is the most important reason for the person behaving in the observed manner?

Principle 10: Infrastructural Functionality. How is information being selected, distorted, prioritized? What are the intensity and duration of the behaviors and feelings involved?

Principle 11: Proximate State and Events. What are the most immediate and closest dysfunctional psychological and physical systems and the results of these dysfunctions when interacting with self and others?

Principle 12: The 15% Principle. This refers to the authors' guidelines that there are often multiple causes for disorders and the percentage of contributions of the causes differs across individuals. For example, 10% of phenotype features may be explained by trait variation, 20% by dysfunctional autonomic systems, 15% by dysfunctional algorithms, 20% by adverse environmental factors, and 35% by attempts to adapt.

Group 3: Intervention Options and Strategies

Principle 13: Identifying Intervention Goals. Intervention can take the form of options and constraints in restoring the person's previous level of functioning, improving the person's functioning, dealing with long-term traits that are maladaptive, improving long-term problems, or any combination of these.

Principle 14: Treating Condition-Contributing Factors, Not Secondary Effects. If possible, treat the main problem—and not the secondary or tertiary ones.

The empirical examination of evolutionary ideas that can be applied to psychological mechanisms is barely 10 years old (Buss et al., 1998.) However, I offer the following to consider if one were to apply evolutionary approaches to mental health therapy. The mental health professional should

1. Have a good foundation in biological evolution.
2. Be familiar with the evolutionary psychology and evolutionary psychiatry literature. This should include (modified from Janicki, 1998) knowledge of the stresses and problems faced by early humans; anatomical, physical, and mental health mechanisms that evolved to deal with these problems; the relationship between the present-day environment and behavior to past environments and behaviors.
3. Have a good foundation in counseling approaches and techniques.

With the preceding as a foundation, the following approaches can be applied:

1. Determine if the behavior is universal. If there is evidence that the behavior disorder (e.g., depression, anxiety, schizophrenia) occurs across cultures, it is likely that there is an evolutionary basis for the behavior. Therefore, an evolutionary perspective may be relevant. Of course, we can expect that the disorder will have different cultural expressions—there will also be different manifestations as a function of gender and age. Obviously, if the disorder is evident in other species (especially mammals, because we are more closely related to them) then this, too, can be another indication that the behavior we see in humans has an evolutionary basis.
2. Determine the possible evolutionary function of the behavior/thought, and so forth. Perhaps a test will eventually be developed to help with this.
3. Inform the client of the possible evolutionary function of the behavior.
4. Work with the client to determine if the behavior can be expressed in a more appropriate, less problematic (i.e., adaptive) way.
5. Work with the family and community members (the latter is more relevant for people from cultures in which the community is important to the individual)—this will help with the development of culturally appropriate solutions.
6. Determine if the behavior can be used in a setting in which the behavior is more acceptable—keeping in mind that antisocial behaviors can be detrimental in the long run.
7. Determine if there are spangrels that can be used in a beneficial way.
8. Determine if the behavior can be modified (exaptation) so that its expression is less detrimental to self and others.

9. Are there other behaviors and feelings that accompany the problem—for example, overreaction, accompanying thoughts? If so, can the reactions be mitigated?

In establishing interventions (this includes drugs), determine the benefits of the intervention compared to the benefits of maintaining the evolutionary-based behavior. Determine if the intervention is in keeping or not with the evolutionary aspects of the behavior and the cultural elements. Those interventions that are in keeping with the evolutionary functions of the behavior and that are in sync with the culture (emic versus etic) will probably be more successful. With the preceding in mind, consider the following hypotheses and procedures:

1. Might behaviors and thoughts that are more primitive (e.g., prelanguage, prelogic, reptilian) be more amenable to behavioral approaches—because behavioral approaches are less language based and have been effectively used at different stages of ontology and have been effectively applied cross-phenogenically? In this framework, might techniques that bypass the frontal cortex—such as relaxation and hypnosis(?)—be more appropriate for problems mainly in the primitive part of the brain? One possible way to delineate whether the problem is in the more primative part of the brain or in the more developed areas such as the cortex and prefrontal cortex would be to examine the area of the brain that is active when the problem manifests itself—for example, through the use of neuroimaging techniques such as positron emission tomography (PET), single photon emission computed tomography (SPECT), magnetic resonance imaging (MRI), and electroencephalography (EEG).
2. Might behaviors and thoughts that are more mediated through the frontal cortex be better amended to approaches and techniques that are more language-based?
3. Develop measures to confirm or rule out the hypothesized evolutionary function of the behavior.
4. Develop criteria to determine if progress and goals are being met.
5. Evaluate the client's progress in general—what are the ramifications to the person—for example, in regard to biological functions, community reactions, or repercussions from family and significant others?
6. Determine if the person's cultural group meets his or her needs; if not, might another group be more conducive to the person's therapeutic process? Determine the functional and dysfunctional aspects of remaining in the group.

In addition to examining the behavior of individuals and the provision of therapy from an evolutionary perspective, one can also add to one's repertoire of understanding the individual and community by learning about the evolutionary development of the community. Drawing from the literature of such social scientists as Durkheim (1933), Toonies (1957), Childe (1951), Steward (1955), White (1959a, 1959b), and Marx and Engels, Axelson (1993) wrote of cultural evolution. He stated that his proposals are especially relevant to industrial and technical societies such as the United States and take into consideration the psychological and social movements of a culture and the effects on the quality of life. He proposes that cultural development occurs in the following stages (Axelson, 1993, pp. 9–10):

1. *Survival: subsistent level of existence.* This first stage entails attending to basic survival needs; cooperation and interdependence are essential. There is recognition that nature controls the environment, and the spirit, mind, and body are interconnected with the environment.
2. *Meeting basic needs: satisfaction of basic economic needs.* The group has its basic needs met and has an increase in the sense of personal control over nature. There is still respect for the environment, and the family and group are still important.
3. *Freedom from economic cares: satisfaction of basic economic needs and acquired wants.* At this stage, the group is no longer in a survival mode, needs are met, and experience has shown the group how to get these needs met. The spirit, mind, and body and environment are no longer as harmoniously in sync as in the previous stages. There is a greater sense of control over the environment, and there is less dependence on the group.
4. *Becoming a self-contained person: overindulgence and satiation of acquired wants.* People are no longer as dependent on each other for their needs and acquired wants; therefore, there is less reciprocity in group interactions. Individualism and competition are more prevalent at this stage, and there is more dissonance among the spirit, mind, body, and environment. There is greater emphasis on accumulating goods and seeking different lifestyles.
5. *Search for meaning and identity: antidote to depression and emptiness of life or life purpose.* There is alienation from one's group and increasing loss of identity—inducing loneliness, depression, and other psychological problems.
6. *Search for remedies: solutions and ways to break out of the conditions.* At this stage, problem-solving behaviors are implemented. The person may seek solutions through self-help groups, applying political and economic pressure, obtaining resources from the government, and so on. If the individual is able to adjust to the new conditions, then maybe stasis occurs.

Understanding of the previous model may provide insight as to when to make interventions in therapy and in communities, and the model may provide explains for behaviors and processes. For example, those at Stages 1 and 2 may be more concerned about survival issues and may be more integrated within themselves, their communities, and environment—making interventions more difficult for the therapist. The model can provide insight into why those at the bottom of the socioeconomic level do not rebel, vote, and get involved in the political process. Stages 3 and 4 can be characterized as the person (or community) experiencing greater confusion within the self and with others. This stage might be a good phase to help provide self-exploration for the person and help the person examine his or her culture. Stage 5 could be a good phase for taking action in terms of therapeutic change, organizing, getting involved in the political arena, and so forth. And stage 6 might be a phase where interactions with the therapist are no longer warranted; people know themselves and are integrated with self and environment.

EXPLANATIONS OF RACISM

From a psychological perspective, there are many explanations for the existence of racism. Axelson (1993) reported the following:

Rigid Personality—There is a personality type that has the same response in different situations. For example, a person gets an initial impression that Native Americans are lazy. The person with the rigid personality will use this same impression for all Native Americans over a period of time and will not change her or his initial impression.

Authoritarian Personality—The authoritarian personality type does not like ambiguity. These people do not use reality testing to modify their biased, inappropriate, or hasty conclusions. They value obedience and conformity and fear self-expression. Like the rigid personality type, they have a predisposed view and have problems restructuring their perceptions. The rigid personality type, the authoritarian personality type, and other personality types may often use displacement and projection as psychological defenses when dealing with minorities.

Projection—The process whereby a person attributes to others the feelings that he or she really feels about those other people. For example, people may have hatred against Asians, but they do not like to admit to themselves that they have these feelings. They therefore feel that Asians hate them—this would justify their hating Asians (because they are reacting to the hatred and are not initiating it).

Displacement—The process whereby a person has feelings about a situation or person, but instead of directing these feelings toward the situation or person that elicits the feelings, the person directs them at another situation or person. For example, a person may get fired from a job, but instead of attacking the boss who did the firing, the person attacks minorities.

Along with the various evolutionary theories to explain racism, one can make the case that there is an evolutionary basis for the exclusion of individuals and groups (Rushton, 1995). The following are some explanations provided by authors.

Stevens and Price (1996) wrote that racism could be an attempt to raise one's status by depreciating others. It could be a mechanism to deal with fears of separation from one's group. It could be a mechanism of maintaining a rank hierarchy in the social system.

Cherry (1994) wrote that we want to perpetuate the genes of our group; therefore, we tend to bond with those who share the same genetic composition as us and to exclude those who are dissimilar. As groups and individuals, it is important to be able to differentiate who is safe or dangerous, what is healthy or not, and so on. This ability to differentiate and generalize enables the group to safeguard itself and to differentiate and conceptualize friend from enemy (Pfenning & Sherman, 1995).

It is possible that during times of scarce resources we tend to hoard and protect our resources because we need the resources to survive and perpetuate ourselves. There is evidence of this in history; for example, the rise of the Nazis occurred during times of economic distress in Germany; the KKK made more inroads during times of economic stress in the United States. Bigotry and prejudice occur during these times because we want to exclude those threatening our resources. During times of abundance these attitudes and behaviors are still there, but they may operate in more subtle and indirect ways.

When one group has more resources than another, then there is a tendency to try to provide explanations and justifications as to why this is the case. Explanations and justifications can include the following: The group possesses more resources because its members deserve it, or because they are better, or are smarter, or their God is better, or they are fitter, or they work harder, or they play by the rules, or they are more virtuous, or are more entitled, or they have to assert their rights (e.g., against reverse discrimination), and so on. These attitudes and behaviors are so ingrained that they often occur without people being cognizant about them—although people against whom they are justifying these attitudes and behaviors are acutely aware of being discriminated against and keep these memories for a long time. The group in control makes the rules and makes sure (consciously or unconsciously) that the rules are stacked in its members' favor. The control and rules can be manifested in such activities as job discrimination, controlling who gets admitted to schools, determining who gets promoted or who gets banks loans, and so on.

Although one group may engage in such activities as racism in order to perpetuate its positions of power, in the long run such behaviors may be detrimental to its interests and to society. For example, it is highly unlikely that the discrimination that is directed toward racial groups is an isolated phenomenon; once these behaviors are unleashed, it is highly probable that they can also be directed against other groups as well—such as those of different religions, political views, gender, and so on. One of the reasons for our capacity to quickly shift the objects of discrimination is that we can easily shift the category of who is in our ingroup and who is in the outgroup (Tajfel, 1970, 1981, 1982; Tajfel & Billig, 1974). We can define who is in the ingroup and who is in the outgroup for relatively trivial reasons (Billig & Tajfel, 1973; Brewer & Silver, 1978; Locksley, Borgida, Brekke, & Hepburn, 1980; Wilder, 1981). Such ways of categorizing people can have enormous repercussions—such as engaging in favoritism toward our ingroup, viewing our ingroup as being superior, having greater identification with and attachment to our ingroup, and so on. And the converse may also occur; for example, those who are in the outgroup may be viewed in a less favorable light, negative attributes may relegated to them, they may be viewed as a homogenous group, and so forth. Discriminatory behaviors can cause instability in the system—those who are being discriminated against may find methods to subvert or change the system and to remove those who are perpetuating the injustice.

Just because we have "innate" exclusionary behaviors does not mean that these exclusionary behaviors cannot be changed. It should be noted that a great deal of the evolutionary literature on group interactions focuses on the competitive aspect—for example, survival of the fittest, striving for dominance, and so on. However, there is another line of research, and some theorists suggest that evolution has also developed mechanisms that promote group interactions: We may have evolved with such behaviors as cooperation and altruism hardwired into our brains (Barkow, Cosmides, & Tooby, 1995; McGrew & Feistner, 1995). It is hoped that this line of research can provide us with further information on the dynamics of human interaction. Such research can shed light on how to overcome the barriers (such as racism) that impede beneficial human relationships.

There are numerous reasons why a group may want to have cohesion, promote harmony, and so forth. Cooperation and cohesion may decrease the need to expend resources allocated for fighting; the resources allocated to war and suppression may be better allocated elsewhere. The promotion of harmony may promote the group's cultural and religious values of living together and not hurting others. The promotion of harmony may spare loss (e.g., of human lives) to the suppressing group: In suppressing another group, the groups being suppressed may defend themselves and hurt the group that is attacking them. Harmony may decrease retribution from the group being attacked.

Groups may want to have cohesion to coordinate their activities to increase economic, political, and military power. Such increases may in turn engender increases in land, food production, technology, people, and so on. (However, one should be aware that if the group's resources run low and reach a critical point [Stevens & Price, 1996], then the mechanisms that promote group solidarity may no longer operate, and competition among groups will facilitate prejudice and racism.)

The proclivity to coordinate our activities to increase our resources by forming alliances can serve as one solution to overcoming racism and prejudice: When we form alliances, our perceptions of who are our friends (ingroup) and enemies (outgroup) are changed. History is replete with examples of how attitudes and behaviors change with changing political and economic alliances. Americans once considered Japanese and Germans their enemies (e.g., the outgroup). When it was to our advantage to form alliances with them, our attitudes and behaviors changed, and we now see them in a more positive light. The key element here is to convince people who are our friends and enemies. When we look at animal behavior, we find that animals can coexist if there isn't competition for resources and when one animal's survival is not at the expense of another. Perhaps we can create these conditions for our society.

To perpetuate our survival, we have evolved to incorporate larger ingroups—from family, to tribe, to clans, to states and nations. We have formed alliances based on region, language, religion, economic interest, political similarities, class, age, gender, and commonality of experience. Those societies that were unable to form alliances to enlarge their power and to form defenses would perish when confronted with larger, stronger forces. Therefore, for our own survival, we need to be more encompassing in who we consider to be in our ingroup.

Because societies and peoples vary in whom they ostracize (e.g., Protestants, Catholics, the Irish, Italians, smokers, and sex offenders have been ostracized), this suggests that whom we ostracize is a choice and that the object of our rejection does not stem from an immutable innate process. Although the "rejection gene" may be innate, whom we reject is mutable.

We are more than instincts. Whom we include or exclude are learned behaviors. Nature has made us malleable. John Calhoun (1967) stated that pathological behavior, by its very definition, denotes an inability to adjust to ongoing conditions. Behavior becomes incompatible with these conditions when the individual fails to fulfill the role that contributes to the success of the biological or cultural system of which he is, or should be, a component part (p. 1). Those societies and individuals who cannot modify their instinctual behaviors to meet the needs of society and the environment are likely to fail and not survive. How we react to racism is a choice, not a predetermined, genetic response.

In terms of evolution, it is critical for our society to develop the ability to incorporate diverse populations, views, and behaviors. It is understandable why we may resent such inclusions. We may be uncomfortable with differences. We may feel economic competition. We may feel threatened by the new people's genes going into our gene pool (which is a ridiculous perspective because all human genes are essentially alike). Our propensity to feel more comfortable with the familiarity of our own kind provides us with known quantities and predictability. But keeping within the constraints of the familiar can be problematic—just as inbreeding within a certain gene pool can engender deleterious recessive chromosomal disorders.

Keeping within the constraints of the familiar and our own kind hinders the diversity of views that is so important to problem-solving. It is almost a universal phenomena that cross-fertilization of ideas, technology, and people has resulted in advances that improve societies. Hybrids of grains have resulted in greater yields. Incorporation of metals from other sources has resulted in better technology with which to compete with our neighbors. The glorious middle kingdom of China was slaughtered by the more modern Europeans and Japanese because the Manchu government refused to incorporate newer ideas and technologies. Like it or not, diversity increases our problem-solving skills and therefore increases our survivability. It is our capacity to incorporate new ways of doing things that has enabled us to be successful as a species.

Culture implements evolution's task of survival and reproduction. If we understand evolution we can gain a better understanding of why behaviors manifest themselves. Understanding of evolution and cultural manifestations may provide us with further information regarding which interventions will be more difficult to implement and sustain, and which will be easier to implement and sustain; in other words, those interventions that are syntonic (in sync) with evolution and culture will probably be more accepted by the client and will more likely be sustained, whereas those interventions that are dystonic (not in sync) with evolution and culture may be more difficult to implement and sustain.

6

---⏷⏵---

Special Populations: Sexual Orientation, Disabilities, Children, Women, and Older Persons

One of the main purposes of this book is to look at some of the issues affecting the mental health of non-White ethnic groups. The economic, political, social, and power aspects are examined because of the enormous detrimental effects of racism on these factors. Within each ethnic group, there are also factors that affect non-White populations—intergenerational conflicts, traditional versus modern views, religious schisms, regional and class differences, and so on. It is important that we explore the various populations within the ethnic communities—we can learn from them, what we learn can be used to help them and others.

Certain groups within minority groups are often burdened by their ethnicity and by society allocating less valence to some particular characteristic they possess. These groups and their issues may be ignored by the power holders and by their own communities. However, in learning about them and their issues we can learn principles and dynamics that we can use to improve our understanding of human behavior; for example, disability studies have indicated that when a person has a disability, people generalize that individual as having other negative characteristics. Similarly, if a person is of a certain ethnic group, certain negative characteristics are generalized to the person. Reid (as cited in DeAngelis, 2001a) noted that in our ignoring gender, class, religion, disabilities, and sexual orientation issues, the real context of people's lives is missed.

The data on such populations as ethnic minority lesbians and gay males, women, those with disabilities, older persons, and children are limited (U.S.

Department of Health and Human Services, 2000). The data that are available on these groups were garnered from research studies conducted at various times, with assorted populations, at a variety of settings. Though there are clear patterns (e.g., poverty and racism can induce stress; therefore, ethnic minorities who are poor and who are discriminated against may have more problems), the data have yet to be accumulated. The reader is encouraged to follow up on the sources from which this chapter draws and to obtain specific information about sample characteristics, methodology, date of research, and so forth.

As mentioned previously, there have yet to be national surveys, with appropriate assessment and approaches, conducted to obtain a clearer picture of the prevalence of mental disorders among the ethnic groups. Once the data are accumulated and analyzed, we can begin the process of more accurately gauging the problems of special populations within the ethnic subgroups. In examining minority data, one should be aware that the prevalence of articles and activity around a certain topic or problem may not necessarily reflect the most important or accurate picture of a group. For example, much of the literature on minority homosexuality discusses the issue of AIDS. However, this is not necessarily the most defining or relevant problem. Similarly, much of the literature on minority adolescents discusses the juvenile justice system. The large amount of attention paid to this aspect of minority youth should not necessarily define them. This does not necessarily mean that these are not problems, but it does mean that the number of articles and conferences held on a certain topic could be more a function of what White society defines as problems and where it is willing to provide funding.

Though we lack accurate mental health data on minority ethnic groups, we do have some data—such as the data on minority health and crime. There are various reasons why we might have more information on some areas of minority populations than on others. Crime and physical and biological problems are easier to measure; thus it might be easier to obtain data on these problems than on mental health problems. Also, there might be greater effort expended to obtain data on minority problems that affect White society groups (such as crime and AIDS). In addition, some advocacy groups are better organized than others. It should be noted that we often make distinctions between health and crime problems and data, and those of mental health. However, health, crime, stress, and mental health problems affect each other in a cybernetic fashion—each can be the cause and effect of the other.

For the reader interested in general guidelines on how to deal with diverse groups, the American Psychological Association has provided "Guidelines for Providers of Psychological Services to Ethnic, Linguistic, and Culturally Diverse Population" (American Psychological Association,

1993). Keep in mind that these are general guidelines and may not necessarily apply to the more specific groups mentioned in this chapter.

SEXUAL ORIENTATION/HOMOSEXUALITY

Most of the cross-cultural studies on sexual orientation issues indicate that little has been written on lesbian, bisexual, transsexual, and transvestite issues. Most of the cross-cultural information on sexual orientation is on male homosexuality. Because this book is focused more on making statements based on data, much of this section will be on male homosexuality. This should not be construed as meaning that the issues of lesbianism and transgender, transsexual, bisexual, and other sexual orientations are less important—there simply is not much data in these areas. When one reads the literature on cross-cultural views of lesbian, bisexual, transgender, transsexual, and transvestite issues, the writers often report that the views on these populations can be extrapolated from information garnered from what has been written on gay males.

It is clear that the depiction of a culture's behavior and values concerning homosexuality is not encompassed in a single, unilateral perspective. The cultures of Africa, Asia, and South America (as is the case for the cultures of Europe) have, and have had, different views and practices in regard to homosexuality. Within a cultural group, there are people who subscribe to different beliefs and practices, at different periods of time. There are differences between religious beliefs and practices. There are differences in espoused values and actual behaviors. There are differences in the spectrum from "conservative" to "liberal" views. There are differences in interpretations. And there are differences between people who subscribe to the spirit of the religion, compared to those who believe they are following the perceived original strictures. Please keep the preceding caveats in mind as you read the following. Because religion can be one key factor in influencing cultural attitudes and values, the following information is provided to help the reader obtain insight into elements that might influence ethnic minorities' attitudes toward homosexuality and people of different sexual orientations.

Christianity, Judaism, and Islam. The monotheistic religions (Judaism, Christianity, and Islam) draw their main tenets from the Hebrew bible. The traditional interpretation of the bible is that it clearly and dogmatically condemns homosexuality. For example, Leviticus 18:22: "You shall not lie with a male as with a woman; it is an abomination." Leviticus 18:30: "So keep my charge never to practice any of these abominable customs which were practiced before you, and never to defile yourselves by them: I am the LORD your God." Romans 1:26: "For this reason God gave them up to dishonorable passions. Their women exchanged natural relations for unnatural." Romans 1:27: "and the men likewise gave up natural relations with women and were consumed with passion for one another, men committing shameless acts with men and receiving in their own persons the due penalty for their error." (Quoted material is from the *Revised Standard Version of the Bible*, 1971.) Of course, these and other biblical statements are controversial, and there is much disagreement in terms of meaning, intent, interpretation, and the weight to which one should give to these biblical statements.

There are some who believe that this stricture against homosexuality has its basis in Judaism's attempt to monopolize the association of sexual activity with procreation and propagation. With the spreading of Christianity and Islam to other countries and cultures, endogenous, traditional values and perceptions have been replaced by these dynamic, insistent, persistent religions' perspective concerning homosexuality. There are wide ranges of beliefs and attitudes in all three religions toward homosexuality.

Islam. Contemporary cultures that subscribe to the Koran believe that it specifically and vigorously condemns homosexuality. However, some believe that there is a distinction between homosexual behavior and thought (Khan, 2001). The behavior is condemned, but people with attraction to the same gender should refrain from acting on their thoughts, and they are encouraged to seek help and guidance from Allah in this lifelong struggle. There is a belief that homosexuality, as with many other behaviors, comes under the rubric of free will (Rashid, 2001), and as such, people have the capacity to exercise free will and should not engage in the sinful homosexual practices.

Hinduism. Homosexuality is a hot issue in India right now. Many claim that the colonization of India by Britain has left a legacy of attitudes and legislations against homosexuality (it is an illegal act in India). Most of the present efforts are directed at the maintenance of these attitudes and laws, although certain small groups want change. Prior to colonization by England, it seems that there was a wide range of practices at different times and places. Regarding what the ancient scriptures say about homosexuality, it seems to be a moot topic. There do not seem to be clear, definitive statements as to its morality or immorality (whereas the Old Testament is clear in its condemnation). There are people who state that the ancient scriptures (e.g., the Vedas) are silent on the subject. Others write that the ancient literature condemned it. And others write that it is condoned. Some state that propagation is the foundation of Hinduism; therefore, homosexuality is an antithesis to this value. Some of those who believe that ancient India condoned homosexuality base their case on the fact that there are many ancient visual depictions of homosexual acts (e.g., temple carvings), as well as literary descriptions (e.g., the Karma Sutra) of homosexuality. What is clear is that in present-day India, homosexuality is not condoned and is often condemned.

Native American. Before the invasion of Europeans and Christianity, many Native American cultures viewed lesbians, gay males, and cross dressers as special beings. Though each Native American culture had its own term for men who acted as women, Europeans used the term *berdaches* to describe them. In the Native American cultures, they were often spiritual leaders, healers, and teachers. They were considered to have the gift of being able to enter both male and female worlds and could serve as liaisons of these worlds to those who lived only in the heterosexual world. Present-day Native American gay, lesbian, bisexual , transgender, and transsexual groups are endeavoring to use the terms *two-spirit* to describe these people—instead of using the traditional *berdache* term. *Berdache* derives from a Persian term, *bardaj*, which is considered by those who advocate the *two spirit* term to be too negative in its connotations—Europeans used it as derogatory term, with connotations implying an effeminate young boy. Parker (2002) wrote, "A study of Indian berdache culture could teach us all a way to break out of the narrow-minded Western model of 'deviance' and allow us to appreciate the beautiful diversity of the human population in our species of humankind wherever they may fall along the spectrum of the beautiful gender rainbow" (p. 2).

Buddhism. Buddhism considers homosexuality a sexual act—just as heterosexuality is. Like heterosexuality, it is considered a right or wrong activity, based on ethical precepts. Lesbians and gay males are considered no more or less libidinous than heterosexuals. Homosexual and heterosexual activities are expected to be guided by moral behavior. Behavior is defined as moral based on the following criteria (Theravada Buddhism): Would you engage in the activity if you would not want it done to you? Does the activity cause harm? Does the behavior help you attain your ethical and moral goals (e.g., to lead a "good life," to be virtuous, to be honorable and decent, to attain a mental state of peace and purity—Nirvana)? Also, is the behavior motivated by good intentions—for example, love, generosity, compassion? If the answer is "no" to the preceding questions, then one would need to examine whether the behavior is moral and ethical.

Actual Practices

Though some religions and cultures proscribe homosexual behaviors, in actual practice these prohibitions are often mitigated. For example, in many cultures, sexual activity with people of the same gender may not define the person as a lesbian or gay male because of such factors as the age at which the activity was engaged in. Hatfield and Rapson (1996) wrote that there is great variation in the acceptance and practice of same-gender sexual activities. They cite authors who found that 64% of tribal societies condone same-gender sexual behaviors at some time; for example, Siwan (African) men and boys consider it the norm to engage in such behaviors; in Azande, Dahomey, !Kung, and other societies in Africa, adolescent girls often engage in same-gender sexual activity. In Morocco, attitudes toward homosexual behaviors are mixed; for example, Hatfield and Rapson wrote that the Zawijas accept homoerotic activities among boys in their early teens. Young men who engage in these activities do not think of themselves as gay and consider themselves as going through a phase. To be a passive (as compared to being dominant) participant in these activities is considered demeaning, and homosexual activities among adult males are considered shameful. Same-gender sexual behaviors among women are considered very rare—perhaps because their sexual activities are strictly controlled.

An excellent source of cross-cultural data is the Human Relations Area Files (HRAF). The HRAF is a depository of cultural anthropology data. A consortium of universities, colleges, and research institutions participates in the accumulation of the data. Most of the files in the HRAF do not contain data on homosexual activities; however, 52 researchers did report on these activities. It was found that male homosexuality was condemned, mocked, and ridiculed in 48% of these societies. It was ignored or not understood in 8% of societies. Twenty-seven percent of the societies found it acceptable. And in 17% it was traditional and well-accepted. In 83% of the societies, less than 20% of the men were reported to engage in homosexual behaviors. In 15% of the societies, 20–50% of the men engaged in homosexual behaviors. In 3% of the societies, at least 50% of the men engaged in homosexual behaviors. Hatfield and Rapson (1996) wrote, "Unfortunately, they almost never mention women's preferences" (p. 120).

In the Chinese culture, Wen (as cited in Hatfield & Rapson, 1996) asked men and women if they ever had homosexual "inclinations" or engaged in pleasurable homosexual behaviors; 1% admitted to having such feelings or acting upon them. Five years later, he surveyed only women and found that 21% had such feelings or had engaged in such behaviors.

Americans were sampled in a survey conducted by the National Opinion Research Center (Davis & Smith, as cited in Hatfield & Rapson, 1996). It was found that 75% thought that homosexual relations were always or almost always wrong; 4% thought it was sometimes wrong, 15% thought it was not wrong; and 6% were not sure.

Among the Europeans, after the heyday of the Greek and Rome cultures, homosexual behaviors were generally disapproved. In present Western cultures, Samson, Levy, Dupras, and Tessier (as cited in Hatfield & Rapson, 1996) wrote that there is variability of attitudes, with the French being more tolerant of sexual diversity and the Americans having a high degree of anxiety about sex. They wrote that there is increasing acceptance of homosexuality throughout the world.

Contemporary U.S. Homosexual Mental Health Data

Although a lot of literature has been published on male homosexuality, there has been little compiled data on minority gay males—and even less on minority lesbians, transsexuals, and those of other sexual orientations. The literature has directed attention at the persecution of lesbians and gay males; the suicide rate of homosexual adolescents; aging lesbians and gay males; the discrimination against lesbians and gay males in housing, marriage, work, and society; benefits; laws; and so on. Most of the published literature on minority lesbians and gay males consists of anecdotal, descriptive, literary, small samples, or "qualitative" materials. The quantitative data on minority lesbians and gay males is mostly in regard to AIDS, HIV—whereas the data on minorities are usually in terms of housing, education, health, social services, employment, poverty, discrimination, drugs, violence, education, and so forth.

The ethnic minority lesbian and gay male may experience more problems than lesbians and gay males who are not ethnic minorities. The following are some of the problems they may encounter. Service providers may not know how to effectively reach the minority gay population. The gay minority member may encounter greater stigma from the minority community. There could be a lack of good educational information and information on resources. There may be suspicion and distrust of the service provider. Service providers may provide differential treatment to gay minorities. There could be insufficient and ineffective resources allocated to minority communities—and the resources that are allocated may fail to trickle down to such subgroups as lesbians and gay males. Tremblay and Ramsay (2000) presented a paper at the 11th Annual Sociological Symposium in San Diego State University, in which they provide a good summary of homosexual mental health problems. Though there are only tangential references to minorities—specifically, African Americans—the information may be helpful in elucidating some of the problems of ethnic minority lesbians and gay males. The following is from their paper.

Proportionally higher rates of depression, suicidal behaviors, anxiety, and HIV have been reported for gay males and African American lesbians and gay males (though HIV and AIDS are now rising at greater rates among heterosexuals and females). They report studies indicating elevated rates of drug and alcohol abuse for lesbians and gay males, African American lesbians and gay males, and bisexuals. These higher incidences appear to be related to the higher rates of personality disorders and emotional problems for lesbians and gay males. The latter elevation may be related to those lesbians and gay males who have not attained the emotionally healthier stage of self-acceptance in their homosexual identity development. Tremblay and Ramsay (2000) go on to say that adult gay males encounter psychological and physical abuse and stigma due to "minority stress."

A survey of adolescents who self-identified as being homosexual, gay, lesbian, bisexual, or engaged in same-gender sexual activity found that gay, lesbian, and heterosexual adolescents who were subjected to harassment based on their assumed "homosexual orientation" were at greater risk for attempting suicide, compared to adolescents who were not subjected to harassment based on their sexual orientation. There have been reports of "feminine" gay males encountering problems integrating into the gay community, and gay people of color encountering racial abuse by the gay community. Personality factors, drugs, stress, and stage of "coming out of the closet" can impact the emotional state of the person with homosexual proclivities.

There are a number of support groups for those of different sexual orientation. For the minority group member, there are pros and cons to joining these groups. Some of the benefits of the activities of these groups include

- Affiliations with these groups provide psychological and social support for minority group members who share the characteristics of these groups.
- Affiliations with these groups allow the minority members to interact on a basis other than ethnicity.
- Some minority communities may not provide support for those with different sexual orientation—support groups can fill this void.

Some of the drawbacks to ethnic minority lesbians and gay males affiliating with these groups include

- These groups are eager to recruit participants to their cause and often want the minority group members to consider their ethnic social, economic, and political needs to be secondary to those based on gender and sexual preference.
- Affiliation with these groups may draw attention to the ethnic minority person—and may result in ostracism and social, economic, and political repercussions.

MINORITIES WITH DISABILITIES

The study of disabilities in a cross-cultural context is relevant to minority mental health because it increases our knowledge of how to help minorities with disabilities, and the attribution and attitudinal studies of disabilities add to increased understanding of perceptions of majority groups toward minorities. In terms of the differences between U.S. ethnic group members with disabilities compared to those living in less economically developed countries, in a simplistic fashion the issues are easy to convey—countries that do not have the resources do not provide resources to help those with disabilities; countries with resources provide resources but have to contend with issues revolving around defining disabilities, deciding who has disabilities, how much and what kind of resources to provide, and providing accessibility. Perhaps more than with any other group investigated in this book, it is difficult (perhaps erroneous) to try to gauge the common mental disorders of those with disabilities. The category of people with disabilities encompasses groups with vastly different problems, characteristics, and types of disabilities. They can range from the young to the very old, from those with one or more of the wide range of learning disabilities to those with one or more of the wide ranges of physical and psychological disabilities. Olkins (as cited in DeAngelis, 2001a) stated that there is little research on the overlap between disabilities and such characteristics as minority status, gender, sexual orientation, child abuse, sexuality, and romantic behaviors.

Minorities have disability rates that are one and a half to two times higher than that of the general population. Of those in the 16 to 64 years age group, African Americans constitute a larger segment of minority persons with disabilities than any other group (Walker, Orange, & Rackley—as cited in Kundu & Dutta, 1995). Minority groups with disabilities are deemed ineligible for rehabilitation services at higher rates than are the general population of persons with disabilities; it takes longer for minorities to obtain eligibility determination; and those who are eligible receive fewer services, the rehabilitation process takes longer, and fewer cases are closed successfully (Atkins & Wright—as cited in Kundu & Dutta, 1995).

International Studies

Two cross-cultural disabilities studies are presented in this section of the chapter. These studies may help us understand some cultural perspectives on disabilities. One study is by Berry and Dalal (1996), and the other is by Westbrook, Varoe, and Pennay (1993). The study by Berry and Dalal (1996) provides information garnered from different international sites. The other study, by Westbrook et al., was conducted in Australia, but the report mentions that the Anglo Australian attitudes were similar to those of "Americans." Westbrook et al.'s study can shed light on the dynamics of cultural groups in the United States because some of the same ethnic groups that emigrate to Australia also come to the United States.

Berry and Dalal (1996) authored a report for the International Centre for the Advancement of Community Based Rehabilitation (ICACBR). They were involved in an international project studying disability attitudes, beliefs, and behaviors. In their report, they presented a review of attitudinal research. The following is some of what they reported. They wrote that Wright (1960) found that people's attitudes toward those with disabilities can range from indifference to positive regard. They report that Yuker (as cited in Berry & Dalal) found that prejudice toward a person with disability is generalized to others with disabilities, and that familiarity with those with disabilities led to more positive attitudes. Age, education, occupation, and economic status did not affect attitudes (Yuker, 1994). Women, as compared to men, had a more positive attitude toward those with disabilities (Siller, Chipman, Ferguson, & Vann, 1967; as cited in Berry & Dalal; Yuker, Block, & Campbell, 1960). Low self-esteem seemed to be related to greater prejudice toward those with disabilities (Eisenman, 1970). There seems to be a generalization and stereotyping effect when some people interact with those with disabilities; that is, the negative evaluation of the condition of disability is generalized to other characteristics that are not demonstrated.

In Berry and Dalal's (1996) studies, one of the factors they investigated was people's attitudes toward those with disabilities. They wanted to determine whether people in their samples had positive or negative attitudes toward those with disabilities. They were also interested in how different cultures viewed the cause of the disability. Their measures were designed to determine the participants' views of the cause of the disability—was the disability the result of one's behavior, was it because of external forces beyond one's control, or was because of "cosmic" forces (e.g., fate, karma)? Their review of attribution theory, in terms of the causes of disabilities, can increase our understanding of perceptions of majority groups toward minorities. Some studies found that when people with disabilities are viewed as being responsible for their disability (internally controlled), more stigma is attached to those people's disabilities (Jones et al., 1984). Mental and behavioral disabilities were often viewed as being more internally controlled than were physical disabilities (Weiner, Perry, & Magnusson, 1988). Individuals who were viewed as having some control over their features or disabilities often elicited anger and neglect from others. When a disability was viewed as not being induced by the person with the disability, then pity was elicited.

According to Kelley's (1972, 1973) attribution theory, we view people's behavior as being internally or externally controlled based on three factors: consistency, distinctiveness, and consensus. Consistency can be defined as the degree to which a person reacts to a particular stimulus in the same manner on other occasions. Distinctiveness can be defined as the degree to which a person reacts in the same manner to other stimuli. And consensus can be defined as the degree to which other people react in the same manner as the person does to particular stimuli. People tend to make inferences of internal attributions when consistency is high, distinctiveness is low, and consensus is low. People tend to make external attributions for a behavior when consistency is high, distinctiveness is high, and consensus is high.

Berry and Dalal (1996) wrote that another attributer could be added to the preceding internal and external factors: cosmic factors. Although cosmic factors are often included in the external factors category, Berry and Dalal, and others, suggest that cosmic factors should be relegated to a separate category. Cosmic factors include making attributions (e.g., of a disability) as the result of karma, "the hand of God," and so forth.

Berry and Dalal (1996) also wrote that another measure was also used in the cross-cultural disabilities studies: relational attitudes. The concept of relational attitudes derives from the research literature on acculturation—that is, the research on the process describing how one person or group adjusts to another. Berry's (1980) theory of acculturation suggests that there are various ways of adjusting when one person or group encounters another culture: assimilation, integration, separation (or segregation), and marginalization. *Assimilation* occurs when group identity has low value, and relationships with the encountered group have high value—one's identity is relinquished and becomes part of the other group. *Integration* occurs when one's group identity is valued and maintained and becomes part of the other cultural group. *Segregation* is present when there is high value placed on one's group identity and a low value on relationships with the other group. Separation can then occur—separation that is either self-imposed, imposed by the group doing the ostracizing, or both. The fourth option is *marginalization*. Under conditions of marginalization, the group considers itself—or is forced to be considered—as alienated from the other group.

> Assimilation implies that persons with [a] disability should be treated exactly like other people, integration implies that persons with [a] disability, while acknowledging their special needs, should be integrated into the larger group. Segregation implies that persons with [a] disability are different and should be treated accordingly. Marginalization implies that persons with [a] disability have no special needs and have no role in the community life. Thus, these four options or modes of adjustment reveal different kinds of attitude that people may have. (Berry & Dalal, 1996, p. 18)

They sampled groups from Canada, India, Bangladesh, and Indonesia. The project was carried out at the following locations: Meadow Lake and Napanee (Canada); Bombay: BDD Chawls, Ellora, Juchandra, and Allahabad: Sirathu and Muradpur (India); Dhaka (Bangladesh); and North Sulawesi (Indonesia). Napanee was selected to provide views representing European-origin thinking about disability. The Meadow Lake Aboriginal (Cree and Dene) sample was selected to represent a rural community similar to those in Asia in terms of socioeconomic status and health resources. The Allahabad and Bombay samples were selected to provide rural/urban contrasts with India. And the Bangladesh and Indonesian rural village samples were intended to provide a comparison with the other rural samples.

The actual results of the data were tentative, and Berry and Dalal found that the meaning of their findings depended on local interpretations of the data and results. However, they found that "it is clear that beliefs and attitudes towards causes, control and responsibility for disability, and relationships with persons with a disability, clearly vary across the samples in this study." They found that the development of programs needed to be tailored to the beliefs and attitudes of the people at the various sites. The report states that in cultures and countries that are trying to maintain basic life functions, and in countries that are experiencing exploitation, unemployment, and degrading conditions, there is severe competition for diminishing resources. Under such conditions, those with handicaps suffer more societal prejudices.

The second study I would like to report on is that by Westbrook et al. (1993). They studied Chinese, Italian, German, Greek, Arabic, and Anglo Australian communities in Australia to determine these groups' attitudes toward disabilities. They surveyed the attitudes of these groups toward people having problems with asthma, diabetes, heart disease, arthritis, amputation of an arm or a leg, cancer, stuttering, facial scars and birthmarks, blindness, deafness, stroke, epilepsy, multiple sclerosis, paraplegia, dwarfism, alcoholism, cerebral palsy, psychiatric illness, mental retardation, and AIDS.

They found significant differences in these communities' attitudes to 19 of these 20 disabilities. No differences were found in the groups' attitudes toward people with arthritis. The German community was significantly more accepting than were Anglo Australians of people with amputation, stroke, cerebral palsy, psychiatric illness, and mental retardation. Compared to Anglo Australians, members of the Italian community were less accepting of those with asthma, amputation, blindness, paraplegia, and AIDS. The Greek community was less accepting of people having problems with asthma, diabetes, heart disease, amputation, cancer, stuttering, blindness, epilepsy, paraplegia, and AIDS. Arab-speaking members were less accepting of those with asthma, diabetes, heart disease, amputation, cancer, stuttering, blindness, epilepsy, paraplegia, alcoholism, and AIDS. Compared to Anglo Australians, members of the Chinese community were more accepting of dwarfism and mental retardation, but less accepting of those with asthma, diabetes, heart disease, amputation, cancer, stuttering, blindness, paraplegia, and AIDS. The average ratings of all communities significantly differed from those of the Anglo-Australians. The German community was significantly more accepting than other communities were, and the other communities were significantly less accepting than were the Anglo Australians. The Arab-speaking members most stigmatized those with disabilities. The four least stigmatized conditions in all communities were asthma, diabetes, heart disease, and arthritis. The four least accepted disabilities in all communities were AIDS, mental retardation, psychiatric illness, and cerebral palsy. Members of the Anglo Australian and German communities were more likely to consider it appropriate for those with disabilities to be integrated into the community. Many members of non–Anglo Australian communities were less likely to utilize community rehabilitation services.

In their survey, Westbrook et al. (1993) found that there is a significant mismatch between the ethnic communities and the mainstream service providers. The authors warn of differences in the attitudes of ethnic service providers—some may be influenced by their ethnic communities and some may be influenced by the effects of their Anglo-based training. It is interesting to note that ethnic community members with disabilities frequently found greater acceptance outside their communities than within them.

Triandis and Hofstede (as cited in Westbrook et al., 1993) and Hofstede (as cited in Westbrook et al., 1993) provided an explanation for some of Westbrook et al.'s (1993) findings. Triandis delineates many societies into those having either individualistic cultures or collectivistic cultures. Individualistic cultures value autonomy, self-reliance, and independence. Collectivist cultures value duty, conformity, cooperation, and sacrifice. Individualistic societies are usually more industrialized and affluent. In surveying collectivistic or individualistic cultures, Hofstede (as cited in Westbrook et al., 1993) found that individualistic cultures had a propensity to think that power in institutions and organizations was more evenly distributed, whereas collectivistic cultures had a tendency to believe that power was more hierarchical. Hofstede also found that collectivistic cultures (with the exception of the Chinese) had higher scores on a scale to avoid uncertainty and ambiguity. Collectivistic cultures dealt with uncertainty and ambiguity by establishing formal rules. They did not tolerate deviant ideas and behaviors. And they believed in absolute truths. In contrast, those from individualistic cultures had lower scores on these factors.

Westbrook et al. (1993) wrote that because there is less of a perceived power distance (hierarchy) between people in individualistic cultures, then those raised in such societies may perceive service providers as being more accessible—that is, there is less distance separating them from the service providers; whereas those who are from collectivistic societies might view service providers as being less accessible, with more distance between them and the service providers. In addition, because collectivistic societies have a tendency to avoid uncertainty and ambiguity, to deal with these by establishing formal rules, to not tolerate deviant ideas and behaviors, and to believe in absolute truths, there may be less acceptance of people with disabilities. Those with disabilities may be viewed as deviating from the norm (in terms of mental or physical norms); this may enhance their ambiguous status, and because collectivistic societies have an alleged tendency to deal in absolute terms, this may result in greater shame and stigma directed toward, and felt by, those with disabilities. Because collectivistic societies tend to have fewer of the advances of technology and its associated ideas, they may be less impacted by science and thus might not adopt a scientific and medical explanation for the causes, process, and prognosis for disabilities. Thus, the beliefs about and prognosis for disabilities may be more negative than those in Anglo cultures, which have greater technical, scientific, and medical knowledge. It should be noted that although the collectivistic cultures may be less apt to use service providers, they also tend to use local support to a greater degree—friends and families are expected to provide greater support.

Another finding of Westbrook et al. (1993) was that AIDS was the most stigmatized disability in all societies. AIDS was more stigmatized in societies whose overall attitude toward people with disabilities was negative. No disability was fully accepted by any group. Attitudes were more positive toward disabilities that were less visible.

The overall rate of disabilities in the U.S. population is 19.4%. The highest rate was for Native Americans (21.9%), followed by that for Blacks (20.0%), then Whites (19.7%); next were Hispanics (15.3%) and Asians and Pacific Islanders (9.9%). For severe disability (defined as an inability to perform a functional activity or role), the overall rate for the U.S. population was 9.6%. The rate of severe disability was highest for Blacks (12.2%), followed by that for Native Americans (9.8%), Whites (9.4%), people of Hispanic origin (8.4%), and Asians and Pacific Islanders (4.9%).

Perhaps the greatest problem for minorities with disabilities is unemployment. For people 18 to 64 years of age, the employment rate of those without disabilities is almost 83%. For those with disabilities, it is about 52%. For non-Whites with disabilities, it is 38.6%. For those with severe disabilities, about 30% are employed. For Hispanics it is about 21.1%. For African Americans it is about 17.8% (Ross, 1999).

There are a number of possible reasons as to why minorities with disabilities have higher unemployment rates, including the following (Ross, 1999):

1. They may encounter greater discrimination due to dual discrimination: because of their ethnicity and because of their disability.
2. Rehabilitation providers may not provide the same level of services to minorities as to Whites.
3. Minorities are not as able to afford to pay for the educational opportunities that are available to them, thus are not as able to compete for jobs requiring education.
4. Minorities may encounter more problems getting transportation to and from work.
5. It may not be as easy for minorities to obtain housing in the vicinity of a work site.
6. There is a lack of work mentors and role models for minorities.
7. Minorities with disabilities often do not have the same opportunities for mainstream job coaching, on-the-job training, and internships.
8. Groups and organizations have a tendency to overlook their capacity to employ minorities with disabilities.
9. Those who support the employment of minorities with disabilities may not be aware of the cultural features of their program design that might hinder the participation of minorities.

ETHNIC MINORITY CHILDREN

In a "Report of the Surgeon General's Conference on Children's Mental Health" (U.S. Public Health Service, 2000) it was noted that the mental health needs of children and their families have created a crises in this country. The following is from that report. It was noted that children's emotional, behavioral, and developmental needs are not being met and that mental health problems can sabotage the child's developmental process.

Mental Problems

The report stated that 1 in 10 children is impaired by mental illness; 1 in 5 receives mental health services. It was estimated that by the year 2020, childhood mental health problems will rise proportionately by over 50%; internationally, they will become one of the most common causes of morbidity, mortality, and disability among children. Children are often either overdiagnosed or underdiagnosed and are often provided treatment of questionable scientific validity.

Offord (as cited in U.S. Public Health Service, 2000) reported that about 16 to 22% of children may have a mental disorder, and 74% of 21-year-olds with mental health problems have previous problems. Although most of the children with mental health problems came from the middle class, the frequency of mental health problems was highest among the very poor. Often those with mental health problems also had comorbid problems. There was evidence that children with mental disorders prematurely terminated and underutilized services.

Kelleher (as cited in U.S. Public Health Service, 2000) stated that in a study of primary care physicians, they identified 19% of the children they saw as having some behavioral or emotional problem. Boys were more likely to be diagnosed with a problem than were girls and young children. Although African American and Hispanic American children were identified and referred at the same rate as other children, they were less likely to receive mental health services, be given psychotropic medications, or have follow-through with treatment.

Young children seemed to have the same prevalence rates for mental disorders as did older children. Certain early indicators (disruptive, aggressive behaviors; family stress; parental behaviors; biological markers— e.g., prematurity) were predictive of future problems. But these were often unrecognized or ignored—unless the problem was severe. Poverty was an important predictor of future problems—22% of children between the ages of birth and 5 years old live in poverty.

Routine standardized developmental and psychosocial assessments of young children and their families were not used often. These instruments could help detect problems—problems that might be exacerbated in the future.

Other Problems

Landsverk (as cited in U.S. Public Health Service, 2000) reported that 482,000 to 710,000 children are in foster care (two or three times more are reported to child protective services and children receiving in-home services). Neglect was the most common reason (50–60%) for the involvement of protective services, followed by physical abuse (20–25%), sexual abuse (10–15%), and physiological/medical neglect (5–10%). The largest group at risk were those from the ages of birth to 5 years old, who were poor, minority, and in female-head-of-household homes. Half the children (birth to 17 years old) in foster care had adaptive functioning problems; 50–65% of children ages birth to 6 had developmental problems; among 2- to 17-year-olds, 50–60% had behavior problems; and among 6- to 17-year-olds, about 40% had some kind of moderate impairment. Children who had been sexually abused were three times more likely to receive mental health services;

those who were neglected were half as likely to receive treatment. African American and Hispanic children were least likely to receive services. The usual focus of the child welfare system was on sexual abuse and physical abuse, whereas the equally damaging problems of neglect were very often ignored.

Telpin (as cited in U.S. Public Health Service, 2000) stated that poor children, minority children, and children with comorbid disorders were disproportionately represented in the juvenile justice system. Within this population, there were high rates of alcohol, drug, or mental disorders; there also seemed to be high rates of comorbid problems. In one study, in Chicago detention centers, two thirds of the girls (650) tested positive for drugs; more than two thirds of the males had one or more psychiatric disorders; nearly 20% of the sample had an affective disorder; rates were higher among females (27.5%); over two thirds of youth with an affective disorder also had problems with substance abuse/dependence (alcohol, drugs, or both); 33 youth (1.8% of the sample) would die violently at their young age.

Canino (as cited in U.S. Public Health Service, 2000) stated that minority children had less access to mental health services. The stigma of mental health problems was greater for minority children. LaPoint (as cited in U.S. Public Health Service, 2000) stated that many end up incarcerated, and there was evidence that poor children and children of color were tracked into the juvenile justice system, whereas their White, middle-class counterparts received health and mental health services.

Takeuchi (as cited in U.S. Public Health Service, 2000) reported that even controlling for such variables as socioeconomic factors, race was a factor that accounted for many of the disparities encountered in terms of children's mental health status and access to care.

> These analyses suggest that simply focusing on income inequality will not resolve racism and its consequences. Racism is a continuous problem and creates a social environment characterized by alienation, frustration, powerlessness, stress and demoralization, all of which can have pernicious consequences on mental health. (Takeuchi, as cited in U.S. Public Health Service, 2000, p. 30)

It was interesting that Takeuchi also stated that educational programs may not be the answer, because research demonstrated that people with racist beliefs had their beliefs reinforced through educational programs designed to reduce such beliefs. "In order to address ethnic and racial inequities in children's mental healthcare, racism must be viewed in a broader context, focusing on institutional racism and the racial hierarchy of society and its systems, including healthcare" (Takeuchi, as cited in U.S. Public Health Service, 2000, p. 30).

Alegría (as cited in U.S. Public Health Service, 2000) presented the case that in order to deal with the disparities in mental heath care, race and ethnic issues have to be addressed—for three reasons. First, the race and ethnicity of the child play a major role in the services they receive. There are racial, ethnic, and cultural differences in the expression and identification of the problem. Service providers may have different criteria for normative behavior. Given a set of aggressive behaviors, Alegría states that African American youth are more often referred to corrections for conduct problems than to psychiatric hospitals. For ADHD, Whites are more often provided with medications, compared to minority group members. Second, there is the problem of identifying the racial and ethnic factors that account for the disparities in the expression of problems and in service delivery. There could be problems in early detection. Service providers may not consider cultural factors. Parents and service providers may not be aware of effective treatments. She stated that although Latino youths are less likely to be defined as having a problem, they have the highest suicide rate. She went on to state that differences in treatment might be affected by insurance status and that minority children have a tendency to receive mental health services thorough the juvenile justice and welfare system—instead of through school or other facilities. Third, racial and ethnic disparities are constrained by institutional, social, political, and market forces. Managed care might put limits on how much and what care can be provided. Alegría states that community and environmental factors need to be examined and changed—factors such as economic problems and violence.

Bilchik (1999) presented the following information at the 46th Annual Meeting of the American Academy of Child and Adolescent Psychiatry. In 1994 adolescents were nearly three times as likely as adults to be the victims of violent crime. In 1997, homicide was the fourth leading cause of death for children ages 1 to 4. It was the third leading cause of death for youth ages 5 to 14. For persons ages 15 to 24, homicide was the second leading cause of death. Children were often victimized by their care providers, with more maltreatment being reported for lower-income and single-parent families. Childhood maltreatment increased the probability of poor school performance, drug use, mental illness, teenage pregnancy, and serious and violent delinquency—by about 25%. Between 1980 and 1996, for youth under age 15, the suicide rate increased by 113% (compared to 9% of the overall rate). A 1998 survey indicated that 54% of all high school seniors had tried illicit drugs; 4 out of 5 seniors had tried alcohol at least once; among eighth graders, 50% reported trying alcohol. Though no figures were provided, bullying was a problem; chronic exposure to bullying contributed to anxiety, depression, fear of attending school, loss of concentration, and so forth. Adults who were exposed to childhood bullying were at increased risk for depression, poor self-esteem, and other mental health problems, and the abused might do the same thing to others. Females were appearing increasingly in juvenile crime statistics—for example, in violent crime, suicide, victimization, and substance abuse. Like males, female delinquents experienced problems with home environments, poverty, and substance abuse. In addition, they were often victims of sexual and physical abuse, involved in abusive relationships, and had to deal with pregnancy and child care. "Fortunately, in recent years, there has been an increasing recognition of the connections among mental disorder, substance abuse, and juvenile crime" (Bilchik, 1999).

Child abuse and neglect have been problems for minority children. Greenfeld and Smith (1999) reported that between 1992 and 1995, child protective service agencies statistics indicated that American Indians and Asian Americans were the only racial or ethnic groups to have increases in the rate of abuse or neglect of children under age 15—the rate for American Indian children was three times greater than that for Asian children. Children have been victims of neglect, physical abuse, sexual abuse, emotional maltreatment, medical neglect, and other forms of verified maltreatment. Nationwide, the 1995 rates reported by child protective service agencies correspond to about 1 child victim of maltreatment for every 58 children of any race—1 per 66 White children, per 30 Black children, per 209 Asian children, and per 80 Hispanic children (from Greenfeld & Smith, 1999)

ETHNIC MINORITY WOMEN

Comas-Diaz and Greene (1994) wrote, "The common denominator of gender and ethnic oppression facilitates connectedness among women of color" (p. 6). In examining the literature on world mental health, one will find a great deal of material on the problems of women. There is no question that women, and especially minority women, bear enormous burdens and that their mental health needs are dire and critical. There is no question that women bear the burden of the horrors of economic, political, social, and cultural oppression. They bear the brunt of war, famine, violence, exploitation, disease, drug abuse, and so on. The United Nations has made women's issues a priority, and numerous groups and individuals have written on the subject of women's problems. The World Health Organization has a website that presents information on the dismal conditions of women in this world at http://www.who.int/dsa/cat98/men8.htm. There are also national efforts throughout the world to improve the plight of women. Many excellent sources provide information on the conditions of women in this country. One of them is the U.S. Department of Health and Human Services' Office on Women's Health. The Office on Women's Health administers the National Women's Health Information Center, which has a website that provides information on women's health (http://www.4woman.gov/). It also has a website on minority women's health (http://www.4woman.gov/owh/pub/minority/index.htm). The information on minority women's mental health is very limited. There are major governmental projects and plans (e.g., National Institute of Mental Health, 1995a, 2000a) to obtain more and better data on a national level.

The National Institute of Mental Health (2000a) provides the following information. They report that gender is the strongest correlate for various mental disorders. With gender, there are associated biological and other socio-psychological factors involved. Women have depressive disorders and most anxiety disorders 2 to 3 times more often than males. Their rate for eating disorders is 8 to 10 times greater than that of men. Males have higher rates of developmental disorders (e.g., autism and attention deficit disorder), substance and alcohol abuse, and conduct disorders. Males and females have equal rates of schizophrenia and bipolar disorders. Women are the main consumers of mental disorders services. Worldwide, major depression, bipolar disorder, schizophrenia, and obsessive-compulsive disorder are among the 10 leading sources of disease-related disability in women.

Common Health Problems of Minority Women by Ethnic Groups

There is a relationship between health problems, ethnicity, poverty, and mental health problems. There could be cybernetic effects, in which problems affect each another. For example, one might not find work because of one's ethnicity; because one can't find work, one may be poor; as a result of being poor, one may not receive adequate health treatment; because one is not getting adequate health treatment, one may have physical problems; because one has physical problems, one may become depressed; because one is depressed, one's immune system is more vulnerable to opportunistic diseases and infections, which induces health problems, which makes it hard to obtain work and insurance; because one can't obtain work, one becomes depressed—and so on.

The following information is from the National Women's Health Information Center (1998). Though there are differences among ethnic groups, Native American, Hispanic, Black, and Asian American women share some health issues that differentiate them from Euro-Americans. Federal policies and social oppression contributed to the poverty and to the poorer health of many members of ethnic groups.

As with the rest of the population, heart disease and cancer are major killers among women of color. African American women have high rates of death from HIV/AIDS, homicide, and unintentional injuries. For Hispanic women, death from HIV/AIDS is high (especially among Puerto Rican women), and there are problems with homicide and unintentional injuries. For American Indian/Alaska Native women, homicide and unintentional injuries are also common causes of death, along with alcohol-related diseases. Tuberculosis among Asian American women is four times that of the general population. Women of color are disproportionately represented among the 15% of the total U.S. population without health insurance.

Asian American Women. Heart disease and cancer are the leading causes of death among Asian American women. Other common health problems for them are tuberculosis, hepatitis B, and cervical cancer. The tuberculosis rate is highest among southeastern refugees from Vietnam, Laos, and Cambodia—the rate of tuberculosis is six times that of the general population. Overall cancer rates are lower among Asian populations, but the number of cervical cancer cases among Asian American women is higher than for Euro-American women. Preventive health care is difficult to provide to Asian American women. Their cultural norms of modesy and their lack of knowledge contribute to their reluctance (especially, recent immigrants) to engage in early detection programs such as those to use Pap smears or breast exams.

American Indian Women. The health status of American Indian women is affected by the fact that rates of poverty and unemployment are higher among American Indians than among other U.S. ethnic populations: 27% live in poverty. This affects their health. For Native American women, the main health problem is heart disease. Sixty percent of them are overweight; they have a sedentary lifestyle, eat high-fat foods, and abuse tobacco and alcohol. They have high rates of diabetes. Alcohol abuse is a leading cause of death and hospitalization for Native Americans ages 45–54. Death due to alcoholism is 10 times the rate of that for other women of color. Violence is reported in 16% of all marital relationships. End-stage renal disease is 2.8 times higher among American Indians than among Euro-Americans. Cervical cancer survival rates are the lowest of all the ethnic groups.

African American Women. Heart disease and cancer are the leading causes of death in African American women—followed by cerebrovascular disease, diabetes mellitus, unintentional injuries, pneumonia, influenza, AIDS, conditions related to pregnancy and childbearing, chronic obstructive pulmonary disease, and homicide. African Americans have more undetected diseases, higher disease and illness rates (from infectious conditions such as tuberculosis and sexually transmitted diseases), more chronic conditions (such as hypertension and diabetes), and shorter life spans than Whites.

Morbidity and mortality rates for Blacks for such conditions as cancer, HIV/AIDS, pneumonia, and homicide exceed those for Euro-Americans. African American females are generally less likely than are White females to report risk behaviors such as smoking cigarettes, consuming alcohol, or using other substances. It has been reported that African American women have the highest mortality rates from homicides and firearm-related events. About one in every three African Americans has a higher incidence of hypertension. They have higher incidents of obesity (50% of African American women are obese), high fat and cholesterol dietary intake, a sedentary lifestyle, and diabetes—these can contribute to heart disease and strokes. The death rate for diabetes is two and a half times that of Euro-American women. African American women have the highest incidences of both low-birth-weight (13%) and very-low-birth-weight (3%) infants. Infant mortality rates were highest for African American babies—7 deaths per 1,000 live births, more than double the rate for White mothers and significantly greater than the rate for all mothers (9 deaths per 1,000 live births.). AIDS is increasing significantly faster for African American women—the death rate from AIDS is 9 times that of White women. Uterine fibroid tumors are also more common in African American women.

Latina Women. Their leading causes of death are heart disease and cancer; the other causes of death among Latinas are cerebrovascular disease; diabetes mellitus; accidents and adverse effects; pneumonia and influenza; conditions originating in the perinatal period; chronic obstructive pulmonary diseases, including asthma; congenital anomalies; and AIDS. There are differences among Latinas in the incidence and severity of diseases and disorders. Lung, cervical, colorectal, and breast cancer are the types of cancers most frequently reported among Latinas. The incidence of breast cancer among Latinas is lower than for White non-Latina women, but Latinas are more likely to die of breast cancer than are White women.

- Latinas die from diabetes at twice the rate of non-Latina whites. Mexican Americans' and Puerto Ricans' diabetes rates are 112% higher than Whites'. The rate for Cuban Americans ranges from 50 to 60% more than the rate for Whites. Mexican Americans and Puerto Ricans have a two to three times greater risk of non-insulin dependent diabetes than non-Latinas. These figures are probably underestimates because of undiagnosed cases.
- Latina women are eight times more likely to get AIDS than are non-Latina White women. Twenty percent of all accumulated AIDS cases among U.S. women are Latinas.
- Some sexually transmitted diseases are more prevalent among Latinas than among other women. Latinas are five times as likely to contract primary and secondary syphilis as are non-Latina whites, and three times more likely to contract gonorrhea.
- Severe chronic depression commonly affects Latinas; about one half of

Hispanic/Latina women reported severe chronic depression—this is similar to the 47% rate of non-Hispanic Black women, compared to 37% of non-Hispanic White women.
- Thirty-three percent of Hispanics have no health insurance; for the poor it is 41%. This is the highest rate of noncoverage of any ethnic group.

The Hispanic population has grown in the past few years and continues to grow. The following information, from the National Center for Health Statistics (2000), provides a more detailed analysis of the many diverse groups encompassed under the umbrella term *Hispanic.*

- The U.S. Hispanic population is made up of 63% Mexican Americans, 11% Puerto Ricans, 4% Cuban Americans, and 22% "other Hispanics."
- Puerto Ricans living on the U.S. mainland fare significantly worse than do other U.S. Hispanics on a number of health indicators.
- More than 1 in 5 Puerto Ricans have reported limitations in an activity. This is compared to about 15% of the Cuban and Mexican population that reported activity limitation.
- About 18% of Puerto Ricans reported themselves to being in either fair or poor health. This compares with 14% of Cubans and 12% of "other Hispanic" groups.
- Eighty-three percent of Puerto Ricans reported that they had seen a physician in the past year. This is compared to 69% of Mexican Americans, 77% of "other Hispanics," and 78% of Cuban Americans.
- Three percent of Puerto Ricans reported they had not seen a physician in the past. This compares to 7% of Mexicans and 4% of Cubans.
- 10.4% of Puerto Ricans reported having to spend time in bed because of illness, compared to 8% of Mexicans and 7.2% of "other Hispanics."
- Puerto Ricans, Mexicans, and "other Hispanics" had about the same rates of lost days from school or work—6.0%, 5.7%, and 6.9%, respectively. This compares to 3.4% of Cubans.
- Of all the Hispanic groups, Cubans reported a higher level of knowledge about AIDS.

Common Health Problems of Ethnic Minority Women by Disease Categories

The following was obtained from the Office of Women's Health (2000).

Asthma. African Americans are hospitalized and die from asthma at three times the rate of Whites. This high rate can be attributed to the conditions under which they have to live, lack of knowledge, and inadequate health care.

Breast Cancer. The rates of breast cancer vary widely among and between ethnic populations. African American women develop breast cancer less often than do Euro-American women. But they have the highest rates death from this disease—compared to all population groups (27.0 per 100,000 women). Hispanic women and American Indian/Alaskan Native women share similar death rates from breast cancer (12.7 and 11.2, respectively). Native Hawaiian women have breast cancer at a rate that is more than 1.5 times that of Euro-American women. Asian/Pacific Islander women's rate of breast cancer deaths is the lowest among all racial/ethnic groups.

Cancer. Women of Vietnamese descent have a cervical cancer rate that is three times higher than that of the second highest group. For Japanese and Korean women, stomach cancer is more common than in other groups (with rates of 15.3 and 19.1 cases per 100,000 women, respectively). Lung and colorectal cancer are higher among Alaskan Native women than in other groups. American Indian women have a particularly higher incidence of cancer of the gall bladder. African American and Hispanic women die from breast cancer at higher rates than do other minority women. African American and Hispanic women are at a higher risk for cervical and colorectal cancer than are other minority women.

Diabetes. Diabetes mellitus is much more prevalent among all four minority groups than among their Euro-American counterparts. It is the fourth leading cause of death for African American, American Indian/Alaska Native, and Hispanic women (especially Cuban, Mexican American, and Puerto Rican). Complications of diabetes—kidney failure, heart disease, stroke, amputations, and blindness—are more prevalent in African American women than in Euro-American women. The rate of diabetes-related kidney failure is higher in American Indian/Alaska Natives and Mexican Americans than in Euro-Americans.

HIV/AIDS. A disproportionate number of minority women in this country—particularly the young and the poor—are infected by HIV/AIDS. Of women living with AIDS, more than 75% are minority women.

For African American women, AIDS is the eighth leading cause of death. It is the second leading cause of death for African American women ages 25–44 within this group; African American women die from AIDS at a 12–13 times higher rate than their Euro-American counterparts. More African American women than women in any other group die from AIDS. For Hispanic women ages 25–44, AIDS is the third leading cause of death. The rate of death from AIDS for Hispanic women is almost three times higher than that of Euro-American women.

There is little HIV and AIDS among Asian American/Pacific Islander women and American Indian/Alaska Native women, but the rates of increase are high.

Heart Disease. Compared to Euro-Americans, death from heart disease is higher among African American and Hispanic women. Asian/Pacific Islander and American Indian/Alaska Native women's rates are significantly lower.

The four major risk factors for heart disease in women are smoking, high blood pressure (hypertension), diabetes, and high cholesterol. African American and Hispanic women experience high rates of heart disease compared to those of other women. African American women have the highest mortality rates from heart disease (155.9 per 100,000) of all American women. African American women have the highest rates of smoking (25.7%) and elevated blood pressure (33.8%) among minority women, and they have a high prevalence of obesity (53%). In addition, a significant percentage of Hispanic women smoke (21%), and obesity is a problem particularly for those of Mexican and Puerto Rican descent. Because American Indian/Alaska Native women are also more obese on average than all women, and smoking is on the increase in this population, heart disease is a significant and growing concern for them as well. Asian American/Pacific Islander women have the lowest mortality rate from heart disease of all population groups. Heart disease, however, is the second leading cause of death for these women.

Lupus. Certain autoimmune diseases are significant problems for some minority women groups. Lupus is more common among minority women than in Euro-American women, and survival rates are lower. Lupus is most prevalent among African American women, who comprise about 60% of all women with the disease. American Indian/Alaska Natives suffer disproportionately from another autoimmune disease, rheumatoid arthritis.

Obesity. Obesity is most common among African American, American Indian/Alaska Native, Hispanic (especially Mexican American and Puerto Rican), and Asian/Pacific Islander (especially Native Hawaiian and Samoan) women. Compared with other populations, women of color, especially African American women, have a high rate of elevated blood pressure, which raises their risk of stroke, heart disease, and kidney disease.

Osteoporosis. All women, regardless of race, are at risk of developing osteoporosis, but to varying degrees. Although African American women tend to have higher bone mineral density (BMD) than do White women throughout life, they are still at significant risk of developing osteoporosis. Asian American women are at high risk for developing osteoporosis. Studies indicate that Asian American and Latino women share many of the risk factors that apply to Euro-American women. Latino women consume less calcium than the Recommended Dietary Allowance in all age groups. Furthermore, as minority women age, their risk of developing osteoporosis more closely resembles the risk among White women. So, as the number of older women in the United States increases, there will be an increasing number of minority women with osteoporosis.

Reproductive Health. Minority women have many cultural and societal issues that may prevent them from receiving adequate reproductive health care. Large percentages of minority women reported that they did not have a Pap test with the past year: 55% of Asian American women, 43% of Hispanic women, and 37% of African American women. (Of Euro-American women, 44% did not have a Pap smear during that time.) In addition, minority women are at high risks for many diseases that greatly affect the reproductive systems, such as ovarian cancer, HIV/AIDS, and STDs.

Sickle Cell Anemia. In the United States, sickle cell anemia affects African Americans and those of Mediterranean descent disproportionately. Every year, about 1 in 400 African American infants are born with this disease, which is genetically passed on. The disease can also occur among non–African Americans. This disease can result in poor physical development, lowered resistance to infections, abdominal pain, swelling and pain in muscles and joints, and reduced life expectancy. In the United States, sickle cell anemia is most common among African Americans. It is estimated that 1 in 12 African Americans has the sickle cell trait.

Smoking. Unhealthy behaviors lead to more than 50% of premature deaths in the United States. The risk behaviors most often leading to premature death and disability are tobacco use, alcohol and drug use, poor diet, and physical inactivity. Lung cancer is the number-one cancer killer of American women, largely attributable to smoking. Native American women have some of the highest smoking rates in the country (44%), compared to White (29%), African American (23%), Hispanic (16%), and Asian (6%) women. In addition, American Indian/Alaska Native women are much more likely than are other women to use cigarettes and smokeless tobacco. On average, smoking rates among African American and Euro-American women are about equal. Hispanic women smoke less than do these two populations, whereas Asian/Pacific Islander women smoke significantly less than other women.

Stroke. Stroke and other cerebrovascular diseases are another leading cause of death for minority women in the United States. African American women have the highest death rate for stroke of all women, at 39.6 deaths per 100,000, in contrast to 22.9 per 100,000, for Euro-American women. Asian American/Pacific Islander women and American Indian/Alaskan Native women have similar mortality rates from stroke as those for Euro-American women. Hispanic women have the lowest mortality rate from stroke (17.3) of all women. Similar to heart disease, major risk factors for stroke include smoking, high blood pressure, and high blood cholesterol.

Substance Abuse. Alcoholism appears to be more common among American Indian/Alaska Native women than among Euro-American women—inducing high rates of chronic liver disease and cirrhosis. Euro-American and African American women drink heavily at the same rates, but African American women are more likely to experience related health problems, such as liver impairments. Their offspring are at greater risk for fetal alcohol syndrome (FAS). Hispanic and Asian/Pacific Islander women appear to drink less alcohol and therefore appear to be at less risk for alcohol-related health problems.

In minority communities, drug abuse is a major problem. With the exception of Asian/Pacific Islanders, drug problems are greater among minority women than among European American women. African Americans and Hispanics (both men and women) are three times more likely to have drug problems than are European Americans. Compared to European Americans, American Indian/Alaska Natives are twice as likely to be in drug treatment. Alcohol and drug use can impact other areas of health: Chronic liver disease or cirrhosis can develop; AIDS can be acquired from injected drug use or sexual contact with an HIV-infected user; or accidents and violence can result.

Violence. Racism and poverty can lead to social anomy—for example, drug abuse, physical abuse, and violence. Violence, emotional abuse, and other assaults on the body and mind can lead to stress, depression, disassociative disorders, and suicide attempts. Although violence is not linked to ethnicity, it is linked to income—women with family incomes of less than $10,000 are more likely to experience violence than are women in families with higher incomes (Craven, 1996).

The following data are from the Bureau of Justice Statistics of the U.S. Department of Justice (Greenfeld & Smith, 1999):

Compared to Whites, Blacks, and Asians, Native Americans were the most likely to be victims of violent crimes (Greenfeld & Smith, 1999, Tables 5 & 7). African American males and females were both as likely to be victims of violence—whereas in other ethnic groups and Whites, males were more likely to be victims of violence than were females (Greenfeld & Smith, 1999, Table 6). Native Americans, Whites, and Asians were more likely to be violently victimized by Whites, but this was not the case for Blacks, who were more likely to be violently victimized by other Blacks (Greenfeld & Smith, 1999, Table 9).

Psychiatric Disorders

The National Institute of Mental Health (1995a) stated that there are a number of factors to consider in examining women' mental health, including biology (e.g., pubertal stage, menopausal status) and psychosocial contexts (e.g., rural and urban environments, poverty, educational status, peer and marital status, and history of abuse). The research on ethnic minority females is limited—for example, in terms of understanding the etiology and prevalence of mental disorders; the clinical course, intervention effectiveness, and service use related to these disorders; and the effects of ethnicity, social class, and sex-role socialization. Because differences have been found among ethnic groups of males in response to high blood pressure medications, this suggests there may be differences in the pharmacokinetics and pharmacodynamics of psychotherapeutic drugs among ethnic groups of women. The document (National Institute of Mental Health, 1995a) goes on to state that genetic epidemiology may help identify genetic and environmental factors contributing to mental disorders and possible prevention strategies.

The Office of Women's Health (2000a) presented the following information on ethnic minority mental health disorders.

Depression. Several psychiatric disorders, including anxiety disorders and mood disorders, disproportionately strike females. Among minority women, depression may be exacerbated by factors such as little education and low income levels, lack of employment, acculturation difficulties, marital and family problems, racism, and single parenthood.

Over a lifetime, Hispanic women have the higher prevalence (24%) of depression. As measured by rates of depression in the past month prior to the data gathering, depression rates for African American women and White women were about the same (6% and 5% respectively)—as compared to about 11% for Hispanic women (Rouse, 1995).

To continue with the Office of Women's Health's (2000a) data: 53% of Hispanic women suffered from severe depression, compared with 37% of European American women. Of the African American women with depression, 47% had severe depression. About 14% of American Indian/Alaska Native female adolescents were described as extremely sad and hopeless; 6% showed signs of serious emotional stress.

Suicide. Suicidal behaviors between ethnic groups and ages are interesting. The differences among the groups raise such questions as, Why do some ethnic groups have higher incidences of suicide than others? Similar questions can be raised as to why there are different rates of suicidal behaviors among the various age groups. Answers to such questions can help us lower the incidences of suicidal behaviors and provide help to those in distress.

- Compared with minority women of all ages, American Indian/Alaska Native women had the highest mortality rate from suicide (4.4); for American Indian/Alaskan Native women between the ages of 15 and 24, the rate was 7.2 per 100,000 persons—making this the highest mortality rate from suicide of all women in this age group.
- Compared to all women, Asian American/Pacific Islander women of all ages had the second highest mortality rate from suicide (3.4); for women over the age of 65, Asian American/Pacific Islander women had the highest mortality rate from suicide (8.8).
- Compared to minority women and compared to all women, Hispanic women of all ages had the lowest mortality rate from suicide (1.7).
- African American women of all ages had a suicide rate of 1.9. For all women over the age of 65, African American women had one of the lowest suicide mortality rates (2.0)—for those 65 years old and older, only American Indian/Alaska Native women had a lower suicide mortality rate.

Eating Disorders. In comparison with White women, eating problems, such as restrictive dieting, bingeing, or purging, seemed to occur as often among Hispanics; eating problems occurred more frequently among American Indians and less frequently among African Americans and Asian Americans.

ETHNIC MINORITY OLDER PERSONS

Risk Factors

The Surgeon General's Report on Mental Health (1999) documented that minority mental health needs were not being met and that minority populations were less likely to receive appropriate mental health care than were members of the population as a whole. The Director of the National Institute on Aging, Richard Hodes (National Institute on Aging, 2001a), has stated "more must be done to redress disparities in health among U.S. minority groups." Life expectancy for African Americans is 69; for Caucasians it is 76. There are disparities in the health indices between minorities and Whites. "We know that the problem can be associated with wealth, income, at-risk behaviors, social and environmental factors, and race and ethnicity." Although Asian Americans' health indices seem to indicate that they are as healthy or even more healthy than Whites, in general, African American, American Indian, and Hispanic ethnic and racial groups do not fair as well compared with their White counterparts on health indices. There are indications that African Americans and Hispanic Americans are at greater risk of having Alzheimer's. Other areas that need to be investigated include cardiovascular disease; cancer; bone, muscle, and joint disorders (such as osteoporosis and osteoarthritis); and vision, hearing, and other sensory disorders. He went on to report that minorities do not have their chronic illness recognized and treated to the same degree as do their White counterparts. This has enormous consequences in terms of immediate and future pain and problems.

A number of factors—including income, ethnicity, and support systems—affected the condition of older persons. Increasingly, people in our society are entering into the category of old age. This is in great part thanks to better medical care and science. The definition of "old," "senior," "elderly," and other labels varies. The definitions used by the Administration on Aging are: "young-old" are defined as those 65–75; the "old" are those 75–85; and the "old–old," are those 85+.

What follows is from the 2001 Report of the Administration in Aging (Administration on Aging, 2001a). As with other mental health data, there are plans to better gather national statistics on the mental health of older persons, from which we can obtain a better picture of the mental health of the older minority.

As one gets older, one can expect to have more infirmities to contend with. Conditions such as depression and Alzheimer's disease tend to increase with old age. It has been found that income, social support, and living arrangements are among the many factors that affect mental health. With decreased income and with less social support, there is an increased risk of receiving inadequate treatment and an increase of mental and physical problems. Married people fair better, emotionally and economically; living alone increases the risk of having problems.

Suicide. The suicide rates for persons 65 and older are higher than for any other age group. The suicide rate for persons 85+ is nearly twice the overall national rate—there are approximately 21 suicides per 100,000 persons among those 85 years of age and older.

Gender. Women on average live 7 years longer than do men; therefore, most of those who are old are women. Older women are more likely than old men to be widowed, to live alone, to be institutionalized, and to receive less retirement income. Because of their greater longevity, old women are also likely to suffer disproportionately from chronic disabilities and disorders, including mental disorders.

Social Support. Social support is important for all groups—including older people. Those without social support are at greater risk of experiencing detrimental mental health. Older people who are gay, lesbian, or bisexual may experience greater problems because they have less social support. They may also be more limited in their use of health care services because they believe health care providers lack sensitivity to their sexual orientation issues.

Minority Status. By 2030, the older minority populations are expected to represent 25% of the older population (compared with 16% in 1998). Between 1998 and 2030, the White population 65 years and older is expected to increase by 79%, whereas older minorities are expected to increase by 226%. Hispanics are expected to increase 341%; African Americans, 130%; American Indians, Native Alaskans, and Aleuts, 150%; and Asians and Pacific Islander Americans, 323%. When interacting with service providers, minorities face language, belief, value, and cultural barriers. "In a number of minority groups, Westernized mental health treatment modalities that tend to be dependent upon verbal inquiry, interaction, and response do not appear to present a comfortable 'fit' with many minority cultural beliefs and practices" (Administration on Aging, 2001a, p. 2).

Income. Poverty is related to mental illness. One of every six (17.0%) older persons is below poverty level. Old people who are vulnerable to being poor are women, African Americans, those living by themselves, the very old, and those living in rural areas. Divorced, 65- to 74-year-old, African American women have a poverty rate of 47%—making them the poorest among the poor.

Physical Health. Most older people report that compared with others their own age, they are in good health; however, most of them have at least one chronic condition, and many have multiple conditions (e.g., arthritis, hypertension, heart disease, cataracts, or diabetes). Although poor health is a key risk factor for mental disorders, service providers often fail to detect these comorbid conditions. Service providers often fail to deal with conditions that augur oncoming mental problems, and once the symptoms manifest themselves, frequently, the symptoms of mental disorders escape detection and treatment. The detrimental effects of drugs and their interaction are of concern in treating older persons. There is still much to be learned about this area, and clients need to be educated. Minorities who have less education or who are not versed in reading English may not understand how to comply with a medical regime—even if they can obtain the drugs and are treated properly.

Stressors and Adaptations. As the older person progresses in age, many chronic stressors may be encountered—for example, retirement or change in status. Adaptations or maladaptations to these can impact on the mental health of the minority person.

Health-Related Events. Health problems may compound quality of life and independence issues and precipitate mental health problems—for example, a broken hip may entail transportation and financial problems. It may entail repeated visits to the hospital and obtaining help for shopping and house maintenance, inactivity, limited social interactions, and so forth—all of which might affect mental health.

Loss of Loved Ones. As one gets older, there are issues of loss and grief. Relatives, friends, or a spouse may die. There may be changes in living arrangements—friends may leave, spouses may enter nursing homes—and loneliness and isolation may ensue.

Chronic Strains. Numerous chronic strains can affect the older individual. There may be the strain of having to relocate. There may be loss of a familiar environment due to changes. Friends and social supports may leave. Neighborhoods may deteriorate. Changes may make it more difficult to reach shopping, health care, and social networks. Relationships may be strained—for example, because of differences in lifestyle and values of children. Financial problems and loss of physical fitness may increase a sense of vulnerability. Being dependent on others and having to take care of others can also be very stressful. These factors may affect mental disposition.

Mental Illness. About 20% of those 55 years and older experience specific mental disorders. "The most common disorders, in order of prevalence, are anxiety disorders, such as phobias and obsessive-compulsive disorder; severe cognitive impairment, including Alzheimer's disease; and mood disorders, such as depression. Schizophrenia and personality disorders are less common" (Administration on Aging, 2001b, p. 6).

Assessment. Diagnosing problems of the older person can be more difficult. The older person may manifest and express his or her problems differently. The service provider may not correctly understand the older person because of generational, cultural, values, and normative standards differences. There is significant underdiagnosis of mental illness by primary care providers when treating older persons.

Treatment. There are a number of unique treatment issues in providing services to older persons. Because of physiological changes, they may metabolize medications differently, and the side effects may differ. Because they often take other medications, there may be unintended synergistic effects. Older adults may forget to take medications or to keep appointments, and they may lack transportation to obtain services.

Delivery of Mental Health Services to Older Adults. Older persons do not use mental health services comparable to their number and to their needs. It is estimated that about half of older persons who admit they need mental health services actually receive them. Among the general population, it is estimated that about 10% have problems with mental health, yet less than 3% of older Americans report seeing mental health professionals for treatment. Older Americans comprise about 13% of the population, yet they account for only 7% of all inpatient services, 6% of community mental health services, and 9% of private psychiatric care.

Stigma. Older people may not receive treatment because they fear the stigma of being treated for a mental disorder. Similarly, their families may be concerned with the stigma of having someone in the family with a mental illness.

Denial of Problems. Older persons may not seek help because they are in denial or because anxiety, depression, memory loss, and dementia may hinder their ability to recognize that they have a problem. Those around older persons may dismiss signs of disorders because they don't recognize them, or they do not want to see that there is a problem, or dismiss the validity of older people's complaints and perceptions.

Access Barriers. Older persons may not be able to afford services. They may not have transportation to service providers' sites. They may be physically and psychological isolated and distant from service providers.

Funding Issues. The funding of services to older persons is often inadequate and fragmented.

Lack of Collaboration and Coordination. Mental health services and services to the aging are often provided by different entities; for example, one facility may provide mental health services, another facility may provide services for those with limited language proficiency, and yet another may provide mental health services. Better coordination of the services would increase the effectiveness of helping older persons.

Gaps in Services. Mental health systems often do not provide the same level of support to older persons as they do to children or adults. The services that are provided are often limited because of reimbursement problems and lack of culturally competent staff.

Workforce Issues. There is a lack of service providers who are knowledgeable in geriatric mental health care, in general. The shortage is even more acute in obtaining staff that are competent in minority geriatric mental health care. As the population ages, the shortage will be even greater.

Diseases and Disorders

The National Institute on Aging (2001b) informs us that there are enormous variations among and between ethnic groups. Hispanics come from a multitude of countries, with differences in values, cultures, traditions, and so on. They come from native South American, American Indian, Black, and White groups. African Americans can come from the one of the many countries and cultures in the Caribbean, Africa, and a multitude of other places. Asians can come from all parts of the world. Heart disease, hypertension, diabetes, Alzheimer's disease, and certain types of cancer have significantly differing rates among minority populations. African Americans have more hypertension and prostate cancer than do Whites. Hispanics have more diabetes and less heart disease. African Americans and Hispanics have higher rates of Alzheimer's than do Whites. African Americans have higher rates of cardiovascular disease. Hawaiian Japanese Americans have lower rates of stroke-related dementia and higher rates of Alzheimer's disease than do Japanese living in Japan. Ethnic groups differ in rates of dementia and in declines in cognitive functions. The differences among and between groups are many. The diversity among minority groups and subgroups will be even greater in the future because of the influx of non-White groups from more diverse areas of the world. "Data are needed on the specific incidence and prevalence rates in different ethnic subpopulations as well as the distribution of subtypes of dementia, genetic and environmental risk factors, and differences in caregiving" (National Institute on Aging, 2001b, p. 19). Age of onset of diseases, process of diseases, and changes in diseases vary across groups. The role of lifestyle, cultural practices, genetics, biological, health care, and a host of other possible factors needs to be examined.

MINORITIES IN RURAL AREAS

There is very little mention in the general literature and in textbooks on minorities in rural areas. This section of the chapter aims to help alleviate the dearth of information in this area. Much of the information that is provided comes from census information. Although there is a time lag between the obtaining of the information and its processing, analyses, and publication, the material does present a picture that is in keeping with general patterns that have been observed. Most of the information in the first part of this section comes from the Department of Agriculture—Rural Economy Division, Economic Research Services: Agricultural Economic Report No. 731 (Swanson, 1996).

Most rural residents face a triple jeopardy for mental illness—being poor, uninsured, and living in isolation (American Psychological Association, 2000). Ethnic minorities are behind rural Whites and urban minorities in many economic and social measures (e.g., occupation, earnings, household incomes, and poverty)—"by almost any measure, rural minority groups were substantially worse off in 1990 than they were in 1980 and, moreover, the disadvantages particular to each group tended to be more pronounced at the end of the decade" (Swanson, 1996, p. 2). Almost 90% of those who live outside of cities are White; minorities make up approximately 15% of the rural population, but consist of over 30% of the rural poor (Swanson, 1996). The probability of being poor for rural Blacks, Hispanics, and Native Americans was three times than that of Whites. The proportion of female-headed families has increased, especially among Black Americans. Joblessness increased in all minority groups but was highest for Blacks and Native Americans. Although the earnings of all rural men declined over the decade, minority men had even lower earnings. Though rural minority groups showed increases in education in the 1980s, proportionally, they are overrepresented in those lacking a high school diploma. Joblessness is higher for minorities than for Whites with the same level of education. In examining the causes of low minority economic and employment levels, Swanson (1996) reported that there was "apparent discrimination when human capital differences are held constant" (p. 3).

Hispanics

The proportion of Hispanics without English-language skills has increased. For rural Hispanics, level of English fluency was the most important determinant of level of income. Hispanics with English fluency and with educational levels comparable to those of Whites had poverty levels that were twice as high. In the last decade, Hispanics had the greatest number of

growth in rural areas. Poverty has increased among rural Hispanics because increases in immigration brought in immigrants working for lower
pay; lack of English proficiency limited their opportunities to better paying
occupations; and a concentration of workers occurred in agricultural work,
which tends to pay less.

Native Americans

Joblessness among working-age Native Americans (21%) is higher than
among any other minority group and has increased. Native Americans in
rural areas tend to work in low-wage manufacturing occupations and in
consumer services. They are overrepresented in lower paying jobs and have
high unemployment.

Blacks

Most rural Blacks live in the southern states. Unemployment was higher in
1990 than in 1980, especially for those with less education. Rural Blacks
with less education are getting poorer. College-educated Blacks earn less
than White college graduates do. Black women are as likely as White women
to work—at each educational level. Black men receive less pay than Whites
do, regardless of level of education, experience, and so forth. Black men
receive less pay compared to Black women and other minorities. In the
1980s, compared to Whites, Blacks were half as likely to have white-collar
occupations, and they were twice as likely to be in service occupations.

Asians

Asians are the smallest ethnic group living in rural areas. There is very
little information about them. About one forth live in Hawaii. Compared to
other groups, they appear to have higher incomes, education levels, and
occupations.

Children

Compared to other groups, rural minority children had the highest levels
of poverty. In 1989, about 16% of rural White children were poor, compared to 50% of rural Black children, 43% of rural Native Americans, and
38% of rural Hispanic children. Although Black and Hispanic women in
married couple families may have an increase in education, smaller families, and a slight decline in poverty for their children, this was offset by the
growth in proportion of children raised in mother-only families, with the
corresponding increase in poverty for them.

In an issue paper on mental health in rural America, the National Rural Health Association (1999) stated that the rural population is different from the urban population in many major factors, such as rural culture, patriotic beliefs, spirituality, family- and community-centered life, independence, and so on. It is interested that the National Rural Health Association uses cross-cultural competencies to provide guidelines to mental health providers in rural areas (APA, 1995). In other words, service providers should do the following:

1. Identify social, economic, political, and religious influences affecting rural communities.
2. Understand the importance of ethnic and cultural influences in rural communities and the importance of the oral tradition.
3. Understand the impact of the interaction between social institutions and ethnicity on the delivery of mental health services.
4. Recognize the impact of the provider's own culture, sensitivity, and awareness as it affects his or her ability to deliver mental health care.
5. Understand alternative treatment sources in the ethnic minority culture. (p. 5).

In another section of the paper, there was a recommendation to investigate the use of telecommuncations in providing services to rural areas. It was clear that those minorities living in rural areas are overlooked, and the focus is on those living in urban areas.

MIDDLE-CLASS MINORITIES

It may seem strange to mention the problems of middle-class minorities. But this group can have problems unique to its socioeconomic attainment. Hollingshead and Redlich (1958) wrote about the problems experienced by marginal people and those who are in transition from one socioeconomic bracket to another. In addition to the usual problems encountered by people in marginal and transitional positions, minorities may encounter problems induced by their ethnic minority background, by the environments they are coming from, and by the environments they are entering into. Almost invariably, when minority members enter the middle-class world, whether in higher education or work, they are entering worlds controlled by, and defined by, White people, who greatly outnumber the minority member. This may engender problems for the minority group member. Much has been written in the psychological literature specifically on the problems of middle-class African Americans (Bagarozzi, 1980; Coner-Edwards & Edwards, 1988; Coner-Edwards & Spurlock, 1988; Cunningham

& Edwards, 1988; Durant & Sparrow, 1997; Feagin, 1991; Feagin & Sikes, 1994; Ford, 1997; Gurin, Miller, & Gurin, 1980; Hochschild, 1993; Jones, 1992; Pinderhughes, 1988; Sampson & Milam, 1975; Steele, 1978). But there is far less in the psychological literature dealing specifically with other ethnic group members of this class—though the psychological literature on socioeconomic and cultural dynamics may provide some insight. For example, the following literature provides examples of socioeconomic and cultural factors that might impact Asian Americans: Kibria, 2000; Kim and Markus, 1999; Kwan, 2000; Tsai, Ying, and Lee, 2000; Yamamoto and Acosta, 1982; Ying, Lee, and Tsai, 2000. The following are examples from the literature on some of the socioeconomic aspects of Native Americans' lives: Cheshire (2001); Garrett and Pichette (2000); Grandbois and Schadt (1994); Moran, Fleming, Somervell, and Manson (1999); Trimble (2000); and Walters (1999). Socioeconomic and cultural aspects of Hispanics' lives are presented by such authors as Bean, Berg, and Van Hook (1996); Bender and Ruiz (1974); Cuellar and Roberts (1997); Gutierrez, Sameroff, and Karrer (1988); Kantor, Jasinski, and Aldarondo (1994); Martinez (1996); Negy and Woods (1992); Santos (1992); Wilkinson and Burke (1984); and Zsembik and Beeghley (1996).

The following describes some of the problems and dynamics of minorities who enter the middle class or who are already in the middle class. Many minority groups come from cultural groups that emphasize adherence to the community and the family. Therefore, minority members from these communities may experience stress from within themselves and from community members that they have to adhere to the values of the community and that they "owe" it to the community to help the community—this may especially be the case with African Americans. Many Hispanics also feel the pressure of having to support their parents and siblings—whereas, within the White middle-class community, the income made by White persons is usually spent on themselves. Often, to attain or retain middle-class status, minorities have to enter White educational institutions and places of employment, and they have to leave their homes and families and encounter different communities. They may have to learn new skills, new ways of communicating and speaking, and new mannerisms. These may be adaptive and functional in their new environments, but may be maladaptive in their ethnic communities. African Americans who are first-generation middle-class occupants may feel the tenuous nature of their newly acquired positions. Those African Americans who come from previous generations of middle-class families may encounter the problem of other Blacks and Whites expecting them to "act Black." As they interact in their new White world, they may encounter stresses that are not as prevalent for their White counterparts—for example, when trying to obtain loans, credit, and housing, their problems may be compounded by racism. As they move around their new communities, they may encounter suspiciousness from police, shopkeepers, and those around them. Asian Americans at work often find that their White coworkers and supervisors have less qualifications and education than they have, yet the Asian American has to take instructions from them. For the Native American, the competitive and hierarchical nature of the White middle class may be the antithesis of their cultural norms of working in harmony and not standing out from their cohorts. Many minorities find that they are the last hired and first laid off. They are often underemployed, with their work and responsibilities not commensurate with their qualifications. Minorities may find that on the job they may have fewer "social credits" than their white counterparts do— that is, their behavior is viewed with more suspicion and scrutiny than behaviors of their White counterparts, and other people have a tendency to make negative interpretations and connotations about their behavior. In reporting on problems of middle-class Blacks, Ford (1997) wrote about limited access and glass ceilings, double standards, exclusion and isolation, powerlessness, voicelessness and invisibility, token status, second guessing, pigeonholing, guilt by association, identity-conflict issues, allegiance issues, survival conflict and guilt issues, and achievement ideology issues.

Numerous other groups within minority communities deserve attention but are often overlooked. These include low-income, unmarried, minority fathers (Coley, 2001) and those people who have combinations of the characteristics of the groups mentioned previously—for example, minority women with disabilities, single minority women, and single minority men raising children. Investigation of these groups can help us understand the dimensions of human nature, and the principles that were learned from other groups can be applied to these groups.

GOALS, PLANS, SOLUTIONS, AND RECOMMENDATIONS

Many of the sources used in this chapter, and in this book, have provided recommendations. Quite often, solutions for one group are apropos for other groups. These solutions often include knowing the culture and cultural expressions of the ethnic group, increasing the number of ethnic group members among the service providers, and increasing funding. The following are some of the plans and solutions to alleviate the problems of those populations mentioned in this chapter.

Gay Males, Lesbian, Bisexuals, and So On

There do not seem to be any national, coordinated plans and goals to deal with gay male, lesbian, and bisexual problems—which means that members of these groups who are also ethnic minorities are even more unlikely to have their needs addressed. Government and other large organizations that deal with the problems of those of a different sexual orientation seem to direct their efforts toward specific issues—for example, preventing AIDS and informing the gay male and lesbian community of risk behaviors and prophylactic measures. The advocacy groups for alleviating gay problems often call for an end to discrimination in jobs and housing, recognition of gay marriages, and the obtaining of equal rights for partners of the same sex—for example, in insurance coverage and state laws to protect gay rights. Many professional organizations, such as the American Psychological Association, have provided education and guidelines to its members on how to interact with and treat gay males, lesbians, bisexuals, and so on. Often the activities to alleviate the problems of lesbians and gay males and those of different sexual orientation are included in programs that promote diversity and tolerance. It seems clear that gay males and lesbians go through an adolescent developmental stage in which they are vulnerable to humiliation, depression, suicide, and acts of violence. It is clear that this population needs help, and effective help is not being provided. For minorities, these pressures are also compounded by discrimination by society, by the gay and lesbian communities, by their own ethnic communities, and—too frequently—by their lower social economic status.

Children

A Report of the Surgeon General's Conference on Children's Mental Health (U.S. Public Health Service, 2000) offers the following national action agenda.

Principles:

1. Promoting the recognition of mental health as an essential part of child health;
2. Integrating family-, child-, and youth-centered mental health services into all systems that serve children and youth;
3. Engaging families and incorporating the perspectives of children and youth in the development of all mental health care planning; and
4. Developing and enhancing a public–private health infrastructure to support these efforts to the fullest extent possible.

Goals:

1. Promote public awareness of children's mental health issues and reduce the stigma associated with mental illness.

2. Continue to develop, disseminate, and implement scientifically proven prevention and treatment services in the field of children's mental health.
3. Improve the assessment of and recognition of mental health needs in children.
4. Eliminate racial/ethnic and socioeconomic disparities in access to mental health care services.

The following is an elaboration of this section of the Report; it is from the "Actions Steps." It is included here because it is the section that provides further information about minority children.

- Increase accessible, culturally competent, scientifically proven services that are sensitive to youth and family strengths and needs.
- Increase efforts to recruit and train minority providers who represent the racial, ethnic, and cultural diversity of the country.
- Co-locate mental health services with other key systems (e.g., education, primary care, welfare, juvenile justice, substance-abuse treatment) to improve access, especially in remote or rural communities.
- Strengthen the resource capacity of schools to serve as key links to a comprehensive, seamless system of school- and community-based identification, assessment, and treatment services to meet the needs of youth and their families where they are.
- Encourage the development and integration of alternative, testable approaches to mental health care that engage families in prevention and intervention strategies (e.g., pastoral counseling).
- Develop policies for uninsured children across diverse populations and geographic areas to address the problem of disparities in mental health access.
- Develop and support mental health programs designed to divert youth with mental health problems from the juvenile justice system.
- Increase research on diagnosis, prevention, treatment, and service delivery issues to address disparities in access to mental health care services, especially among different racial, ethnic, gender, sexual orientation, and socioeconomic groups.

5. Improve the infrastructure for children's mental health services, including support for scientifically proven interventions across professions.
6. Increase access to and coordination of quality mental health care services.
7. Train frontline providers to recognize and manage mental health issues, and educate mental health care providers about scientifically proven prevention and treatment services.
8. Monitor the access to and coordination of quality mental health care services.

Women

The National Women's Law Center, FOCUS on Health & Leadership for Women at the University of Pennsylvania School of Medicine, and the Lewin Group (as cited in the Office of Women's Health, 2000c) provided the following analysis and recommendations.

- America's policy makers are letting women down with inadequate, ineffective, and inconsistent health care policies that too often focus on illness rather than on health. There is a need to change the framework of women's health—health should be defined as well-being, rather than as simply the absence of disease. Factors that affect women's health include prevention, income level, education, and environment.
- There are intolerable gaps in health care policy at the state and national levels.
- Too many women lack health insurance coverage or have inadequate insurance coverage. Nearly 1 in 7 women (14%) does not have health insurance.
- The states and the nation have not done enough to address many women's lack of access to health care and to health care providers. Nearly 1 in 10 Americans (9.6%) lives in an area where there are few or no health care providers.
- The states and the nation have not focused enough attention on preventive measures, such as smoking cessation, nutrition, physical activity, and screening for diseases and conditions.
- The nation and the states have not focused sufficient attention on reproductive health, mental health, or violence against women.
- Federal and state health policies do not address the health needs and priorities of women in racial or ethnic minorities, lesbians, and low-income women.
- More research needs to be done on women's health and the conditions that affect them.

The Office of Women's Health (2000d) stated that substantial numbers of minority women distrust the health care system and perceive it as hostile and insensitive. Many minority women are single parents. They often seek traditional, ancestral, or spiritual healing. Many experience racial, ethnic, and gender discrimination. They are often dissatisfied with their health care plans and service providers. There are often cultural, religious, economic, social, ethnic, power, and gender differences between themselves and those who provide them with services. In regard to solutions more specific to ethnic minority women, the Office of Women's Health (2000d) has offered the following:

I. The health care system needs to be changed.
1. *Medical practice.* There are inadequate numbers of primary care physicians, especially in rural or urban low-income areas in which many minority women live. There is an absence of nearby health care facilities. Physicians often do not speak the language or understand the culture of their patients.

   Minority women often receive treatment in facilities with high volumes of clientele (e.g., community health centers, hospital outpatient clinics). Such settings inhibit doctors spending time with patients and provide less preventive care, education, and counseling.
2. *Medical education.* Lack of cultural competence hinders understanding and effective communication between the physician and ethnic minority women. This hinders appropriate diagnoses and treatment. The provision of services from community-based care is needed by minority women in underserved communities.
3. *Medical research.* Very limited numbers of minority women participate in research studies. Consequently, data that are gathered are inadequate and misrepresent these minority women; thus, conclusions and generalizations about the ethnic group cannot be made.
4. *Medical leadership.* Too few women and minorities serve as administrators and service providers. This results in the ethnic minority women's needs not being addressed. Stereotyping and language barriers can occur. Communication problems can occur; for example, health care materials may be written at inappropriate literacy levels. The lack of women and minorities as administrators and service providers prevents the development of health care services that are relevant to the social, cultural, and health needs and practices of minority women.

II. Economic barriers need to need to be addressed and removed.
1. *Income levels.* Minority women are more likely to have lower incomes and to live in poverty than are Caucasian women. Minority women tend to have less formal education than do Caucasian women. Minority women with similar levels of education as Caucasian women earn less money and have fewer assets. Minority women hold a disproportionate share of low-wage jobs, and they have higher unemployment rates. Low income is strongly associated with the decreased use of health services and poor health outcomes. Poor women often delay treatment, resulting in more serious problems when they resort to service providers. Early prevention, education, and intervention are needed.
2. *Health insurance.* Compared with Caucasian women, more minority women are uninsured or rely on public funds for support. Compared

with Caucasian women, minority women are less likely to have private health insurance. Medicare and Medicaid programs provide limited coverage and frequently do not meet all of these women's health care needs. The gaps in socioeconomic status and health insurance coverage between Caucasian and minority women appear to be growing.

3. *Social and cultural barriers.* Ethnic minority women often lack the social and economic power to counter the U.S. health care system's cultural values. They often encounter discrimination and the lack of culturally appropriate services. They need child care, transportation, and a host of other services.

Older Persons

Identify environmental and lifestyle factors and health behaviors that directly influence physical and mental fitness and risk of disease. Already, it has been found that diet, exercise, safety, and other factors promote health and reduce the risks of disease and disability.

This is from the National Institute on Aging's (2001a) *Strategic Plan to Address Health Disparities Fiscal Years 2000–2005*, "Research Goals to Reduce or Eliminate Disparities" (Goals A–C).

A. Research Goals to Reduce or Eliminate Health Disparities
  A1. Advance understanding of the development and progression of diseases and disability that contribute to health disparities in older racial and ethnic minority groups.
  A2. Develop new or improved approaches for detecting or diagnosing the onset or progression of disease and disability among older ethnic and racial minorities.
  A3. Develop new or improved approaches for preventing or delaying the onset or progression of disease and disability among older racial and ethnic minorities.
  A4. Develop new or improved approaches for treating disease and disability.

B. Research Infrastructure Goals
  B1. Support research training and career development.
  B2. Provide support for institutional resources.

C. Public Information, Outreach, and Education Goals
  C1. Develop research-based information resources.
  C2. Communicate research-based information to increase public awareness.
  C3. Transfer knowledge to health care providers.

This is from the National Institute on Aging's (2001b) *Draft NIA Strategic Plan for Fiscal Years 2001–2005*, "Reduce Health Disparities Among Older Persons and Populations" section, Research Goal C, Subgoals 1–3 and D, Subgoals 1–3.

Research Goal C:
Subgoal 1: Increase Active Life Expectancy and Improve Health Status for Older Minority Individuals
   a. Analyze disease prevalence and course in minority populations and subpopulations.
   b. Increase inclusion of minorities/subpopulations in research.
   c. Develop preventive and interventional strategies for healthy aging appropriate for diverse populations.
   d. Improve culturally appropriate health care delivery.
   e. Develop strategies for information dissemination.
   f. Improve health behaviors and health promotion strategies.
Subgoal 2: Understand health differences associated with race, ethnicity, gender, environment, socioeconomic status, geography, and culture.
   a. Study normal aging processes in special populations.
   b. Determine the effects of early life factors on adult health.
   c. Develop necessary data related to health differences and causes.
   d. Promote clear and functional definitions of race, culture, and ethnicity.
   e. Determine the relative influences of race, ethnicity, economic status, education, and work experiences in health.
Subgoal 3: Monitor health, economic status, and life quality of older persons and inform policy.
   a. Study over time population changes and underlying causes of health and function of older persons.
   b. Provide information useful for policy.
   c. Produce data on burdens and costs of illness, healthy life expectancy, longevity, and mortality trajectories.
   d. Monitor population aging and the global burden of disease.

Population aging is not unique to the United States. As advances in sanitation, nutrition, and medical care are spread over the world, the global burden of disease has been shifting from infectious diseases to diseases of more industrialized societies, including heart disease, hypertension, diabetes, and cancer. The perspective of international studies helps increase understanding of American population aging through comparison with that of different systems.

Although many of the disparities in adult health and life expectancy across nation, county, race, occupation, and social class are well documented, causal mechanisms are less well understood. Understanding these differences is critical for developing behavioral and public health interventions. Future research efforts will focus on developing better cross-national and sub-national databases on health outcomes, risk factors, and SES structural factors, such as societal inequality. (National Institute on Aging, 2001b)

Research Goal D:

Enhance Resources to Support High Quality Research

Subgoal 1: Train and attract a diverse workforce of new, mid-career, and senior researchers necessary for research on aging.

Subgoal 2: Develop and sustain a diverse NIA workforce and a professional environment that supports and encourages excellence.

Subgoal 3: Develop and distribute research resources.

It has been mentioned a number of times in this chapter that major governmental projects are underway to improve data gathering on minorities. It should be pointed out that having plans, conducting research, and obtaining data do not solve problems. This is just the beginning of the process of alleviating the problems of minorities. Gathering data does not mean that services are provided. Gathering data does not mean that recommendations and guidelines are implemented. Gathering data does not mean that political, economic, bureaucratic, and other interests will not sabotage efforts to improve the conditions of minorities. Gathering data does not mean that even if funds are allocated for minority needs, the funds will actually be spent to help minorities. All too often, funds are absorbed by administrative and other costs, which results in very little trickling down to those who need the services. The ultimate criteria are whether or not the needs of the community members are being met. Plans, data, and research need to be used and implemented. Effective, parsimonious systems need to be developed that improve the status of the minority older persons, women, children, those with disabilities, and those of different sexual orientation. These systems will need to generate momentum and facilitate self-maintained improvements.

The alleviation of problems entails systemic, multiple approaches, with the key ingredients being:

1. The minority community itself needs to be responsible for its own activities. It needs to develop systems that allow it to have and to exercise responsibility. Society needs to educate and train community members to do so. Society needs to prevent the sabotaging of activities that facilitate community development.

2. There need to be multiple systems working for the development of economic, social, and political systems and for the empowerment of the minority members.
3. The interventions must develop and maintain self-perpetuating systems that meet human need—for example, the need for security, the need for belonging, the need to feel useful.
4. The ethics and morality conducive to social development must be reinforced and supported—the church and schools are already doing this, but more needs to be done.
5. At the present time, the needs of males have to be addressed. They appear to be one of the keys to improving social and economic conditions. Unemployed males engage in much of the criminal, violent, drug, and other destructive and costly (e.g., court and prison) activities. If they were employed, they might feel more productive and useful and might have the economic basis to raise their families. They would be able to obtain funds through regular employment rather than through illegal activities. This in no way suggests that women's employment, development, and services should not also be focused on. But many of the services directed toward women's needs have fostered dependency. It is necessary to develop systems for them as well as for males, to meet their economic needs.
6. Minority members need to obtain entrepreneurial skills. The minority members who have been able to survive and prosper in this culture are those who have entrepreneurial skills.

The mental health therapist's role is to facilitate the previous guidelines in individual counseling, in group therapy, in community action, and in training others. This does not mean that traditional counseling approaches and techniques should not be used. It means that they should be used and coordinated with the previous guidelines.

7

◄○►

World Mental Health—
It Isn't the Fault
of the Minorities and the Poor

An argument can be made that the conditions of the ethnic poor in an affluent country like the United States in no way share commonalties with conditions of the poor in the poverty-stricken areas of Africa, South America, Asia, and other parts of the world. However, when one examines the conditions of these groups, one is impressed by the commonalties that are shared. Within each country, the ethnic poor frequently have disproportionately higher levels of unemployment, police abuse, drug abuse, violence, schools of poorer quality and resources, and so on. Members of dominant groups throughout the world often share many of the same negative perspectives of their respective ethnic members, resulting in discrimination and detrimental stereotypes. It has been found that the mental health of minorities and women in the United States is affected by racism and sexism; similarly, throughout the world, societies' reactions to socioeconomic status, gender, age, color, ethnicity, religion, sexual orientation, and minority status can induce mental problems or exacerbate vulnerable and dysfunctional factors (Lefley, 1999)—such as child abuse and crime.

WHY STUDY THE CONDITIONS OF OTHER
CULTURES IN THE WORLD?

The following are some reasons why we should study the conditions of ethnic minority groups and the poor in other parts of the world:

1. Many of the problems encountered by the poor and ethnic minorities in other countries are also endemic in poor and minority communities in the United States. These problems include substance abuse, violence, crime, lower rates of employment, depression, anxiety, PTSD, and a host of other maladies.
2. In examining the conditions of people in similar circumstances in other parts of the world, one may be able to discover new and different ways of solving problems.
3. Looking outside of one's culture may provide new perspectives for viewing problems within one's own culture. When one examines phenomena from within one's own culture, there are biases that one is not aware of. These biases may hinder better perspectives, definitions, and solutions to problems. For example, it is almost a universal phenomenon that the conditions of minorities in each community and country are viewed as a result of characteristics particular to the ethnic group. That is, the minority group is responsible for its conditions. However, when one examines the conditions of minorities in various parts of the world, it becomes clearer that the conditions of minorities have less to do with genetic and cultural dispositions of the group and more to do with the dynamics of power. For example, after the European Americans' conquest of the Native Americans, pathological labels were attributed to Native Americans and their culture (e.g., many Native American were stereotyped as being lazy and alcohol abusers, and their communities were labeled dysfunctional and desultory). Yet these same descriptors were not as prevalent before the conquests (they were more often described as savages, heathens, etc.). Before the conquest, when they had power, many of these peoples had their own intact political, economic, military, and social systems. These systems were functional and had sustained them for hundreds, if not thousands, of years—testimony to the Native Americans' capacity to develop systems to meet the needs of their societies and the individuals in them. The experience of the Scots and Irish can also serve as an illustration of how negative characteristics are ascribed to ethnic groups, but when circumstances change, these characteristics prove to be inaccurate. There was a period in the history of the Scots and Irish when they were stereotyped (e.g., by the English) as lazy and dissolute in their native countries, but when they came to the United States, these characteristics proved to be no longer viable. The peasants of Russia and members of "untouchable" groups of India had disparaging attributes associated with them. But when they came to the United States, these attributes were no longer associated with them, and their former conditions and status became elevated. Before the formation of Israel, many Arabs and Europeans viewed Jews with condescension as being weak and pathetic, but after the formation of

Israel, Jews were viewed as having formidable military skills. Within the United States itself, when groups such as the Italians and Jews first came to this country, they were viewed as having dysfunctional characteristics (e.g., Jews and Italians were diagnosed as "feeble-minded"— Kamin, 1977) that were the result of their culture and "race." But when their conditions improved and with their increased power, they were no longer viewed in the same negative light. The poor of the streets of Bombay, Liverpool, Moscow, and New York have a lot in common. Their perceived shortcomings are not necessarily the result of characteristics endogenous to themselves or to their cultures; instead, their perceived shortcomings are frequently the result of social, economic, and political forces outside their communities.

WHY AND HOW DO INEQUITIES EXIST?

There are a number of posited reasons as to why the poor exist and why societies define some groups as minorities. The following are some of the explanations:

1. Under a hierarchical, competitive system—such as capitalism—one is bound to have a pyramidal structure, with some people on the top and many on the bottom. As part of this system, one needs to have a non-working, inexpensive, low-maintenance, auxiliary work-pool (the poor). Such a work-pool can serve as a reminder to workers of their vulnerability if they don't work. It can also serve to replace workers as needed. It can serve as a source to hire and lay off work during fluctuations in the economy, and so on.
2. There is the genetic drift theory, which posits that in every society there are people with genes that are not as functional for that particular society; therefore, people with these genes filter to the "bottom" of society. The previous two theories have more to do with providing explanations for the existence of the poor. The next two can provide explanations for why minorities exist and why they receive the treatment that they do.
3. Minorities exist to validate the values of the ruling group (a sociological perspective). If you recall, the allocation of minority status is not determined by the number of people in the "subordinate" group; rather, it is determined by the group in power. The group in power allocates minority status to certain groups that do not have power. Besides using skin color or cultural differences to delineate the two groups, the group in power provides negative characteristics to the minority groups—for example, they are lazy, they are dirty, and so forth. Such allocation of labels to the minority group validates social values and perceptions: The

group in power has characteristics that are the converse of the minority groups'; for example, the group in power would therefore be defined as hard-working, clean, and so on.

4. There is an innate tendency within us to scapegoat others (an intrapsychic perspective—Frazer, 1998). There are a number of reasons for this—for example, by blaming our problems on others, we can objectify and focus our problems, and therefore we can do something about the problem—by attacking others. Another explanation is that it is easier to blame our problems on others rather than accept responsibility for our problems. There is also the theory that we may harbor resentment against minority groups because they are different. We value group cohesion and we value those who are similar to us. We view those who are different as a threat to cohesion and to our values. In order to justify our negative feelings of them, we define them as a being a threat to us; therefore, our perceptions and treatment of them are warranted.

5. From an evolutionary perspective, one could posit that the allocation of minority status and the conditions of the poor are the result of competition for resources. The more resources a particular group has, the greater the likelihood of survival. Resources can be obtained, maintained, and increased through power and dominance over others. Therefore, the more power and dominance a group has over other groups, the greater the survival probability. Those who can place themselves at an advantage over others will do so and will promote their own interests. The accompanying unequal distribution of resources results in some people being richer and others being poorer. If we identify with a particular group, we will want that group to have more power and resources and to stymie the other groups that are not similar to us.

In addition to the previous, there may also be historical factors operating at any given time and place that might differentiate ethnic minorities and the poor from others. For example, Whites may have a different group history than non-Whites. The non-White groups of the world often share some commonalities. Often, they were conquered or controlled by European powers under the colonial, imperialistic, or mercantile model. Gerzina (1999) wrote that racism was part of imperialism and colonialism. As one group dominated another, the subjected group was often associated with negative moral, cultural, or intellectual traits, whereas the dominant group was associated with positive traits. In the present day, Western culture permeates the world and carries many of the biases and perceptions of Europe and the United States. This can result in differential treatment of Whites and non-Whites. Because of these historical factors, non-Whites have much in common with each other, and Whites have much in common with each other—with the concomitant differentiation between the haves and the have-nots.

Comas-Diaz (2000) identified three factors in preserving racism: evolutionary, psychological, and ethnopolitical. From an evolutionary perspective, she cited Lawrence A. Hirschfeld (1996), who wrote that racial differentiation occurred at an early age and resulted in a preference for one's own race through projection, identification, and disidentification. From psychology, she drew from the ideas of Carl G. Jung. Jung wrote that people have a darker or evil side to their being (defined as the shadow part of personality); how they work with this side of their being depends on the culture. Jungian psychology presents the view that to U.S. Whites, people of color represent the shadow part of their being. U.S. Whites project onto people of color their disowned, inferior side. Thus, hatred and scapegoating of this aspect of their being can occur. This brings us to the third part of Comas-Diaz's explanation for racism: ethnopolitical. Because people of color are the shadow aspect of U.S. Whites, people of color can be repressed, exploited, and traumatized. "As conquered enemies, Native Americans, African Americans, Latinos, and Asian Americans have been subjected to repression by the U.S. government, which has designated them as savages, slaves, and colonized entities" (Comas-Diaz, 1994). "People of color are often exposed to imperialism and intellectual domination at the expense of their cultural values" (Said, as cited in Comas-Diaz, 2000, pp. 1319–1320). The domination can incur a number of reactions on the part of the ethnic member; for example, there could be the Stockholm syndrome, whereby people of color identify with their oppressors, suppress their own people, and maintain the power of the dominant group; or one's self and one's culture could be disowned—this could result in detrimental developmental, psychological, physical, and spiritual problems. Problems can include depression; loss of self and community; somatic disturbances; shame, rage, and stress; loss of power, trust, and safety; dysfunctional relationships and self-concept; loss of hope; and demoralization. Self-hatred could be projected onto other people of color—because one cannot safely attack the dominant group. Bezruchka (2001) wrote that our hierarchical structure, with its features of power, domination, and coercion, induces resignation, resentment, submission, heart attacks, and a host of other pathologies.

Although the previous provides explanations for the existence of minorities and the poor, and for the way they are treated, there are reasons why they continue to exist. These could be based on political, ideological, or moral grounds (Encyclopaedia Brittanica, 1997). For example, the elimination of the minority or poor group could incur moral and ethical dissonance among some members of the dominant group's social values—for example, values of not killing or hurting weak, vulnerable people. The cost of eliminating the minority group could outweigh the benefits; for example, the group to be eliminated might strike back and make the assaults of the dominant group costly; or the group in power might not want to contend with domestic and international organizations that sympathize with and support the ethnic group that is to be eliminated. Another possible reason for allowing the minority group to exist is that it can provide services that are needed; for example, it can provide cheap labor or its members have skills that are useful. Of course, if a group is small enough and offers no relevant threat, then it may be allowed to exist by the dominant group.

In their book *Haves and Have-Nots*, Curtis and Tepperman (1994) explain how inequalities exist. They divide their reasons into three major categories: economic, power, and status inequalities. The following is a description of what they have written on these categories.

Economic Inequalities

There are a number of theories for the existence of economic inequalities. Roberto Michels (1968) wrote that inequalities exist because humans have leaders and leaders by definition entail concomitant processes that maintain their power and differentiate their interests from those they represent or control. Rousseau, Marx, and Engels (Olsen, 1970) argue that class systems and private property induce economic differentiations. Another explanation of economic inequities is that society rewards those they value; therefore, the valued persons and groups have more. Inequities facilitate the process whereby those with more wealth, power, and prestige have greater access to opportunities that occur by virtue of their positions. These opportunities serve to consolidate and expand their positions.

Curtis and Tepperman (1994) go on to provide explanations for the mechanisms that account for inequalities. These mechanisms limit the opportunities for those with less from having access to more. The mechanisms to promote inequalities are exclusion, disability, decoupling, and scarcity. *Exclusion* is the mechanism of simply excluding people from resources (e.g., not hiring a minority job applicant to a position)—the controlling powers simply do not allow certain groups to have the same opportunities as others. *Disability* is the mechanism whereby certain categories of people are discouraged from competing for positions because of some perceived shortcomings or prohibitive differences (e.g., the employer may perceive that there are differences that are a hinderance; the minority member may choose not to apply for positions because they feel their values are not in sync with the potential employer's; they may perceive that the employer will not hire them because the employer believes the potential applicant's values are too much in conflict with the employer's; there may be feelings of alienation, distrust, low aspirations, group pressure, self-blame, etc.). These thoughts and feelings disempower the individual.

Decoupling is the process whereby the "have-nots" are disconnected from the networks that provide opportunities to improve their condition (e.g., the "haves" have networks that allow them to be more aware of job opportunities, whereas the "have-nots" are out of the loop and are decoupled from such information and opportunities). *Scarcity* is the final mechanism that can explain the reasons why some people have more than others: There are limited resources; therefore, those with more power keep the resources (e.g., jobs, higher wages) to themselves and do not distribute to the "have-nots."

Curtis and Tepperman's (1994) studies indicated that inequalities increase with population size, economic surplus, and social complexity. They state that inequalities will occur in societies with market economies, vested interests, and hierarchies.

Power Inequalities

The power to dominate others has four aspects: differentiation, inequality, legitimization, and symbolization. *Differentiation* is the process whereby those with power establish ways to differentiate themselves from those they control. They attempt to convince those they control that the inequity that results from their dominance is legitimate—for example, is ordained by God, is logical, and so forth. They develop *symbols* to remind those they dominate who is in charge and who is to submit. The methods of differentiation can take different forms and entail the establishing of social distinctions among people; for examples, bosses wear ties, workers wear uniforms. Differentiation is often accompanied by social *inequality*; that is, on and off the job, by virtue of the job, there are differences in power, respect, lifestyle, opportunities, and so on. *Legitimatization* is needed to justify the differences and inequities between the haves and the have-nots. This can be accomplished through various means, such as the "haves" conveying the perception that their position is legitimate because they have the position (justification by virtue of the position). Or, the position is legitimate because they are endorsed by others (e.g., the boss selected them; therefore, it is legitimate). Another rationale is that their position is legitimate because they are more "naturally" suited for the position. Positions can be legitimized based on legal grounds—for example, the police officer has the right to stop us and take away our liberties. Persons wielding power could also legitimize differences by inducing the belief that inequities exist because they need the power in order to influence political and social forces that impact on their constituents.

Brian Martin (1994) wrote, "individual productivity has a relatively low impact on career performance in large-scale organizations. Advancement depends greatly on jockeying for position, for example by forming alliances, obtaining credit for collective work and increasing evaluation of particular types of contributions" (p. 326). He found that promotion to higher status positions in bureaucracies is not based on ability, skills, or merit. Promotion is based on compatibility with those in the right positions and associating with the right people. Consequently, ethnic minorities are not likely to be promoted because, despite having ability, skills, and merit, they do not have the opportunity to associate with the "right people" and establish compatible relationships. However, it is important for bureaucracies and semi-bureaucracies to foster the impression that those in higher-status positions are promoted because of their merit. It is important that the perception exists that there is a correspondence between merit and higher attainment. The preceding impressions are important to foster in lower participants because lower participants need to accept the legitimacy of those with power. However, Martin's research indicates that the truth of how individuals attain their positions of power does not correspond to the perceptions of legitimacy they try to convince others of.

Status Inequities

Status inequalities occur as another mechanism to differentiate those with power from those who do not have power. Status inequality can take many forms. It can take the form of the people with power having access to those with power (underlings lower in a hierarchy have to follow a chain of command that does not allow them access to those higher in the echelons); they may attend status meetings with higher-status titles (e.g., "executive" meetings or "leadership" meetings); they may dress in a more prestigious fashion; they may have better locations and furnishings in their offices; they may sit themselves at meetings in positions considered to reflect hierarchy (e.g., at heads of tables); their manner of speech may reflect their power (e.g., they may make comments like, "I will be doing evaluations of you"); and so forth.

The preceding factors help shed light on the dynamics of power and provide information on the elements at work in the lives of minorities and the poor. These elements are not just economic, social, and political in their causes and effects. They can also have enormous repercussions on mental and physical health. The next section describes some of the main efforts to obtain mental health epidemiological data on these effects on a worldwide basis—and in the United States. Such data can delineate common problems experienced by various groups in the world and can increase our understanding of where and how to provide help to alleviate suffering.

WORLD MENTAL HEALTH OF MINORITIES AND THE POOR

To allow for international comparisons of data, the World Health Organization (WHO, 1992) helped develop the International Classification of Diseases (ICD). It is a system for classifying various forms of morbidity (departure from healthiness or well-being). It classifies diseases, injuries, and causes of death. It is used in many countries. It is revised approximately every 10 years. The ICD-10 has extensive material on mental and behavioral disorders. The most recent version of the *Diagnostic and Statistical Manual,* or *DSM-IV,* developed by the American Psychiatric Association, was designed to coordinate its terminology with that of the ICD-10.

Another measure that has been developed is the DALY (Disability Adjusted Life Years). The DALY is used by WHO and by the researchers with the World Health Project. DALYs were developed to measure the effects of problems. A great deal of the recent work on the condition of minorities and the poor has used this system of measurement. This is discussed next.

World Health Organization and the World Mental Health Project

Epidemiological Terms, Criteria, and Data for Cross-Cultural Analyses. In comparing groups across societies, it is important to have definitions, instruments, databases, and so on that are common to all participants. The Mental Health section of the World Health Organization has provided definitions, instruments, diagnostic terms and criteria, and epidemiological data for cross-cultural analyses. For the interested reader, these are provided at the World Health Organization's website: http://www.who.int/dsa/cat98/men8.htm.

Disability-Adjusted Life Years—DALYs. The World Health Organization (WHO) and the World Mental Health Project have been involved in obtaining worldwide mental health data. Another group that has been gathering data on world mental health is the World Bank (1993). The 1993 World Bank's World Development Report tried to quantify the global burden of disease. The World Bank worked with health economists to develop DALYs. The World Bank recognized that improvement of economic conditions could improve mental health. And improvements in mental health can improve economic conditions; for example, a healthy worker will have fewer work days lost due to sickness. The World Health Organization (WHO) is part of the United Nations. The World Mental Health Project, working with WHO, is coordinated by the Department of Social Medicine of Harvard's Medical School. The World Mental Health Project places particular emphasis on obtaining data on the mental health of minorities and the poor. It was founded in 1995 after the publication of the book *World Mental Health: Problems and Priorities in Low-Income Countries* (Desjarlais et al., 1995). The data that are provided allow for comparisons between the "established market economies" (that is, the industrialized countries such as the European countries, Australia, Japan, and the United States) and the countries that are not as industrialized and that are economically poor. The project draws on research from anthropology, economics, clinical studies, and epidemiology and provides an analysis based on physical, psychiatric, social, and cultural factors that contribute to mental illness and social problems.

Both WHO and the World Mental Health Project work with DALY data. DALYs measure the total effects of a particular problem. One DALY is one year of healthy life lost. Components that constitute the DALYs include the age at which disease or disability occurs, how long its effects last, and its impact on quality of life. Each condition is assigned a disability weighting from zero (perfect health) to one (death). The weighting figure is multiplied by the years lived in that state of health and is added to the number of years lost because of the condition. Projections of the future burden of the condition are discounted at the rate of 3% for each year, and in the calculation of the burden over a lifetime, childhood and old age are given less weight. If the condition can shorten one's life, "premature" death values are based on comparisons with a standardized model of life expectancy. The use of DALYs is not without its critics (Groce, Chamie, & Me, 2001)—one of the main criticisms is that DALYs devalue those with disabilities.

The DALYs of selected illness categories in the established market economies—the category in which the United States is in—are provided in this section. This information was obtained from Table 1 of the Surgeon General's Report on Mental Health (1999a). The following is a percentage breakdown of the burden of each disease, as defined by DALYs (that is, as measured by years of life lost to premature death and years lived with a disability of specified severity and duration [Murray & Lopez, 1996]): 18.6%, all cardiovascular conditions; 15.4%, all mental illness (includes suicide); 15.0%, all malignant disease (cancer); 4.8%, all respiratory conditions; 4.7%, all alcohol use; 2.8%, all infectious and parasitic disease; 1.5%, all drug use.

On a worldwide basis, the World Bank has presented the following data on the percentage of DALYs lost (all the DALYs figures presented in this section can be found in the World Bank, 1993): 34%, behavior-related illnesses (communicable and noncommunicable); 18%, other noncommunicable diseases; 9.5%, maternal/perinatal; 9.0%, respiratory; 8.1%, mental health problems; 5.8%, cancer; 5.3%, other communicable diseases; 4.4%, heart disease; 3.2%, cerebral-vascular; 2.6% malaria.

Compared to other diseases, mental illnesses make up approximately 8.1% of DALYs of the health problems in this world. When one examines the 8.1% of DALYs lost to mental health, the following is a breakdown of the percentages of DALYs lost in each mental health category (World Bank, 1993): 17.3%, depressive disorders; 16.4%, other; 15.9%, self-inflicted injury; 12.7%, Alzheimer's/dementia; 12.1%, alcohol dependence; 9.3%, epilepsy; 6.8%, psychosis; 4.8%, drug dependence; 4.7%, PTSD.

The inclusion of epilepsy in the mental health category is interesting because most mental health workers in the United States do not give epilepsy much attention. However, epilepsy can be more of a problem in less developed countries. In these less developed countries, although epilepsy is a problem in and of itself, it is also a marker for and harbinger of other problems. In industrialized countries, epilepsy has a prevalence rate of about 4 to 8 per 1,000 people. In developing countries, the prevalence can be three to five times higher. In such countries, epilepsy has been associated with higher rates of a host of medical problems, including increased rates of cerebral palsy, mental retardation, abnormal pregnancies, postnatal CNS infection, and brain injuries. Childhood epilepsy is associated with a four-fold increase in risk for psychiatric disorders, and those with epilepsy induced by brain lesion were four times more likely to have psychopathology.

In terms of the overall DALYs of the health problems of the world, another category is related to mental health: behavior-related illnesses (communicable and noncommunicable). These are problems induced by human activities and include disabilities due to violence, diarrheal diseases, malnutrition, tuberculosis, sexually transmitted diseases, and motor vehicle and other unintentional injuries. Behavior-related illnesses account for 34% of the DALYs lost.

Desjarlais et al. (1995) report that with improvements of conditions, in both industrialized and underdeveloped countries, and with increased life expectancy, there is also an increase in depression, schizophrenia, dementia, and other forms of chronic illness. Economic growth and improvements, and changes in social conditions, have been accompanied by increases in alcoholism, drug abuse, and suicide. With economic progress and with increased longevity, there has been an increase in social, psychiatric, and behavioral pathologies. In ethnic minority communities and with the poor, violence, abuse, dislocation, poverty, and exploitation are among the many problems encountered. The use of DALYs is new to the field of measurement, and DALYs have yet to be developed for U.S. minorities and the poor, making it difficult to make comparisons with the DALYs that have been gathered for minorities and the poor in other parts of the world. However, the alcoholism, drug abuse, domestic violence, crime, and other pathologies associated with many ethnic and poor communities in the world can also be found in many U.S. ethnic and poor communities. It can be expected that the DALYs for the U.S. ethnic and poor communities will be greater than those of the rest of the United States—a possible indicator of this comes from the Executive Summary of the Fogarty International Center (Fogarty International Center, 2000):

> In the United States, health disparities are evident within and among population groups. Genetic and environmental factors, nutrition, access to health education and services, behavior, and other factors are implicated in varying degrees as contributors to these disparities. (p. 1)

The World Health Organization (2000) reports that the United States ranks 37th on health care, despite the fact that we spend a lot more per person on health care than any other country does. The low ranking for the United States can be attributed to the health care that is provided to minorities and the poor.

The Pan American Health Organization's (2000) epidemiological report of the United States showed that

> While chronic disease conditions are the leading causes of death for both minority and nonminority persons over 45 years of age, minority populations (African-Americans, Hispanics, Native Americans, and Asian American/Pacific Islanders) incur a disproportionate share of death, illness, disability, and adverse health conditions. Commonly used health indicators such as life expectancy at birth and infant mortality rates show continued widening of the health gap between minority and majority populations. Poverty is a major contributing factor to the disparities in health status. (pp. 5–6)

The Kaiser Family Foundation (2000) examined the health insurance coverage and access to physician services among African Americans, Latinos, Asian Americans and Pacific Islanders, and American Indians and Alaska Natives. From the Foundation's website, one can obtain more specific data on these groups. Among the Foundation's findings are

> Racial and ethnic groups in the United States continue to experience major differences in health status compared to the majority white population. Although many factors affect health status, the lack of health insurance and other barriers to obtaining health services markedly diminish minorities' use of both preventive services and medical treatments. (p. 1)

To obtain a summary of epidemiological data on U.S. mental health, see the Surgeon General's Report on Mental Health (1999c). The diagnostic instrument that is used to gather the data in the Surgeon General's Report on Mental Health is the *Diagnostic and Statistical Manual.*

FINDINGS AND SOLUTIONS

Desjarlais et al. (1995) agree with the World Bank's efforts to deal with health problems. That is, through the publication of World Bank's Development Reports (World Bank, 1993), the World Bank tried to impact policy makers. It advocated for further investments into health care. It sought cost-effective ways to improve health care, reduce poverty, develop human resources, empower women, and expand educational opportunities. Although Desjarlais et al. (1995) agreed with the preceding World Bank aims, they also stated that there should be greater focus on mental health issues, with more attention given to violence, alcoholism, drug addiction, child abuse, homelessness, discrimination, and dislocation.

Desjarlais et al. (1995) found the following in their analyses of the World Bank's data:

- Social environments have an impact on mental health. Even for problems that are genetic and hereditary, the provision of support services can help mitigate or exacerbate the problems; for example, untreated schizophrenia is likely to last longer and have a greater detrimental effect than schizophrenia that is treated; domestic violence, drug and alcohol abuse, the narcotics trade, prostitution, crime and street violence, and child abuse and abandonment are some of the many social factors that impact the mental health of ethic communities and the poor.
- There are multiple interacting factors involved in behavioral disorders and social problems; for example, suicidal behaviors may be linked to exposure to violence, depression, availability of weapons, social conditions, and cultural milieu. Social conditions could be linked to depression, which could be linked to drug abuse and medical problems, which could be linked to addiction, prostitution, HIV infections, and child and partner abuse, which could be linked to suicide.
- Problems occurred in clusters rather than as single entities; for example, victims of violence might have PTSD problems as well as depression. Community violence can be associated with PTSD and depression. Children who grow up in environments where there is crime, violence toward women and children, and drug abuse may experience depression as adults.
- Problems have a tendency to induce other problems; for example, abused children may abuse others; drug abuse may lead to HIV infections, domestic violence, and prostitution.
- Key social forces can impact social and psychiatric problems; for example, repressive gender practices can be devastating to women's mental health; empowering them and educating them can improve their mental health.

Investments in poor communities can break the cycle of poverty. Economic policies that isolate communities from financial and social resources can facilitate social and psychiatric morbidity.

• Desjarlais and colleagues found that the delineation of world problems into those of developed and developing nations cannot be easily done—developed and developing nations share many of the same problems, though some nations have more or less of particular problems. For example, increased population growth is often accompanied by social pathologies such as destruction of cultural systems, economic restructuring, breakdown of family structures, and so on. Desjarlais et al. (1995) wrote,

> Development often creates poverty side by side with wealth, producing the social origins of suffering for many as well as rising living standards for some. The new forms of poverty, along with social ills they produce, are challenges to social justice and human rights. Only when economic development is linked to a global concern for equity and human rights can it eliminate a key source of the new morbidities. (p. 262)

• In analyzing problems and providing solutions, it is of critical importance to consider the culture of the people involved. Local culture may have its own definitions of mental illness and problems; traditional cultural practices and beliefs should be considered. Local systems should be developed and its inhabitants trained. Services and systems should be locally controlled and administered. Local strengths and resources should be developed, and weaknesses should be remedied. Economic and structural inequities should be eliminated. And it is fundamental to any problem-solving efforts to consider that the well-being of the individual is fundamentally connected to the well-being of the community.

• Desjarlais and colleauges found that the provision of mental health services can be effective and affordable.

• They also advocated for the involvement of policy makers—"policies that encourage gainful employment, reduce poverty, protect the environment, improve the quality of leisure, and provide universal basic education, primary health care, decent housing, and adequate nutrition are all prima facie beneficial" (Desjarlais et al., 1995, p. 270).

• Early detection and education and prevention programs should be instituted.

• Effective treatment and prevention programs for alcohol and drug abuse are important.

• Programs should be developed to deal with the causes and consequences of collective and interpersonal violence.

• Psychological and social problems should be given at least as much attention as are medical problems.

Desjarlais et al.'s (1995) report of the connection between environment and mental illness is not new. Brearey (1978) reported that the medical profession has long realized not only the connection between the environment and health (e.g., living with others who have tuberculosis increases one's chances of getting tuberculosis), but also the connection between the environment and mental health. However, the mental health professions are less likely to see the connection between environment and mental health. There are a number of reasons for this, including the following. Mental health professionals are trained to provide therapy in the context of one-to-one sessions, and occasionally in group settings; therefore, they are less likely to be aware of, and be concerned with, the effects of the environmental context on the person's problems. Also, mental health professionals' environments are more secure than those of the poor and minorities; therefore, they are not as concerned with environmental factors (except in cases where these affect them, such as in cases of domestic sexual, physical, and mental abuse). In addition, mental health professionals try to stay in the middle and upper class by serving these classes; these classes have their environmental needs met; therefore, environmental factors are not as much as a concern for them in therapy. Another factor that may be relevant is that it is not to the economic, social, and political benefit of mental health professionals, and policy makers, to have healthy systems in poor and minority communities—mental health professionals and policy makers make their money and retain their positions by delivering services, and not by developing individuals and communities that are self-sustaining. Therefore, it is in their best interest to maintain the status quo. Also, policy makers come from the middle and upper classes. They see things from their own social and economic perspectives; consequently, they fail to see the need to develop and implement mechanisms and programs for the growth of healthy poor and minority communities.

The following are some of the findings of the National Institutes of Health Fogarty International Center's (Fogarty International Center, 2000), *Executive Summary of Strategic Plan for Fiscal Years 2000–2003, for Reducing Disparities in Global Health*:

- Many low- and middle-income nations are undergoing technological changes. They are making the transition from traditional technologies to such technologies as fiber-optics and satellite telecommunications networks. Networks such as these will evolve and become the main technological ingredients in the scientific and health-care systems in these countries. There is a need to consider how these emerging technologies in low- and middle-income nations can be applied to such areas as gathering and analyzing epidemiological data, improving clinical work, and developing programs for distance learning. There is a need to consider how these technologies can be applied to the scientific collaboration of information and to software and computing.

- There has been vigorous study of the factors involved in economic development. However, very little attention has been directed toward examining the relationship among health, demographic data, and economic development. Recently, economists and public health officials have been investigating the relationship between national growth and health. In addition, they are studying the relationship between health and productivity on an individual level. These studies indicate that if we have a better understanding of the determinants and consequences of public health, it will increase our understanding of the long-term influences on economic development and will improve the formulation of policy makers. Investments in health-related technological development can benefit from research into the relationship among health, poverty, and productivity.
- Attention should be given to increasing the number of underrepresented minorities in research; efforts should be made to target members of these groups during their formative years in academia.
- There needs to be an increase in the training of professionals from low- and middle-income nations in the theoretical and practical ethical aspects of cross-cultural research.

The Surgeon General presented a summary of the mental health of the United States (Surgeon General's Report, 1999d). The section of a report titled *Overview of Cultural Diversity and Mental Health* specifically addressed the issues of ethnic minorities. Ethnic minorities are defined as those in four major racial or ethnic groups: African American (Black), Asian/ Pacific Islander, Hispanic American (Latino), and Native American/American Indian/Alaska Native/Native Hawaiian (grouped together as "American Indians"; Center for Mental Health Services, 1998). Drawing on the research of others, the following is some of what was reported:

- Ethnic minorities differ from each other and from society in regard to culture. "Culture" is defined as the beliefs, norms, values, and shared heritage of a group. The cultures of many minority racial and ethnic groups often differ greatly from European cultures. Individuals within each culture may differ in language, acculturation, gender, age, class, spiritual beliefs, and so on (Lu, Lim, & Mezzich, 1995). In addition, many people have multiple ethnic or cultural identities.
- Minorities often differ from the "general" U.S. population in economic, social, and political status. The most obvious difference is in income. Poor minority families are three times more likely than are White families to be below the federally established poverty line. Although some Asian Americans are somewhat better off financially than other minority groups

are, as a group they are one and a half times more likely than Whites are to live in poverty. Minority women and children are affected more than others are by poverty (Miranda & Green, 1999).

- Lower socioeconomic status is strongly linked to mental illness. People in the lowest socioeconomic bracket are about two and a half times more likely than those in the highest strata to have a mental disorder (Holzer et al., 1986; Regier et al., 1993b). Greater stress seems to be a factor associated with lower socioeconomic conditions. Poor women are exposed to more frequent, threatening, and uncontrollable life events than the general population (Belle, 1990).
- The mental health system is not serving ethnic minorities at acceptable levels (Neighbors et al., 1992; Takeuchi & Uehara, 1996; Center for Mental Health Services [CMHS], 1998). A number of barriers hinder minority groups from trying to obtain services. Those minority group members who succeed in obtaining services may receive inappropriate services.
- There is research that indicates many minority group members fear and are uncomfortable with the mental health system (Lin, Inui, Kleinman, & Womack, 1982; Sussman, Robins, & Earls, 1987; Scheffler & Miller, 1991). "These groups experience it as the product of white, European culture, shaped by research primarily on white, European populations. They may find only clinicians who represent a white middle-class orientation, with its cultural values and beliefs, as well as its biases, misconceptions, and stereotypes of other cultures" (Surgeon General's Report, 1999d, p. 1).
- Culturally competent service providers are needed. As much as such these providers are needed now, the need will be even greater in the near future because of the enormous demographic changes that will occur (Center for Mental Health Services, 1998; Snowden, 1999; Takeuchi & Uehara, 1996).
- The main reasons for the inadequate services to minorities have to do with clinical, cultural, organizational, and financial factors.
- Culture impacts whether a person seeks mental health services and how the person responds to treatment.
- Culture determines how we respond to everyday problems.
- Religious beliefs and practices often determine whether a person obtains mental health services. Religion and spirituality play important roles in the lives of many racial and ethnic group members. Religion impacts their health and well-being. Many believe that well-being, good health, and religious commitment or faith are closed interrelated (Priest, 1991; Bacote, 1994; Pargament, 1997; Taylor, 1986).
- Culture influences the way a person experiences mental problems. It may even influence whether or not a person experiences mental problems.
- Signs of distress may be expressed through culture-bound syndromes.

- African Americans, Latinos, Asian Americans, and Native Americans have close ties to their families and communities. This is part of their sense of identity and provides comfort in the face of discrimination.
- There is a need for culturally appropriate assessment tools and better measures to determine when an ethnic group member warrants treatment.
- There are major differences in the use of mental health facilities. Some ethnic minority groups are underrepreesented in outpatient facilities, and other minority groups are overrepresented in outpatient facilities.
- The mental health system is not designed to meet the mental health needs of ethnic minorities. This seems to be the result of cultural differences and organizational, financial, and diagnostic reasons.
- There is a great deal of evidence that ethnic minorities do not use specialized, outpatient mental health treatment as much as Whites do (Gallo, Marino, Ford, & Anthony, 1995; Leong & Lau, 1998; Snowden, 1999; Sussman et al., 1987; Vega & Kolody, 1998; Vega et al., 1998a; Zhang, Snowden, & Sue, 1998).
- There are many reasons why ethnic group members are not as likely to seek treatment from mental health providers. Studies with African Americans indicate that the reasons include lack of time, fear of hospitalization, and fear of treatment (Sussman et al., 1987).
- Clinician bias may result in underdiagnosis, overdiagnosis, or misdiagnosis of ethnic group members with mental disorders. One reason for this is that mental health therapists rely on their subjective judgments and on the behavioral signs and symptoms of the client, instead of relying on more objective methods such as laboratory tests.

In terms of recommendations to improve the mental health of those in the United States, the Surgeon General's Report (1999b) offers the following suggestions: Continue to Build the Science Base; Overcome Stigma (of mental illness); Improve Public Awareness of Effective Treatment; Ensure the Supply of Mental Health Services and Providers; Ensure Delivery of State-of-the-Art Treatments; Tailor Treatment to Age, Gender, Race, and Culture; Facilitate Entry Into Treatment; and Reduce Financial Barriers to Treatment.

The Surgeon General's Report is aimed at improving the mental health of all citizens in this country. There is no doubt that minorities can benefit from these recommendations. However, some sections of the report mention minorities specifically. The following are excerpts of those parts of the report that mention minorities.

Ensure the Supply of Mental Health Services and Providers
The fundamental components of effective service delivery include integrated community-based services, continuity of providers and treat-

ments, family support services (including psychoeducation), and culturally sensitive services. Effective service delivery for individuals with the most severe conditions also requires supported housing and supported employment. . . . the goal of services must not be limited to symptom reduction but should strive for restoration of a meaningful and productive life.

Across the Nation, certain mental health services are in consistently short supply. These include the following: Wraparound services for children with serious emotional problems and multisystemic treatment. Both treatment strategies should actively involve the participation of the multiple health, social service, educational, and other community resources that play a role in ensuring the health and well-being of children and their families.

Ensure Delivery of State-of-the-Art Treatments

"State-of-the-art" treatments, carefully refined through years of research, are not being translated into community settings. As noted throughout this report, a wide variety of community-based services are of proven value for even the most severe mental illnesses. Exciting new research-based advances are emerging that will enhance the delivery of treatments and services in areas crucial to consumers and families—employment, housing, and diversion of people with mental disorders out of the criminal justice systems. Yet a gap persists in the broad introduction and application of these advances in services delivery.

Tailor Treatment to Age, Gender, Race, and Culture

This report presents clear evidence that mental health and mental illness are shaped by age, gender, race, and culture as well as additional facets of diversity that can be found within all of these population groups—for example, physical disability or a person's sexual orientation. The consequences of not understanding these influences can be profoundly deleterious.

To be effective, the diagnosis and treatment of mental illness must be tailored to individual circumstances, while taking into account, age, gender, race, and culture and other characteristics that shape a person's image and identity. Services that take these demographic factors into consideration have the greatest chance of engaging people in treatment, keeping them in treatment, and helping them to recover thereafter. The successful experiences of individual patients will positively influence attitudes toward mental health services and service providers, thus encouraging others who may share similar concerns or interests to seek help.

Members of racial and ethnic minority groups account for an increasing proportion of the Nation's population. Mental illness is at least as prevalent among racial and ethnic minorities as in the majority white population [Regier et al., 1993]. Yet many racial and ethnic minority group members find the organized mental health system to be uninformed about cultural context and, thus, unresponsive and/or irrelevant. It is partly for this reason that minority group members overall are less inclined than whites to seek treatment [Sussman et al., 1987; Gallo et al., 1995]. . . . There is an insufficient number of mental health professionals from racial and ethnic minority groups [Peterson et al., 1998], a problem that needs to be corrected. (pp. 1–11)

This chapter has presented worldwide information on the mental health of minorities and the poor. It has also presented information on minorities and the poor in the United States. It should be apparent that minorities and the poor in other parts of the world share some common dynamics and problems with those in the United States. The solutions delineated in other parts of the world might also be applied to the United States, and the solutions to problems in the United States might be applied to other parts of the world. Undoubtedly, there are differences between U.S. minority ethnic group members and other ethnic groups in the world—just as there are differences within and among minority groups in the United States. Nevertheless, there are enough commonalties between the U.S. minority populations and populations in other parts of the world to warrant the sharing of information to solve common problems.

Much can and should be done in the study and treatment of mental disorders throughout the world. The need is especially pressing for ethnic minorities and the poor. They constitute enormous populations in the world—in fact, they are the majority in numbers, and they will grow further in the future (National Intelligence Council, 2000). There are challenging problems to contend with: problems in the development and refinement of terms, definitions, concepts, and assessment tools; and problems in the delineation of problems, determining a meaningful course of action to alleviate the problems, implementing the solutions to the problems, and developing systems to maintain and expand on the gains that have been made. Although the United Nations has worked on these problems, these are just incipient steps.

The study and treatment of these populations should be accompanied by actions. We have enough information, some of which has been presented in this chapter, to start in certain directions—for example, provide women with support, and promote local development. As the World Bank reports, the helping of the disfranchised of the world is in the economic best interest of the world. Once these communities are developed, they will have the income to serve as markets for trading partners. The present costs of crime, poverty, mental diseases, health problems, and so on drain huge resources from countries. These inequities are also often the main reasons for social upheaval—the dispossessed want to force the holders of power to have a more equitable allocation of economic, social, political, and military power.

The use of the military and police to suppress the discontent has required massive resources from national budgets.

The alleviation of mental health problems, and the conditions that induce them, can help the economies of communities, countries, and the world. The interaction with other scholars and activists throughout the world can bring us closer to each other and enable us to help each other. If we do not develop the underdeveloped populations, the more militaristic elements of the world might take up the banner for them. If we do not improve conditions, drug lords will continue to introduce illegal drugs into communities to help them deal with the effects of poverty. If we do not do more, our problems will expand and our lives will be significantly affected. Already, vast numbers of people are affecting neighboring countries by crossing into their borders to escape poverty and oppressive elements.

It should be clear that racism and discrimination play an important role in hindering the development of ethnic minority and poor populations. By not allowing the prejudicial aspects of our thoughts and behaviors to influence our actions, we can be of service to others and ourselves.

8

—◄o►—

Concluding Remarks

SCHOLARSHIP AND ACTION

Many have offered ethical standards, training guidelines, statements of competencies, and solutions to minority mental therapy (e.g., Axelson, 1993; Ponterotto, Casas, Suzuki, & Alexander, 1995). This book shares one of the perspectives taken by Sue (Ponterotto, Casas, Suzuki, & Alexander, 1995), "Counseling professionals need to recognize that counseling does not occur in isolation from larger events in our society. All of us have a responsibility in understanding the political forces and events that affect not only our personal but professional lives as well" (p. 628). I take it a step further and say, "Lets do something about it."

We need people of action. It is hoped that the new generation of mental health professionals will take a more active role in improving the conditions of those who encounter racism and those who are poor. It is hoped that they will develop and implement new and better ways of delivering mental health services. It is hoped that the new non–European American mental health professionals will be trained as scholars, as well as agents of change. They need to be able to analyze the needs of non–European American communities from a new perspective. Such perspectives should engender new models that are relevant to non–European American members and expand our present repertoire of approaches and techniques. Presently, many non–European American scholars are all too often used like any other scholars; that is, they are trained to use standard approaches and techniques to deal with non–European American problems, and they leave the implementation of their ideas and findings to others. This has to change.

The new ethnic scholars will need to know what the Europeans Americans know—and more. The new ethnic scholars must have therapeutic, as well as organizational and leadership, skills. They will need to know how corporations, organizations, and communities operate and know how to make an impact on these. They will need to know how to work on a governmental and international level.

They will need to develop new and different ways of gathering minority data. They will no longer depend on data provided by White institutions and administrators. They will need to have strong investigative skills.

Research is necessary to investigate the positive aspects of minority culture, values, perceptions, skills, and behaviors. This should be shared with other minorities. Research must be done, and shared with other minorities, on how to deal with the stresses of racism. The delineation of these natural or developed coping skills can help all groups. It would be beneficial to all if we knew effective skills for dealing with racism, poverty, being marginal, having a perceived low locus of control, and having to deal with the many other difficult aspects of life.

Although research is needed to shed light on effective coping skills, we should not ignore the study of psychopathology across cultures. Draguns and Phillips (1972) offered the following reasons to study psychological problems across cultures: (a) to complete the taxonomy of human disturbances; (b) to contribute to the understanding of the plasticity and variety of human attempts at coping beyond the level of people's adaptive resources; (c) to discover common features of maladaptive responses across cultures; (d) to contribute to the development of better conceptual models; (e) to learn about the pressures society brings on its members; (f) to gain some insight across time by studying present behaviors; (g) to learn, given particular situations, what responses have been used; (h) to learn more about therapeutic interventions; (i) to learn how (and why) members of different cultures react differently to identical techniques; (j) to learn about the features of therapy that transcend cultures; and (k) to learn the parameters and robustness of our therapeutic tools. It is obvious that cross-cultural studies have important contributions to make. They are the very essence of human interactions. It behooves us to explore this area of knowledge.

Vega and Rumbaut (1991) wrote, "Research is needed to identify protective factors that appear to decrease the prospect of suffering from serious mental health problems, or from related manifestations such as alcohol or drug abuse, within diverse ethnic minority groups. In particular, recent findings that certain immigrant groups exhibit lower levels of psychiatric symptoms than do majority group natives thus present researchers with a problem in search of explanations" (p. 379). They also recommend that "research needs to move beyond the usual correlational analyses of reported symptoms and sociodemographic variables, to take social and historical contexts fully into account" (Ruiz, as cited in Vega & Rumbaut, 1991, p. 379). They wrote that we need to distinguish cultural acculturation processes from personal disorganization and psychological distress. And we need to investigate psychiatric signs, symptoms, and dysfunctions within diverse ethnic minority communities.

It is difficult to perceive things differently and to change (Kuhn, 1970).

It is recognized that if mental health professional educators were to shift from developing clones of themselves, many other problems would ensue. For example, mental health professional educators might need to deal with the ambiguity of having to evaluate student performance and activities in areas that are new and different and that are beyond their expertise. Mental health educators will have to leave behind their homogeneous world and learn to deal with conflicting values, cultures, behaviors, approaches, techniques, and other uncomfortable and unfamiliar factors. They will need to share their power with non-White ethnic groups.

As reported earlier (Desjarlais et al., 1995; Curtis & Tepperman, 1994), there is evidence that as a country develops, there is an increase in mental disorders. This phenomena needs to be examined further. Are the findings of Desjarlais et al. (1995) and Curtis and Tepperman (1994) valid? If so, what are the conditions that produce mental problems? Desjarlais et al. (1995) reported that when conditions improve in both industrialized and underdeveloped countries, there is also an increase in depression, schizophrenia, dementia, forms of chronic illness, alcoholism, drug abuse, and suicide. Are violence, abuse, dislocation, poverty, and exploitation the reasons why these psychiatric problems occur? Or is the reason, as indicated by Curtis and Tepperman (1994), that inequalities increase with population size, economic surplus, social complexity, and with market economies, vested interests, and hierarchies—resulting in conditions that are not conducive to mental health? Is there a paradoxical effect, in which our quality of life deteriorates in some way with further development of the country? Does development expose people to "unnatural" conditions? Does the loss of traditional social, economic, and political conditions produce social and psychological anomy? Are the changing roles and transitions too stressful? Does Rousseau's romanticized visions of the "noble savage" have validity? These are just some of the many questions that the ethnic scholar can act upon.

THERAPY AND ACTION

Kiselica and Robinson (2001) traced the development and issues in advocacy for social justice work in counseling. They drew on the writings of Baker (1981, 2000), Kiselica (1995, 2000), Kiselica and Ramsey (2001), and Lee (1998) to provide the following as being influential: Du Bois's works on racism and civil rights; Parsons's work with immigrants, which became the foundation of career counseling; Snaches's challenges to the validity of culturally biased standardized tests that were used with African Americans and Hispanics; Horney's challenges of the appropriateness of the male-dominated psychoanalytic field's perceptions of women; Carl Rogers's argument that psychology should be used to solve social problems; Massimo and Shore's approaches to juvenile delinquency; Vontress's strategies to social change; Guthrie's book that called attention to the fact that Western European bias permeates American psychology; Menacker's activist counseling theory for applying counseling to environmental and institutional changes; Krumboltz and Peltier's urging for counselors to provide their services in the client's own milieus; and Gunnings's risk-oriented counseling that calls for counselors to confront policy makers who affect the lives of others.

Kiselica and Robinson (2001) cite the following attributes and skills that are necessary for a counselor to work on social issues. The counselor should have the capacity to understand the needs of people who suffer and have a commitment to help them. Counselors should have the verbal and nonverbal communication skills to listen, understand, and respond empathetically to those who suffer and have the capacity to advocate for their clients and effectively deal with people in power. They should have an understanding of the multiple systems that impact a client—from the intrapsychic to the social, economic, political, educational, family, cultural, community milieus. Counselors should be able to intervene on an individual level to help their clients, as well as provide interventions to groups (e.g., in group therapy and to groups that impact those in therapy), and intervene with organizations and systems that affect the client. The counselor should know how to use the media, technology, and the Internet to advocate for social causes. And counselors should be able to have assessment and research skills to determine the effectiveness of their efforts.

Those involved in providing relevant and effective counseling services to minorities and the poor will encounter resistance from administrators and fellow counselors. Institutions will exert social, economic, and political sanctions against those trying to institute meaningful changes. The counseling and psychological professions should provide services to help counselors who are working with the poor and are discriminated against. The help could be in the form of providing free counseling services to those who experience burn-out; free legal services; and political backing to counselors who encounter harassment from colleagues and whose jobs are threatened because of their activities.

Those of us who are in the professions that purport to help others often use the public and people who suffer as a means to obtain grants and to obtain funds and resources for ourselves and for the agencies we work for—we engage in self-aggrandizing altruism. Democracy, the church, and capitalism have marginalized the suffering of minorities and the poor and have placed the needs of disenfranchised in the tangential part of our consciousness and activities. Surely, we in the counseling profession can develop systems to help those who suffer, as well as help therapists who help those who suffer. Surely, we can do more than offer platitudes, and special issues of journals that are ineffectual and result in anemic activity. Surely, we can develop services that have a measurable impact on improving the social, economic, or psychological health of those who are ostracized and who are considered to be on the periphery of our economy.

The new therapists need to expand their approaches and techniques. They need to explore. They need to determine which is the best course of action to alleviate the suffering that our clients encounter. It is essential that the new ethnic mental health professional learn the traditional approaches and techniques—and then explore new ones. If the new ethnic mental health professional were to simply assume the perceptions of European Americans, it could be detrimental to the ethnic groups that are served. The beliefs, values, and perceptions of European Americans, when conveyed in therapy, might be detrimental to the non–European Americans' self-affirmation, definitions of normality, conceptualization of the world, axiology, time orientation, goals, epistemology, definitions, ontology, and definitions of reality (Akbar, 1991, 1991a; Banks & McGee, 1995), ability to diagnose (Baldwin, 1991; Smart & Smart, 1997; Westermeyer, 1987); and ethics (Pedersen, 1997). In his summary, Ivey (1995) wrote, "Humanistic, psychodynamic, and cognitive-behavioral theory have brought us many ideas and innovations. We need not discard them, but we need to review them anew as culturally derived phenomena. How can we adapt them to the culturally diverse future we all face?" (p. 70). Multicultural counseling and therapy (MCT) and the approaches developed for working with cross-cultural populations deserve serious consideration.

INSTITUTIONAL SKILLS

The ethnic minority therapist works and lives in a sea of institutions. The therapist will need to know how to negotiate, survive, and thrive in such an environment. The therapist will need to impart these skills to the client. Perhaps one of the skills that warrant the therapist's inclusion in her or his repertoire is knowledge and application of Nash's equilibrium (Balkenborg & Schlag, 2001; Binmore, 1990; Cressman, 1992; Hammerstein & Selten, 1994; Hofbauer & Sigmund, 1998; Kuhn & Nasar, 2001; Maynard Smith, 1982; Monderer & Shapley, 1996; Nachbar, 1990; Weibull, 1995). Nash's equilibrium has been found to be helpful in analyzing and predicting behaviors in economics, political science, evolutionary biology, and many other fields. Because minorities and minority counselors may need to interact with Whites, institutions, administrators, and social and economic systems, it may behoove the minority therapist to know this model of bargaining, of negotiating, and of predicting human behavior. Game theory (from which equilibrium theory is an extension) and Nash's equilibrium can be applicable to cooperative and noncooperative behaviors.

The therapist will need to contend with the institutional resistance that will inevitably occur as new and different activities are advocated. There is no question that a multitude of attempts will be made by institutions to sabotage, discredit, detract, derail, and criticize the minority mental health professional's activities. The minority mental health professional's job and position will be threatened. Unless the minority mental health professional is of strong character and is courageous enough to withstand the onslaught of these attacks, it is essential that this individual belong to associations that will provide support. These will need to be organized with strong legal, financial, and popular backing. Such supporters can also serve the function of ensuring that the minority mental health professional adheres to ethical and moral values and behaviors.

Technology and Information

With the advent of computers, the Internet, and the myriad of newer technological and electronic modes of transmitting and receiving information, it is now possible for community members, scholars, researchers, and activists to exchange ideas and learn from each other. Researchers can have direct access to community members, and community members can have direct access to researchers. Educators can now readily reach into communities and homes through the Internet and through other electronic technologies. Community members can use these same technologies to have access to vast amounts of information. They can share with each other and with other communities. International interactions can expand the horizons of minority communities, the poor, those who provide services to them, and those who study them.

Research can be done by community members and by practitioners. With the advent of computers and the more expeditious manner of information accumulation and distribution, and with the advent of friendly statistical programs (personal computers can now do the statistical gathering and analysis of data that were previously done by large university mainframes), increased numbers of professionals and lay people have the tools to contribute data and to do research—this should be encouraged.

COUNSELING MODELS

A number of approaches have been offered for the provision of relevant mental health services to cross-cultural populations (Berg-Cross & Chinen, 1995; Cross, 1995; Daniels & D'Andrea, 1996; Pedersen, 1985, 1988;

Ponterotto et al., 1995; Triandis, 1980). Some of these (e.g., MCT) have been presented in this book. I would like to add another: In determining whether a therapeutic approach will work across cultural populations, one should consider whether the approach and technique (a) are culturally syntonic and (b) have an evolutionary function.

Syntonic/Dystonic

Cross-cultural therapeutic models, approaches, and techniques can be viewed from a syntonic/dystonic framework. Culturally syntonic means that the approach is in keeping with the culture's values, behaviors, expectations, and so forth. Culturally dystonic would mean that the approach is out of sync with the culture. Of course, most developers of therapies view their therapies as being culturally syntonic with other cultures. However, one has to be careful that one is not deluding oneself into a false belief that one's approach is culturally syntonic. This would be a common assumption because therapeutic approaches are usually developed by people who are not aware of the full spectrum of people's behaviors, values, culture, and so forth. The models and approaches are developed by people whose education has been dominated by a particular school of psychology and by those with a limited range of interactions with other peoples. Therefore, a careful evaluation would need to be done to determine whether the approach is culturally syntonic. Perhaps people who are knowledgeable about the culture could be consulted. In an attempt to determine whether an approach might be viable in a cross-cultural application, perhaps an analysis could be done to determine if the approach is similar to that used by indigenous members of the community. Research could be conducted to determine if the approach has been used effectively with the same, or similar, populations. I propose that the models, approaches, and techniques that are more culturally syntonic would more likely be accepted by its recipients.

Because this book advocates the use of science as a measure, the reader might consider the viability of using behavioral and neobehavioral approaches. These approaches have been successful in demonstrating their effectiveness (American Psychological Association, 1993). The behavioral approaches have demonstrated success across species and with humans across the developmental life span—from children to older persons. In demonstrating success across species in changing behaviors, the assumption is that the approach should also be applicable to humans across cultures. It should be noted that behavioral approaches are less intrusive than many of the other approaches that entail in-depth exploration of feelings and the psyche. Criticisms of behavioral models and approaches may include (a) humans are more than animals, and what has been found to be effective for other species may not be applicable to humans; (b) humans are far more complex than other animals, and therefore the superficiality of this model makes it inappropriate for explaining and changing behavior; and (c) this model and these approaches ignore the importance of language and culture—two elements that are characteristic of our species and that may even set us apart from other species. My reply is that the language and culture that differentiate us from the other animals also differentiate one group of people from another, making it difficult communicate. We need approaches and techniques that transcend language. The behavioral approaches can be applied to animals and humans who do not speak, thus making it appropriate to be used across cultures. In addition, behavioral approaches are more in keeping with a scientific approach to therapy. There is documented evidence that it works. It is replicable. It has a data bank from which to draw upon. It is more readily modifiable with new evidence of what works and what does not work.

Evolutionary

The evolutionary model has received very little attention in the counseling and psychology therapeutic literature. The reason for the inclusion of the evolutionary model in this discussion is because it has been found to be an effective theory to explain a great deal of human biological and behavioral phenomena. It has been found to be applicable across time and place for most living creatures on this planet. Thus, it appears to have relevance in the study of human behavior across cultures. For those interested in helping people of different cultures, this model would be worth pursuing to determine its applicability to counseling and therapy.

It should be noted that the behavioral and evolutionary approaches were not emphasized in my master's and doctoral programs. The behavioral approach was taught to me in a perfunctory fashion, and I had no exposure at that time to the evolutionary model. I began to use these approaches based on my investigations of what is needed to effectively work cross-culturally, rather than the approaches being derived from my training and background.

CONTRIBUTIONS OF OTHER CULTURES

Chapter 2 presented some of the differences between European Americans and non–European Americans. Differences between groups could potentially enrich the lives of everyone involved. These differences do not necessarily need to be a source of dissonance and dissention. One of the points made in this book is that ethnic cultures have positive contributions to make to the American social fabric.

If the data from various studies are accurate, perhaps we can learn from ethnic groups. Such knowledge might improve our mental and physical health. We cannot assume that our values, perceptions, and customs are the best in the world. We cannot assume that the learning process goes in only one direction—from us to them. We cannot assume that learning from others will not help us attain our goals of improving our lives in very meaningful, relevant ways. There is evidence that our society makes people physically and mentally sick. Bezruchka (2001) wrote that support, friendship, cooperation, sociability, and egalitarian systems—which are antithetical to our competitive, hierarchical, capitalistic system—are conducive to health. Perhaps we can learn from the ethnic cultures that promote harmony and cooperation. We find that Mexicans (and mainland Puerto Ricans) who come to the United States develop increased rates of psychopathology (Regeser-Lopez, & Guarnaccia, 2000). Are there elements and systems in the United States need to be changed in order to promote our well-being? Greenfield and Smith (1999) reported data that indicate that Asian groups have lower rates of violence and child abuse and neglect. The Office of Women's Health (2000) reported lower rates of breast cancer for African American and Asian women; lower rates of smoking, alcohol and drug abuse, and heart disease for Asian Americans; lower suicide rates and mortality rates from stroke for Hispanic women; lower suicide mortality rates for African American and American Indian/Alaska Native women over 65; and lower rates of eating problems among African Americans and Asian Americans. The Surgeon General's Report on Mental Health (1999) stated that Asian Americans' health indices seem to indicate that they are as healthy or even more healthy than Whites. Again, if some of these findings are accurate, perhaps we can learn from various cultures the behaviors and values that can improve our lives.

Authors cited in this book have provided material on contributions that non–European Americans can make. The following is a summary of what some of them have written. What is said about cultures here is by no means comprehensive or exhaustive. The statements are gross generalizations and do not apply to all members of an ethnic group or to an entire culture; similarly, the statements do not exclude some European cultures and members from having some of the behaviors and values associated with non-European cultures. The purpose here is to illustrate that other cultures can contribute to the mental health of all of us by expanding our horizons about the range of human behaviors, by providing us with a wider repertoire of solutions to deal with our problems, and by helping us understand the influences that impact our clients.

Although studies have found differences between minorities and whites, perhaps each group has something to learn from the other. This can enhance each group's repertoire of how to interact with the world and solve problems. Non–European Americans can learn from European Americans—indeed, are forced to learn from European Americans—but perhaps European Americans can also learn from non–European Americans. The following are some examples of what European Americans can learn from non-European cultures.

Horwitz and Scheid (1999) report that some cross-cultural researchers have developed hypotheses that the more benign psychiatric outcomes that appear to occur in developing countries (compared to those in industrialized, developed countries) may be the result of relatively lower stress and greater social support. They report that traditional societies offer cultural belief systems that externalize causality of psychiatric problems (e.g., it is "God's will," or karma), thus lessening individual and family blame. Traditional societies may offer the patient greater opportunities for reintegration and normalization of roles. And such societies may provide extended kinship networks that help buffer the impact of mental illness on the patient and on care providers (Leff, Lefley, Lin, & Kleinman, as cited in Horwitz & Scheid, 1999). Other explanations for benign outcomes include the following: In traditional societies, psychosis may be seen as a temporary condition, accompanied by expectations of recovery (Waxman, as cited in Horwitz & Scheid, 1999). In Western societies, mental illness can result in self-depreciation or depreciation of the person by society (Estroff, as cited in Horwitz & Scheid, 1999). Such reactions could engender attempts to deny illness, reject medications, and ward off the dependency status of mental illness. In individualistically oriented Western societies, the loss of autonomy that can result in having a psychiatric condition can be more debilitating and threatening than for family-oriented cultures in which the individual thinks of herself or himself as part of a family system. In traditional collectivistic societies, there may be less social isolation, a more tolerant family milieu, and more extended family support than that found in Western nuclear families (Leff, as cited in Horwitz & Scheid, 1999).

From the studies of Sue (1995a), European Americans can learn that they do not need to consider time in a linear fashion and do not have to be controlled by time and schedules. They might benefit by expanding their definitions of what constitutes a family and consider a definition that incorporates extended members of the family and those who may not have genetic commonality. Perhaps European Americans can benefit from knowing that not all mental problems are resolved through exploring internal conflicts. Some problems can be induced by elements in their environment. And instead of looking at the world from an empirical, symbolic, logical, cause-and-effect, linear, rationalistic, or reductionist analysis of phenomena, a non-European's nonlinear, wholistic view and approach to the world can sometimes provide a more objective and meaningful perspective.

Peng and Nisbett's (1999) study of those from Chinese cultures and those from European American cultures in the United States shows that perhaps European Americans have something to learn. They can learn to deal with contradictions by taking a compromising, moderate perspective instead of a polarizing, categorical, extreme perspective.

According to Irvine and York's (1995) report of the differences between European Americans and African Americans, perhaps European Americans can learn to be more field-dependent rather than being field-independent. They could benefit from responding to the whole, rather than to the parts, and could engage in inferential reasoning, rather than deductive or inductive reasoning. They could approximate space and numbers, rather than adhering to exactness. They could focus on people rather than on things; be more proficient in nonverbal than in verbal communications; learn with variation and kinesthetic instruction; attend to social over nonsocial cues; and learn to proceed from top-down processing, rather than from bottom-up processing.

Based on work by Baruth and Manning (1992), Casteneda and Gray (1974), Grossman (1984), and Ramirez and Castaneda (1974), perhaps European Americans can learn elements of Latin American culture. They can learn in groups, be sensitive to the opinions of others; remember faces and social words, be more extrinsically motivated, learn by doing, use concrete representations rather than abstract ones, and attend to people.

According to Baruth and Manning (1992), Bradley (1984), McShane and Plas (1982), Sawyer (1991), Swisher and Deyhle (1989), and Tharp (1989) (as cited in Irvine and York, 1995), perhaps European Americans can learn from Native Americans to attend more to visual, spatial, and perceptual information, rather than to verbal; learn privately, rather than publicly; and use mental images to remember and understand words and concepts, rather than using word associations. They can watch and then do, rather than use trial and error; learn by nonverbal mechanisms, rather than by verbal ones; and learn experientially and in natural settings. European Americans might benefit from learning more from a generalist orientation, being interested in people and things; valuing conciseness of speech, slightly varied intonations, and limited vocal range; and perceiving wholistically and visually.

Perhaps cross-cultural studies could be of value to European Americans because these induce an examination of assumptions and practices. Cross-cultural studies induce us to examine such areas as free will—What are the dynamics of this and what are the implications for individuals and society? And eating disorders—What role does our society play in this problem? Perhaps European Americans can learn from ethnic families (Schwartz, Barrett, & Saba, 1985) to be less preoccupied with mainstream American values and be more concerned with their families; have less aversion to fatness, be less concerned with mainstream interest in achievement and success, and be less ambitious, competitive, appearance-conscious, success driven, and prone to compare self and family to others.

Perhaps European Americans can learn from Asian, African, and Native American conflict-resolution styles (Gabrielidis, Stephen, Ybarra, Pearson, & Villareal, 1997) and place more emphasis on the group, compared to individualistic cultures like that of the United States, which place more emphasis on the individual.

Perhaps European Americans can benefit from learning the emotional content of communication, rather than focusing on the articulation and logic of the communication (Chang, 1994; Liem, Lim, & Liem, 2000; Sata, 1973). Studies that indicated ethnic differences in the reaction to drugs (e.g., Lin, Anderson, & Poland, 1997) may increase our awareness that we cannot assume that everyone reacts the same to drugs—there are different drug reactions among European Americans, as well as between European and non-European groups. The pursuit of solving the problems engendered in diagnosing ethnic minority mental health disorders can improve our diagnostic skills in general—thus the diagnostician, as well as European and non-European populations, can benefit.

Because European Americans enter and leave relationships easily (Hui & Triandis, 1986), perhaps they can learn from those from non-Western cultures how to have relationships that are more intimate and longer-lasting. Perhaps European Americans can learn from African Americans to spank for the benefit of the child, rather than for parent-oriented reasons (Whaley, 2000). By the way, I do not think children should be spanked at all.

From ethnic studies (Surgeon General's Report, 1999) on the mental health of racial and ethnic minority populations, we find that there are different ways of defining mental health and different reactions to those with mental health illness. Perhaps European Americans can learn from ethnic groups alternative definitions of mental health and healthier reactions to those with mental problems. Similarly, there are different cultural expressions of mental illness. Perhaps increasing the range of expressions of mental illness ("idioms of distress") can help those with mental illness. Ethnic minorities' use of the extended family, mutual aid systems, voluntary organizations, and clubs may be of value to European Americans to emulate. Understanding help-seeking behaviors and barriers to serving minorities can help improve services to all populations. Understanding how to deal with ethnic fears of hospitalization, fear of treatment, the stigma of mental illness, denial of problems, self-reliance, utilization of treatment, help-seeking behavior, compliance with treatment, premature termination of treatment, and responses to medications can benefit everyone.

Europeans have solved their societies' internal problems by killing their opponents, forcing them to leave the country, or having opponents voluntarily leave their home country. Europeans have been able to leave their countries and spread throughout the world because of their superior technology and weaponry. But the world has changed. The monopoly the West once had on advanced technology has been broken. Many Second and Third World countries now have advanced technologies. With the cessation of the colonial system, with other countries' greater resistance to being conquered, and with the rise of nationalism, Europeans will find that they can no longer solve their problems through emigration and conquest. They may need to learn how to live with each other. Perhaps they can learn from the Asian and African cultures. These cultures have had intact cultures that have lasted for much longer periods of time than those in Europe. Perhaps European Americans can learn to be more concerned about others, engage in less dichotomized thinking, be more inclusive in their thinking, be more concerned with harmony, and learn that there are many paths to the truth.

In the process of improving racial categorizing and dealing with the abuses of minority research and data reporting, we will discover more effective methods that can benefit all of us. Such discoveries might be applicable to improving the way we categorize in general, as well improving the detection of, and providing resolution to, abuses in research and data reporting.

Our research on the way minorities deal with racism can also benefit others. For example, such research might add to our repertoire of more effective, or alternative, approaches and techniques for dealing with stress.

Ramseur's (1991) factors that are central to African American psychological health might benefit others as well. For example, it might be of value for European Americans to maintain a positive self-image, have connections to the community, maintain an accurate perception of what is happening in the environment, cope with stressors and adapt to the environment, have emotional intimacy with others, maintain a sense of competence, and work productively.

It has been found that although the incidence and prevalence of schizophrenia are the same in most countries, the recovery rate in less developed countries is significantly better; for example, 63% of those with schizophrenia in less developed countries were in remission and 16% suffered social impairment, compared to 37% in remission and 42% with social impairment in industrialized countries (Warner, as cited in Lefley, 1999, p. 573). This raises the question of whether certain factors in less developed countries might mitigate the course of schizophrenia and whether developed countries can apply these factors to people with schizophrenia in their own countries.

Can Hayles's (1991) observations of the strengths of African American families be applied to European American families? That is, would it help European American families to have kinship and extended family networks; work toward harmony, cooperation, and interdependence; accept differences; foster internal development, work, and achievement orientation; adhere to tradition; have strong male and female bonds; have adaptable and flexible roles; develop support to deal with stressors (e.g., obtain emotional support from others and appreciate one's roots); respect and utilize the skills and wisdom of senior family members; and emphasize children?

As with the improvements in racial categorizing and dealing with the abuses of minority research and data reporting, the development of assessment tools that are more sensitive to cultural factors can be of value to European Americans. Such improvements will provide ideas and ways to improve assessment in general. For example, Grieger and Ponterotto's (1995) six components of worldview and acculturation that can be used for assessing the ethnic person's readiness for counseling can also be used to examine all populations' readiness for counseling. This involves assessing the person's knowledge of counseling and what it entails; the family's attitude and knowledge of counseling; the client's and family's attitude toward helping and counseling; the degree to which the client is acculturated into European American, middle-class values and norms; the degree to which the family is acculturated into European American, middle-class values and norms; and finally, the client's and family's attitude toward acculturation. In general, the acculturation questions can help the therapist determine the client's readiness and knowledge of counseling and acceptance of the expectations of counseling and middle-class values.

Alexander and Sussman's (2000) report on the use of alternative therapeutic approaches might be helpful for dealing with European Americans as well. That is, European Americans might also benefit from the use of music, food, art, play, dance, and folk tales as therapeutic techniques.

The role of politics and power in counseling, and the study of the characteristics of those who teach and provide therapy to minorities, needs to be examined, scrutinized, and monitored. We should maintain constant vigilance on these matters. Politics and power permeate our society, our lives, our profession, and the lives of those we serve. Politics and power determine what we do, whom we treat, how we treat, how resources are allocated, and impact a host of other factors. Our profession and our society can benefit from our examination of ethical behaviors, allocation of resources, and characteristics of our teachers, students, and service providers. Such examination can allow us to correct injustices, discrimination, prejudice, and other crimes against humanity.

The novel and creative approaches in the use of technology and computers with ethnic and poor populations can benefit everyone. Technology and computers can be used to overcome barriers, enhance communications, and tailor interactions to cater to the client's learning style and needs. Such uses can improve the provision of services to everyone. Similarly, using technology and computers to promote the sharing of ideas among peoples, and to teach and to learn, can help minorities and everyone else.

The delineation of effective evolutionary psychological approaches for the provision of treatment to minorities can surely be applied to other populations. Fabrega's (1997) guidelines for diagnosing sickness and providing treatment (healing) across cultures and McGuire and Troisi's (1998) principles for therapeutic treatment from an evolutionary psychiatric perspective can be recommended in the provision of services to everyone. Of course, my guidelines for the applications of evolutionary approaches to mental health therapy should be seriously considered.

Axelson's (1993) study on cultural evolution can increase our awareness of the factors that surround our clients' everyday lives. Such an understanding can provide insight into elements outside the therapist's office that might enhance or sabotage therapeutic efforts. Knowledge of the culture can help therapists determine which approaches and techniques to use—the ones that are culturally syntonic will have an increased probability of working, and those that are culturally dystonic may have a lower probability of working.

Investigations into the causes of, dynamics of, and solutions to racism can help promote insight and techniques for dealing with intolerance. Because every group has diversity—for example, diversity of class, income, strengths and weaknesses, gender, sexual orientation, religion—such information can help all groups live in greater harmony.

Our insights into and solutions for poverty can help provide information on how to deal with the poor. Such improvements can help us meet our ethnical and moral responsibilities, alleviate suffering, and contribute to the development of healthy societies.

Desjarlais et al.'s (1995) findings on world mental health problems can shed light on the dynamics of mental health problems in this country— for the poor, as well as the nonpoor. For example, they report that multiple interacting factors are involved in behavioral disorders and social problems; problems occur in clusters, rather than as single entities; problems have a tendency to induce other problems; and key social forces can impact social and psychiatric problems. Such information is of value to us. Their findings that increased development may be accompanied by increased pathology raise important questions as to the effects of increased development, our societies' goals, and the role that mental health professionals can play—for example, should we be ringing the warning bell and advise our leaders of the consequences to society's mental health?

Some of the ethnic attitudes, values, and behaviors that might be helpful for European Americans to consider can include the following:

- Many Asian cultures consider humans to have many aspects to their being (e.g., each of us has aspects that are good and bad, male and female, etc.). Might such a perspective be psychologically healthier than viewing ourselves in unilateral terms—for example, we are good, we are bad?
- When Native Americans returned from war, some used rituals to help the warriors cleanse themselves of the effects of war. Might such rituals help our soldiers and survivors of sexual assault deal with post-traumatic stress?
- Many ethnic groups have a rich history in the use of herbs. Might such knowledge help all of us know more about ourselves and enable us to better take care of ourselves and others?
- Some Native Americans believe that there are many aspects to the sacred—including the jokester and the clown. Might it improve our mental health and enhance our relationship with the sacred to view God as having more multiple dimensions, rather than just being solemn, serious, vengeful, and loving?
- Some Native Americans believe there are three sexes: male, female, and "homosexual." Would such a perception help us understand and improve our dealing with people of different sexual orientations, instead of viewing them as practicing deviant behavior?
- Might the Asian's, African's, and Native American's concern for others be of value to teach all children, instead of teaching them the European American approach of focusing on themselves?
- Many religions use dance (e.g., Islam's dervishes) as a method to interact with God. Could Europeans benefit from including this in their worship repertoire?
- Native Americans and many other ethnic groups consider God to be everywhere, and nature is considered part of God—and therefore should not be exploited. Might such a view help European Americans have a better relationship with nature (instead of viewing it as a source to be exploited)?
- Similarly, many Buddhists consider all living things to be sacred and feel that all living things should be respected. Might such a perspective help us all feel more comfortable in the world and with our fellow creatures?
- Some cultures (e.g., Native American) consider mental illness part of the divine. Might different perspectives such as this enable us to relate better to mental illness—and help those with mental illness to feel less of its stigma?
- It was found that when Western approaches were modified, Chinese American clients were better served; for example, if the intake process was shortened, educational information was provided early in treatment,

short term therapy was used, pharmacotherapy was conservatively applied, the therapist was available to all members of the family, clients were not necessarily seen on a regular basis, and termination was not applied (Takeuchi, Uehara, & Maramba, 1999). Might such findings be of value when applied to other groups?

Other contributions from ethnic cultures can include the following:

- Achievement is not defined in monetary terms (from the Hindu and Buddhist perspectives).
- Sex is not associated with sin (e.g., from the pre–European Asian perspective).
- Corporal punishment should not be used on children (e.g., early accounts of Native American child-training practices).
- Charity is important (e.g., from the Islam religion).
- There is respect for scholarship (e.g., from Chinese values).
- Self-control is important (e.g., from Zen Buddhism).
- People should abstain from tobacco (e.g., from the Islam religion).
- One does not have to be a White, thin, blond female to be attractive; just being a female is in and of itself attractive (from the African American culture).
- Vegetarianism can improve our health (e.g., from Hindu and Buddhists dietary habits).
- Being exposed to the foods of other cultures can increase our options of selecting healthier foods (from knowledge of the foods of ethnic cultures).
- Interacting with different cultures increases awareness of different ways of doing things (from interacting with ethnic minorities).
- "Aberrant" behavior is not a clinical disorder, but rather is a natural or idiosyncratic expression (from knowledge of many ethnic cultures).
- As minority groups gain greater presence in the United States, they will increase interactions with each other. We can all deal with our conflicts in the competitive, capitalistic manner that we have learned so well from our White compatriots, or we can draw those elements from our various cultural heritages that will solve our problems in a cooperative, communal manner, with a more equitable distribution of wealth among the groups.

I do not deny that there are dysfunctional elements and behaviors in non-European groups—there certainly are, just as there are in European groups. I merely point out that the dominant group, the White group, can learn a lot from minorities—to the benefit of everybody.

UNIVERSAL PERSPECTIVE

An important aspect of cross-cultural therapeutic work is delineating which approaches are appropriate for particular populations and which transcend culture. For example, in terms of universals, in his study of the active ingredients in cross-cultural treatments, Frank (1991) found that a key element was the client's belief in the mental health professional: If the client believes in the effectiveness of the mental health professional, then the probability is increased that the treatment will work for the client. Axelson (1993) wrote that authentic interpersonal relations are the key to effective interactions with minorities. He wrote that there are universal structures and functions we encounter across cultures: a family unit, marriage, parental roles, education, medicine, activities to meet physiological needs (e.g., work), and forms of self-expression that meet psychological and spiritual needs. He goes on to state that "All human beings possess basic emotions and feelings, but learned ways of expression may vary from culture to culture. Basic emotions are stimulated in different ways by particular cultural environments. The group norms tend to set the type and pace of allowable expression" (Axelson, 1993, p. 162). An approach is likely to be more effective if it takes into consideration universal structures and functions. These include family and community dynamics, psychological and spiritual needs, and basic emotions and feelings.

The approaches and techniques delineated by ethnic scholars in the United States can be models from which peoples of the world can benefit. Instead of the present approaches created and practiced by and for U.S. European, middle-class people, the delineation of universals in counseling can make this country a source from which other countries can draw and learn.

It is my hope that the new ethnic mental health professionals will offer not only new approaches and techniques, but also new values: a willingness to serve others, a willingness to extend themselves beyond their ethnic group and gender and to work with all peoples; a willingness and capacity to apply scientific approaches to their work; and a willingness and capacity to use their intellect in the search for knowledge. The new ethnic mental health professionals will be able to delineate effective and ineffective therapeutic contributions of other cultures; their values will be such that the best of our profession will be drawn to working with people in the greatest need, with the poor, and with the disadvantaged. The new ethnic mental health professional will give recognition, accolades, and rewards to those who serve people who are in the most need of our services. The new ethnic mental health professional can serve as a model for other professionals to emulate. Perhaps what is needed is a national academy to train minority mental health workers. Participants in this academy can be trained to have the values and skills to deliver effective services to minorities. They can form networks among minority communities. They can be part of the international growth of advocacy and self-help movements that are occurring throughout the world (Lefley, 1999). They can provide leadership in the formation of different systems. The present training institutions are too enmeshed in mimicking the status quo to provide a cadre with the values and services to more effectively help minorities. Takeuchi, Uehara, and Maramba (1999) wrote that there are three service models: clinical, welfare, and advocacy empowerment. Present systems deliver clinical services and sometimes they have a welfare component. Perhaps the new ethnic mental health professionals can add the advocacy empowerment component to their services.

During each era, we become jaded to inequities, injustices, policies, and behaviors that are detrimental to populations and societies. During each era, pathologies are normalized and accepted. These pathologies that are normalized can take the form of acquiescence at the maltreatment of laborers and the working class at the beginning of the industrial age. They can take the form of forcing the Chinese to import drugs during the Opium Wars. They can take the form of ignoring the cruelties inflicted on the Scots and the Irish by the English in their efforts to control the former. They can take the form of persecuting Jews and gypsies in Europe. The list of accepted normalized cruelty is extensive.

This country also contributed generously to the list of human pathologies. This country accepted and normalized the slavery of African Americans, the genocide of Native Americans, to the cruelties and discriminations inflicted on Asians Americans—and the list goes on and on. Those who were aware of these injustices and who spoke out against them were marginalized and condemned—the abolitionists, suffragettes, labor organizers, Quakers, and so on. We need to be aware of social pathologies in our everyday lives and in the world around us. We, in the mental health professions, deal with the affects of these pathologies—we are in a position to speak and advocate for the amelioration of conditions that contribute to the problems we encounter in therapy. We have responsibilities, just as people in other professions have. For example, mechanics may see many cars that have accidents because of structural features and thus are in a position to advocate for the improvement of features in cars that consistently contribute to the destruction of lives. Medical doctors may see factors that contribute to health problems (e.g., smoking, obesity, drug and alcohol use); they are in a position to inform the public of these dangers. Many people work in occupations where they have the knowledge to recognize certain detrimental aspects of products and activities. They can, and should, educate the public of these problems. Not only can they, and should they, do so, but they are ethically bound to get actively involved in protecting the public. So, too, if mental health professionals know of factors that take enormous tolls on the citizens of this country, they have a duty not only to educate and inform the public of what is happening, but to take a more active role in instituting changes.

Not only bombs and bullets kill and destroy lives; a society that serves the interests of one ethnic group at the expense of others can be just as destructive. Racism does not necessarily wear a white robe and hood; it can wear formal attire and a smile, as it perpetuates the status quo and destroys lives. Brutality is not necessarily exercised in the form of obvious fascistic oppression; it can be exercised by insidious social, political, and economic systems that result in ruined lives, poorer mental and physical health, and greater mortality and morbidity in innocent populations that do not warrant such treatment. It can take the form of lives lived in despair. It can take the form of parents watching their children face the prospect of limited opportunities and discrimination because they are not part of the preferred group. It can take the form of higher poverty rates for one group, compared to another. It can take the form of better education for one group and not another. It can take the form of a judiciary that allows greater opportunities for justice for one group over another. It can take the form of one group growing fat, while other groups suffer malnutrition. It can take the form of good intentions and talk of support that are not implemented by meaningful action. It can take the form of professional organizations serving their own interests and using the spurious rationale of providing better services to the public and the poor. It can take the form of people who are so concerned with the status quo and with stability that their failure to act and rectify inequities induces revolts and mass social trauma from those who seek economic, social, and political redress. Passivity, ignorance, and concern for self as a response to inequities and injustices are factors in the crimes against humanity. For the benefit of society, I hope the mental health field will take a leading role in correcting the inequities and injustices of our times. There is so much that needs to be done.

References

Adebimpe, V. (1981). Overview: White norms and psychiatric diagnosis of Black patients. *American Journal of Psychiatry, 138,* 279–285.

Adler, J., Wingert, P., Wright, L., Houston, P., Manly, H., & Cohen, A. D. (1992, February, 17). Hey, I'm terrific! *Newsweek,* 46–51.

Administration on Aging. (2001a, January 10). *Older adults and mental health: Issues and opportunities—Chapter 1: Background (Older Americans and their characteristics).* (Online). Retrieved February 20, 2002, from the World Wide Web: http://www.aoa.gov/mh/report2001/chapter1.html.

Administration on Aging. (2001b, January 10). *Older adults and mental health: Issues and opportunities—Chapter 1: Background (The mental health of older Americans).* (Online). Retrieved February 20, 2002, from the World Wide Web: http://www.aoa.gov/mh/report2001/chapter1.html.

Akbar, N. (1991). Mental disorder among African Americans. In R. L. Jones (Ed.), *Black psychology* (pp. 339–352). Berkeley, CA: Cobb and Henry.

Akbar, N. (1991a). Paradigms of African American research. In R. L. Jones (Ed.), *Black psychology* (pp. 709–725). Berkeley, CA: Cobb and Henry.

Alarcon R. D. (1995). Culture and psychiatric diagnosis: Impact on *DSM-IV* and ICD-10. *Psychiatric Clinics of North America, 18,* 449–465

Alexander, C. M., & Sussman, L. (2000). *Creative approaches to multicultural counseling.* (Online). Retrieved February 20, 2001, from the World Wide Web: http://cc.byu.edu/courses/sw660/readings/ CreativeApproaches.htm.

Alsup, R. E. (2000). *Liberation psychology: A visionary mandate for humanistic, existential, and transpersonal psychologies.* (Online). Retrieved February 20, 2001 from the World Wide Web: http://www.sonoma.edu/psychology/os2db/alsup1.html.

Alter, J. (1999, September 20). Bridging the digital divide. *Newsweek,* 55.

Amante, D., VanHouten, V., Grieve, J., Bader, C., & Mangules, P. (1977). Neuropsychological deficit, ethnicity, and socio-economic status. *Journal of Consulting and Clinical Psychology, 43*(4), 524–535.

American Counseling Association. (1995). *ACA Code of Ethics and Standards of Practice.* Alexandria, VA: Author.

American Counseling Association. (2000, June). *Helping to ensure your views are heard* (pp. 22, 29). Alexandria, VA.: Author.

American Psychiatric Association. (1994*). Diagnostic and statistical manual of mental disorders* (4th ed.). Washington, DC: Author.

American Psychological Association. (1992). *Ethical Principles of Psychologists and Code of Conduct.* Washington, DC: Author.

American Psychological Association. (1993, January). Guidelines for providers of psychological services to ethnic, linguistic, and culturally diverse populations. *American Psychologists, 48*(1), 45–48.

American Psychological Association (1993, October). *Task force on promotion of psychological procedures* (A report adopted by the Division 12 Board). Washington, DC: Author.

American Psychological Association. (1995). *Caring for the rural community: An interdisciplinary curriculum.* Washington, DC: Office of Rural Health.

American Psychological Association. (1996, May, June). *When policy-makers misuse psychological data.* Washington, DC: Author. (Online). Retrieved February 20, 2001, from the World Wide Web: http://www.apa.org/monotor/may96/misuse.html.

American Psychological Association. (2000, August). *Training for psychologists and other mental health professionals.* Washington, DC: American Psychological Association (APA Online/Public Policy Office). (Online). Retrieved September 22, 2001, from the World Wide Web: http://www.apa.org/ppo/issues/ebspsychsamhsa.html.

American Psychological Association Office of Ethnic Minority Affairs. (2000). *The handbook for increasing ethnic minority membership participation in state psychological association and APA divisions.* Washington, DC: Author. (Online). Retrieved June 1, 2002, from the World Wide Web: http://apa.org/pi/oema/handbook/introduction.html#existing.

American Psychosomatic Society. (1995). *Toward an integrated medicine: Classics from psychosomatic medicine, 1959–1979.* Washington, DC: American Psychiatric Press.

Amnesty International. (1999). *United States of America: Police brutality and excessive force in New York City police department* (AI Index: AMR available from International Secretariat, 1 Easton Street, London, WCX 8DJ, United Kingdom). London: Author.

Andersen, B. L., Kiecolt-Glaser, J. K., & Glaser, R. (1994). A biobehavioral model of cancer stress and disease course. *American Psychologist, 49*, 389–404.

Andreoli, T. (1994, June 20). Experts probe major influences in marketing to minorities. *Discount Store News, 33*(12), 12.

APA Research Office. (2000). *1997 APA directory survey.* American Psychological Association. (Online). Retrieved February 20, 2002, from the World Wide Web: http://research.apa.org/whoweare.html.

Arbib, M. A. (1972). *The metamorphic brain.* New York: Wiley.

Armstead, C. A., Lawler, K. A., Gorden, G., Cross, J., & Gibbons, J. (1989). Relationship to racial stressors to blood pressure responses and anger expression in Black college students. *Health Psychology, 8*, 541–556.

Aron, A., & Corne, S. (Eds.). (1994). *Writings for a liberation psychology: Ignacio Martin-Baro.* Cambridge, MA: Harvard University Press.

Arthur, D. (1995, June). The importance of body language. *HR Focus, 72*(6), 22–23.

Association of Research Libraries. (1998). *Transforming libraries–Distance learning (Issue 6)*. (Online). Retrieved December 20, 2000, from the World Wide Web: http://www.arl.org/transform/index.html.

Atkinson, D. R., Ponterotto, J. G., & Sanchez, A. R.(1984). Attitudes of Vietnamese and Anglo-American students toward counseling. *Journal of College Student Personnel, 25,* 448–452.

Atkinson, D. R., & Thompson, C. E. (1992). Racial, ethnic, and cultural variables in counseling. In S. D. Brown & R. W. Lent (Eds.), *Handbook of counseling psychology* (pp. 349–382). New York: Wiley.

Attneave, C.(1982). American Indians and Alaska Native families: Emigrants in their own homeland. In M. McGoldrick, J. Pearce, & J. Giordano (Eds.), *Ethnicity and family therapy* (pp. 55–83). New York: Guilford.

Austin, N. L., Carter, R. T., & Vaux, A. (1990, May). The role of racial identity in Black students' attitudes toward counseling and counseling centers. *Journal of College Student Development, 31*(3), 237–244.

Axelson, J. A. (1993). *Counseling and development in a multicultural society*. Pacific Grove, CA: Brooks/Cole.

Azar, B. (1998a, May). Federal agencies encourage more cross-disciplinary work. *APA Monitor, 29*(5). (Online). Retrieved November 11, 2000, from the World Wide Web: http://www.apa.org/monitor/may98/cross.html.

Azar, B. (1998b, May). Melding expertise, furthering research. *APA Monitor, 29*(5). (Online). Retrieved November 11, 2000, from the World Wide Web: http://www.apa.org/monitor/may98/meld.html.

Azar, B. (1998c, May). Report calls for more interdisciplinary research. *APA Monitor, 29*(5). (Online). Retrieved November 11, 2000, from the World Wide Web: http://www.apa.org/monitor/may98/research.html.

Azar, B. (1998d, May). Sharing data with other fields yields important discoveries. *APA Monitor, 29*(5). (Online). Retrieved November 11, 2000, from the World Wide Web: http://www.apa.org/monitor/may98/net.html.

Bacote, J. C. (1994). Transcultural psychiatric nursing: Diagnostic and treatment issues. *Journal of Psychosocial Nursing, 32,* 42–46.

Badcock, C. (1991). *Evolution and individual behavior*. Cambridge, MA: Basil Blackwell.

Bagarozzi, D. A. (1980, April). Family therapy and the Black middle class: A neglected area of study. *Journal of Marital & Family Therapy, 6*(2), 159–166.

Baker, S. B. (1981). *The school counselor's handbook*. Boston: Allyn & Bacon.

Baker, S. B. (2000). *School counseling for the twenty-first century* (3rd ed.). Columbus, OH: Merrill.

Baldry, C. (1999, August). Space–the final frontier. *Sociology, 33*(3), 535.

Baldwin, J. A. (1991). African (Black) psychology: Issues and synthesis. In R. L. Jones (Ed.), *Black psychology* (pp. 125–135). Berkeley, CA: Cobb & Henry.

Balkenborg, D., & Schlag, K. H. (2001, September 11). *On the evolutionary selection of Nash equilibrium components*. (Online). Retrieved March 20, 2002, from the World Wide Web: http://www.ex.ac.uk/~dgbalken/papers/asym.PDF.

Banks, J., & McGee, C. (Eds.) (1995). *Handbook of research on multicultural education*. New York: Macmillan.

Banton, M. (1980). The idiom of race: A critique of presentism. In C. Marrett & C.

Leggon (Eds.), *Research in race and ethnic relations* (vol. 2). Greenwich, CT.: Jai Press.

Barbarin, O. (1983). Coping with ecological transitions by Black families: A psychosocial model. *Journal of Community Psychology, 11,* 308–322.

Barkow, J. H. (1989). *Darwin, sex, and status: Biological approaches to mind and culture.* Toronto: University of Toronto Press.

Barkow, J. H., Cosmides, L., & Tooby, J. (Eds.). (1995). *The adapted mind: Evolutionary psychology and the generation of culture.* New York: Oxford University Press.

Barnes, E. J. (1980). The Black community as a source of positive self-concept for Black children: A theoretical perspective. In R. Jones (Ed.), *Black psychology* (pp. 106–138). New York: Harper & Row.

Barrera, A. (1993, Fall). *Distance education: The challenge for a multicultural society.* (Online). Retrieved June 20, 2000, from the World Wide Web: http://www.ncbe.gwu.edu/ncbepubs/focus/focus8.htm.

Baruth, L. G., & Manning, M. L. (1992). *Multicultural education of children and adolescents.* Boston: Allyn & Bacon.

Bean, F. D., Berg, R. R., & Van Hook, J. V. W. (1996, December). Socioeconomic and cultural incorporation and marital disruption among Mexican Americans. *Social Forces, 75*(2), 593–617.

Behar, L. B. (1997, May). The Fort Bragg evaluation: A snapshot in time. *American Psychologist, 52*(5), 557–559.

Bell, D. (1992). *Faces at the bottom of the well: The permanence of racism.* New York: Basic.

Belle, D. (1990). Poverty and women's mental health. *American Psychologist, 45,* 385–389.

Bender, P. S., & Ruiz, R. A. (1974, October). Race and class as differential determinants of underachievement and underaspiration among Mexican-Americans and Anglos. *Journal of Educational Research, 68*(2), 51–55.

Bennett, S. (1994). The American Indian: A psychological overview. In W. Looner & R. Malpass (Eds.), *Psychology and culture* (pp. 35–39). Boston: Allyn & Bacon.

Berg-Cross, L., & Chinen, R. T. (1995). Multicultural training models and the person-in-culture interview. In J. G. Ponterotto, J. M. Casas, L. A. Suzuki, & C. M. Alexander (Eds.), *Handbook of multicultural counseling* (pp. 333–356). Thousand Oaks, CA: Sage.

Bergin, A. E., & Garfield, S. L. (1986). *Handbook of psychotherapy and behavior change.* New York: Wiley.

Bergin, A. E., & Garfield, S. L. (1994). *Handbook of psychotherapy and behavior change.* New York: Wiley.

Bermúdez, A., & Palumbo, D. (1994, Winter). Bridging the gap between literacy and technology: Hypermedia as a learning tool for limited English proficient students. *Journal of Educational Issues of Language Minority Students, 14,* 165–84.

Berry, J. W. (1980). Acculturation as varieties of adaptation. In A. Padilla (Ed.), *Acculturative theory, models and some new findings* (pp. 9–25). Boulder, CO: Westview.

Berry, J. W., & Dalal, A. (1996, October). *Disability attitudes, beliefs and behaviours:*

Report on an international project in community based rehabilitation (Report). Kingston, Ontario, Canada: Queen's University, International Centre for the Advancement of Community Based Rehabilitation. (Online). Retrieved March 22, 2002, from the World Wide Web: http://meds.queensu.ca/icacbr/dabb.txt.

Berry, J. W., Kim, U., Power, S., Young, M., & Bujaki, M. (1992). Acculturation attitudes in plural societies. *Applied Psychology: An International Review, 38,* 185–206.

Berry, J. W., Poortinga, Y. H., Segall, M. H., & Dasen, P. R. (1992). *Cross-cultural psychology: Research and applications.* Cambridge, England: Cambridge University Press.

Bertenthal, B. (1998, May). A new age of discovery. *APA Monitor, 29*(5). (Online). Retrieved November 11, 2000, from the World Wide Web: http://www.apa.org/monitor/may98/ss.html.

Beutler, L. E., Crago, M., & Arizmendi, T. G. (1986). Research on therapist variables in psychotherapy. In S. L. Garfield & A. E. Begin (Eds.), *Handbook of psychotherapy and behavior change.* New York: Wiley.

Bezruchka, S. (2001, February 26). Is our society making you sick? *Newsweek, 14.*

Bhattacharyya, M. (1998). Creating a new research agenda on race, gender, and class impacts on educational achievement and underachievement: A workshop on race, gender, class, and student achievement. *National Educational Research Policy and Priorities Board,* Washington, DC.

Biafora, F. A., Taylor, D. L., Warheit, G. J, Zimmerman, R. S., & Vega, W. (1993, August). Cultural mistrust and racial awareness among ethnically diverse Black adolescent boys. *Journal of Black Psychology, 19*(3), 266–281.

Biafora, F. A., Jr., Warheit, G. J., Zimmerman, R. S., Gil, A. G., Apospori, E., & Taylor, D. (1993). Racial mistrust and deviant behaviors among ethnically diverse Black adolescent boys. *Journal of Applied Social Psychology, 23,* 891–910.

Bickman, L, (1996). A continuum of care: More is not always better. *American Psychologist, 51,* 689–701.

Bickman, L., Guthrie, P. R., Foster, E. M., Lambert, E. W., Summerfelt, W. T., Breda, C. S., & Heflinger, C. A. (1995). *Evaluating managed mental health services: The Fort Bragg experiment.* New York: Plenum.

Bierber, I. (1972). Sex and power. In J. Masserman (Ed.), *The dynamics of power* (pp. 120–134). New York: Grune & Stratton.

Bilchik, S. (1999, October 21). *History of juvenile justice and mental health: Future partnership for children.* 46th Annual Meeting of the American Academy of Child and Adolescent Psychiatry, Chicago, Illinois. (Online). Retrieved February 20, 2001, from the World Wide Web: http://ojjdp.ncjrs.org/about/spch991021.html.

Billig, M., & Tajfel, H. (1973). Social categorization and similarity in intergroup behavior. *European Journal of Social Psychology, 3,* 27–52.

Binmore, K. (1990). *Essays on the foundations of game theory.* Cambridge, MA: B. Blackwell.

Blauner, R. (1969). Internal colonialism and ghetto revolt. *Social Problems, 16,* 393–408.

Bloomfield, C. L., & Fairley, I. R. (1991). *Business communication—A process approach.* San Diego, CA: Harcourt Brace Jovanovich.

Bolles, R. C., & Beecher, M. D. (1988). *Evolution and learning.* Hillsdale, NJ: Erlbaum.

Bowerman, R. G., & Glover, D. E. (1988). *Putting expert systems into practice*. New York: Van Nostrand Reinhold.

Boyce, N. (2001, January 15). Truth and consequences. *U.S. News and World Report*, 40.

Boykin, A. W., & Toms, F. D. (1985). Black child socialization. In H. P. McAdoo & J. L. McAdoo (Eds.), *Black children: Social, educational, and parental environments* (pp. 33–51). Beverly, CA: Sage.

Bradley, C. (1984). Issues in mathematics education for Native Americans and directions for research. *Journal for Research and Mathematics Education, 15*(2), 96–106.

Brearey, P. (1978). *The social context of health care*. London: Robertson.

Brewer, M. B., and Silver, M. (1978). In-group bias as a function of task characteristics. *European Journal of Social Psychology, 8*, 393–400.

Brigham, J., & Weissbach, T. (1968). *Report of the National Advisory Commission on Civil Disorders*. New York: Bantam.

Brigham, J., & Weissbach, T. (Eds.). (1972a). *Racial attitudes in America: Analysis and findings of social psychology* (pp. 107–110). New York: Harper & Row.

Brigham, J., & Weissbach, T. (Eds.). (1972b). *Racial attitudes in America: Analysis and findings of social psychology* (p. 80). New York: Harper & Row.

Brody, T. M. (1994). Absorption, distribution, metabolism, and elimination. In T. M. Brody, J. Larner, K. Minneman, & H. Neu (Eds.), *Human pharmacology: Molecular to clinical* (2nd ed., pp. 49–61). St. Louis: Mosby-Year Book.

Broman, C. L. (1996). Coping with personal problems. In H. W. Neighbors & J. S. Jackson (Eds.), *Mental health in Black America* (pp. 117–129). Thousand Oaks, CA: Sage.

Bullock, S. C., & Houston, E. (1987). Perceptions of racism by Black medical students attending White medical schools. *Journal of the National Medical Association, 79*, 601–608.

Buss, A. H. (1988). *Personality: Evolutionary heritage and human distinctiveness*. Hillsdale, NJ: Erlbaum.

Buss, D. M., Martie G., Haselton, M. G., Shackelford, T. K., Bleske, A. L., & Wakefield, J. C. (1998, May). Adaptations, exaptations, and spandrels. *American Psychologist, 53*(5), 533–548.

Butterworth, G., Rutkowska, J., & Scaif, M. (1985). *Evolution and developmental psychology*. New York: St. Martin's.

Cacioppo, J. (1994). Social neuroscience: Autonomic, neuroendocrine, and immune responses to stress. *Psychophysiology, 31*, 113–128.

Caianiello, E. R., & Musso, G. (1984). *Cybernetic systems: Recognition, learning, self-organizations*. New York: Wiley.

Calhoun, J. (1967). Ecological factors in the development of behavioral anomalies. In J. Zubin & H. Hunt (Eds.), *Comparative psychopathology: Animal and human*. New York: Grune and Stratton.

California Scientific Software. (1993). *Brainmaker*. 10141 Evening Star Drive, #6, Grass Valley, CA 95945; (916) 477-7481.

Career Information System [Computer software]. (1998). Eugene, OR: University of Oregon.

Carpenter, S. (2001, September). Boosting the number of ethnic-minority reviewers for APA journals. *Monitor on Psychology, 82.*

Castelnuovo-Tedesco, P. (1991). *Dynamic psychiatry: Explorations in psychotherapy, psychoanalysis, and psychosomatic medicine* (Series: Emotions and behavior monographs; No. 10). Madison, CT: International Universities Press.

Casteneda, A., & Gray, T. (1974). Bicognitive processes in multicultural education. *Educational Leadership, 32,* 203–207.

Cebrzynski, G. (1998, June 8). Commitment to minority marketing leads to $$. *Nation's Restaurant News, 32*(23), 80.

Center for Mental Health Services. (1998). *Cultural competence standards in managed care mental health services for four underserved/underrepresented racial/ethnic groups.* Rockville, MD: Author.

Chale, E. M. , & Michaud, P. (1997). *Distance learning for change in Africa.* (Online). Retrieved June 20, 2000, from the World Wide Web: http://www.idrc.ca/acacia/outputs/op-chale.htm.

Chancer, L. S. (1992). *Sadomasochism in everyday life: The dynamics of power and powerlessness.* New Brunswick, NJ: Rutgers University Press.

Chang, E. (1994). Myths and realities of Korean–Black American relations. In E. Y. Yu (Ed.), *Black–Korean encounter: Toward understanding and alliance* (pp. 83–89). Los Angeles: Institute for Asian American and Pacific Asian Studies.

Chapple, E. D. (1970). *Culture and behavior.* New York: Holt, Rinehart, & Winston.

Cheatham, H. (1990). Empowering Black families. In H. Cheatham & J. Stewart (Eds.), *Black families: Interdisciplinary perspectives.* New Brunswick, NJ: Transaction.

Cheatham, H., Ivey, A., Ivey, M., & Simek-Morgan, L. (1993). Multicultural counseling and therapy. In A. Ivey, M. Ivey, & L. Simek-Morgan (Eds.), *Counseling and psychotherapy: A multicultural perspective* (pp. 92–123). Boston: Allyn & Bacon.

Cherry, A. L. (1994). *The socializing instincts: Individual, family, and social bonds.* Westport, CT: Praeger.

Cheshire, T. C. (2001, May). Cultural transmission in urban American Indian families. *American Behavioral Scientist, 44*(9), 1528–1535.

Childe, V. G. (1951). *Social evolution.* New York: Schuman.

Chunn, J., Dunston, P., & Ross-Sheriff, F. (1983). *Mental health and people of color.* Washington, DC: Howard University Press.

Clark, R., Anderson, N. R., Clark, V. R., & Williams, D. R. (1999). Racism as a stressor for African-Americans: A biopsychosocial model. *American Psychologist, 54*(10), 805–816.

Clarkson, J. D. (1981). Theories about cultural areas. In *The new encyclopaedia Britannica* (Macropaedia) (Vol. 5, pp. 364–368). Chicago: Encyclopaedia Britannica.

Cocking, R. R. (1979). New directions in the assessment of children's language. In M. N. Ozer (Ed.), *A cybernetic approach to the assessment of children: Toward a more human use of humane beings* (pp. 11–66). Boulder, CO: Westview.

Cohen, A. (Ed.). (1974). *Urban ethnicity.* London: Tavistock.

Cohen, S., & Herbert, T. B. (1996). Health psychology: Psychological factors and physical disease from the perspective of human psychoneuroimmunology. *Annual Review of Psychology, 47,* 113–142.

Coleman, H. L. K. (1995a). Conflict in multicultural counseling relationships: Sources and resolution. *Journal of Multicultural Counseling and Development, 23*(3), 195–200.

Coleman, H. L. K. (1995b). Strategies for coping with cultural diversity. *The Counseling Psychologist, 23,* 722–740.

Coley, R. L. (2001). (In)visible men: Emerging research on low-income, unmarried, and minority fathers. *American Psychologist, 56*(9), 743–753.

Colony. (1973). In *Encyclopaedia Britannica* (Vol. 6, p. 85). Chicago: Encyclopaedia Britannica.

Comas-Diaz, L. (1994). An integrative approach. In L. Comas-Diaz & B. Greene (Eds.), *Women of color: Integrating ethnic and gender identities in psychotherapy* (pp. 287–318). New York: Guilford Press.

Comas-Diaz, L. (2000, November). An ethnopolitical approach to working with people of color. *American Psychologist, 55*(11), 1319–1325.

Comas-Diaz, L., & Greene, B. (1994). Overview: An ethnocultural mosaic. In L. Comas-Diaz & B. Greene (Eds.), *Women of color: Integrating ethnic and gender identities in psychotherapy* (pp. 3–9). New York: Guilford.

Coner-Edwards, A. F., & Edwards, H. E. (1988). The Black middle class: Definition and demographics. In A. F. Coner-Edwards & J. Spurlock (Eds.), *Black families in crisis: The middle class* (pp. 1–9). Philadelphia: Brunner/Mazel.

Coner-Edwards, A. F., & Spurlock, J. (Eds.). (1988). *Black families in crisis: The middle class.* New York: Brunner/Mazel.

Cooper, R. S. (1993). Health and the social status of Blacks in the United States. *Annals of Epidemiology, 3,* 137–144.

Cornell, D. G., Peterson, C. S., & Richards, H. (1999). Anger as a predictor of aggression among incarcerated adolescents. *Journal of Consulting and Clinical Psychology, 67,* 108–115.

Corsini, R. J. (1977). *Current personality theories.* Itasca, IL: Peacock.

Corsini, R. J., & Wedding, D. (1995). *Current psychotherapies.* Itasca, IL: Peacock.

Cose, E. (1993). *The rage of the privileged class.* New York: HarperCollins.

Cosmides, L., & Tooby, J. (1995). Cognitive adaptions for social exchange. In J. H. Barkow, L. Cosmides, & J. Tooby (Eds.), *The adapted mind: Evolutionary psychology and the generation of culture.* New York: Oxford University Press.

Cosmides, L., & Tooby, J. (1997). *Evolutionary psychology: A primer.* (Online). Retrieved June 20, 2000, from the World Wide Web: http://www.psych.ucsb.edu/research/cep/primer.htm.

Craven, D. (1996, December). *Female victims of violent crime* (NCJ-162602). U.S. Department of Justice, Office of Justice Programs, p. 3.

Crawford, J. (1997). *Best evidence: Research foundations of the bilingual education act.* (Online). Washington, DC: National Clearinghouse for Bilingual Education. Retrieved June 20, 2000, from the World Wide Web: http://www.ncbe.gwu.edu/ncbepubs/reports/bestevidence/research.htm.

Cressman, R. (1992). *The stability concept of evolutionary game theory.* Berlin: Springer Verlag.

Cripe, L. I. (2002, Winter/Spring). Limitations of records reviews. *Clinical Neuropsychology Newsletter 40, 20*(1), 7–8, 29–30.

Crocker, J., & Major, B. (1990). Social stigma and self-esteem: The self-protective properties of stigma. *Psychological Review, 96,* 608–630.

Cross, W. E., Jr. (1971). Negro-to-black conversion experience: Toward a psychology of black liberation. *Black World, 20*(9), 13–27.

Cross, W. E., Jr. (1978). Models of psychological nigrescence: A literature. *Journal of Black Psychology, 5,* 13–31.

Cross, W. E., Jr. (1985). Black identity: Rediscovering the distinction between personal identity and reference group orientation. In M. Spencer, G. Brookings, & W. Allen (Eds.), *Beginnings: The social and affective development of Black children* (pp. 155–173). Hillsdale, NJ: Erlbaum.

Cross, W. E., Jr. (1995). The psychology of nigrescence: Revising the Cross model. In J. G. Ponterotto, J. M. Casas, L. A. Suzuki, & C. M. Alexander (Eds.), *Handbook of multicultural counseling* (pp. 93–122). Thousand Oaks, CA: Sage.

Crow, T. J. (1986, October). The continuum of psychosis and its implication for the structure of the gene. *British Journal of Psychiatry, 149,* 419–429. Royal College of Psychiatrists, England.

Crow, T. J. (1990). Nature of the genetic contribution to psychotic illness—A continuum viewpoint. *Acta Psychiatrica Scandinavica, 81,* 401–408.

Crow, T. J. (1995a, July). A Darwinian approach to the origins of psychosis. *British Journal of Psychiatry, 167*(1), 12–25. Royal College of Psychiatrists, England.

Crow, T. J. (1995b, September). Aetiology of schizophrenia: An evolutionary theory. *International Clinical Psychopharmacology, 10* (Suppl. 3), 49–56.

Crow, T. J. (1995c, October). A continuum of psychosis, one human gene, and not much else: The case for homogeneity. *Schizophrenia Research, 17*(2), 135–145. Elsevier Science Publishers, B.V., Netherlands.

Crow, T. J., Done, D. J., & Sacker, A. (1995). Childhood precursors of psychosis as clues to its evolutionary origins. *European Archives of Psychiatry and Clinical Neuroscience, 245,* 61–69.

Crow, T. J., & Harrington, C. A. (1994). Etiopathogenesis and treatment of psychosis. *Annual Reviews of Medicine, 45,* 219–234.

Cuellar, I., & Roberts, R. E. (1997, May). Relations of depression, acculturation, and socioeconomic status in a Latino sample. *Hispanic Journal of Behavioral Sciences, 19*(2), 230–238.

Cui, G. (1997, Winter). Marketing strategies in a multi-ethnic environment. *Journal of Marketing Theory & Practice, 5*(1), 122–134.

Cummins, J., & Sayers, D. (1995). *Brave new schools: Challenging cultural illiteracy through global learning networks.* New York: St. Martin's.

Cunningham, W. B., & Edwards, H. E. (1988). Group psychotherapy: An alternate form of treatment. In A. F. Coner-Edwards & J. Spurlock (Eds), *Black families in crisis: The middle class* (pp. 255-269). Philadelphia: Brunner/Mazel.

Curtis, J., & Tepperman, L. (1994). *Haves and have-nots: An international reader of social inequity.* Englewood Cliffs, NJ: Prentice-Hall.

Cushner, K., McClelland, A., & Safford, P. (1992). *Human diversity in education.* New York: McGraw-Hill.

Dana, R. H. (1993). *Multicultural assessment perspectives for professional psychology.* Boston: Allyn & Bacon.

D'Andrea, M. (1992, October). The violence of our silence. *Guidepost, 35*(4), 31.

D'Andrea, M. (1993, August). *Dealing with racism: Counseling strategies.* Paper presented at the annual meeting of the American Counseling Association, Atlanta.

D'Andrea, M. (1999, May). Alternative needed for the *DSM-IV* in a multicultural-postmodern society. *Counseling Today, 44,* 46.

D'Andrea, M., & Arredondo, P. (2000, August). Dignity, development & diversity—speaking truth to power: Dealing with difficult challenges. American Counseling Association, *Counseling Today, 30,* 37.

D'Andrea, D., & Daniels, J. (1991). Exploring the different levels of multicultural counseling training in counselor education. *Journal of Counseling & Development, 70,* 78–85.

D'Andrea, M., & Daniels, J. (1995). Promoting multiculturalism and organizational change in the counseling profession. In J. G. Ponterotto, J. M. Casas, L. A. Suzuki, & C. M. Alexander (Eds.), *Handbook of multicultural counseling.* Thousand Oaks, CA: Sage.

D'Andrea, D., Daniels, J., & Heck, R. (1991). Evaluating the impact of multicultural counseling training. *Journal of Counseling & Development, 70,* 143–150.

Danet, B. N. (1965). Prediction of mental illness in college students on the basis of "nonpsychiatric" MMPI profiles. *Journal of Consulting Psychology, 29,* 577–580.

Danieli, Y. (1997, Winter). International handbook of multigenerational legacies of trauma. *PTSD Research Quarterly, 8*(1), 1–8.

Daniels, J., & D'Andrea, M. (1996). MCT theory and ethnocentrism in counseling. In D. W. Sue, A. E. Ivey, & P. B. Pedersen (Eds.), *A theory of multicultural counseling and therapy* (pp. 155–173). Pacific Grove, CA: Brooks/Cole.

D'Arcy, J. (1999, February 1). Who's keeping track of school diversity law? Cheshire case exposes weaknesses in state monitoring. *Hartford Courant,* A1.

Dashefsky, A. (1975). Theoretical frameworks in the study of ethnic identity: Toward a social psychology of ethnicity. *Ethnicity, 2,* 10–18.

Davis, E. (1990). *Representations of common sense knowledge.* San Mateo, CA: Morgan Kaufmann.

Dawes, R. M. (1998, October). The social usefulness of self-esteem: A skeptical view. *Harvard Mental Health Letter, 15*(4), 4–5.

DeAngelis, T. (2001a, April). Thwarting modern prejudice. *Monitor on Psychology, 32*(4), 26–30.

DeAngelis, T. (2001b, November). Understanding and preventing hate crimes. (American Psychological Association) *Monitor, 32*(10), 60–63.

DeLeon, P., & Williams, J. G. (1997, May). Evaluation research and public policy formation: Are psychologists really willing to accept unpopular findings? *American Psychologist, 52*(5), 551–552.

Desjarlais, R., Eisenberg, L., Good, B., & Kleinman, A. (1995). *World mental health: Problems and priorities in low-income countries.* Oxford: Oxford University Press.

De Vos, G., & Romanucci-Ross, L. (Eds.). (1975). *Ethnic identity: Cultural continuities and change.* Chicago: University of Chicago Press.

Dhanarajan, D. (1997). *Convergence of distance and conventional education: International perspectives.* (Online). Retrieved June 20, 2000, on the World Wide Web: http://www.col.org/speeches/cambridge97.htm.

Dineen, T. (1996). *Manufacturing victims: What the psychology industry is doing to people.* Montréal: R. Davies.

DiNitto, D. M., & Dye, T. R. (1987). *Social welfare: Politics and public policy.* Englewood Cliffs, NJ: Prentice-Hall.

Dolson, D. P., & Mayer, J. (1992, Winter-Spring). Longitudinal study of three program models for language-minority students: A critical examination of reported findings. Bilingual Research Journal: *Journal of the National Association for Bilingual Education, 16*(1–2), 105–157.

Domhoff, G. W. (1971). *The higher circles: The governing class in America.* New York: Vintage.

Domhoff, G. W. (1978). *The powers that be: Processes of ruling-class domination in America.* New York: Random House.

Domhoff, G. W. (Ed.). (1980). *Power structure research.* Beverly Hills, CA: Sage.

Domhoff, G. W. (1990). *The power elite and the state: How policy is made in America.* New York: Aldine de Gruyter.

Domhoff, G. W. (1996). *State autonomy or class dominance? Case studies on policy making in America.* New York: Aldine de Gruyter.

Domhoff, G. W., & Dye, T. R. (Eds.). (1987). *Power elites and organizations.* Newbury Park, CA: Sage.

Dovidio, J. F., & Gaertner, S. (1986). *Prejudice, discrimination, and racism.* Orlando, FL: Academic Press.

Dovidio, J. F., Gaertner, S. L., Kawakami, K., & Hodson, G. (2002, May). Why can't we just get along? Interpersonal bias and interracial distrust. *Cultural Diversity and Ethnic Minority Psychology, 8*(2), 88–102.

Draguns, J. G., & Phillips, L. (1972). *Culture and psychopathology: The quest for a relationship* (pp. 1–24). Morristown, NJ: General Learning Press.

Dubois, J. (1996). National statistics and trends towards distance education. (Online). Retrieved June 20, 2000, from the World Wide Web: http://pegasus.cc.ucf.edu/~cfche/d-plan.html.

Durant, T., & Sparrow, K. (1997, January). Race and class consciousness among lower and middle class blacks. *Journal of Black Studies, 27*(3), 334–351.

Durkheim, E. (1933). *The division of labor in society* (G. Simpson, Trans.). New York: Cromwell-Collier & Macmillan.

Dye, T. R. (1971). *The politics of equality.* Indianapolis: Bobbs-Merrill.

Dye, T. R. (1976). *Who's running America? Institutional leadership in the United States.* Englewood Cliffs, NJ: Prentice-Hall.

Dye, T. R. (1998). *Understanding public policy.* Upper Saddle River, NJ: Prentice Hall.

Dye, T. R. (1999). *Power and society: An introduction to the social sciences.* Fort Worth, TX: Harcourt Brace College Publishers.

Dye, T. R. (2000). *Politics in states and communities.* Upper Saddle River, NJ: Prentice Hall.

Dye, T. R. (2001). *Top down policymaking.* New York: Chatham House.

Dye, T. R., Gibson, L. T., & Robinson, C. (1999). *Politics in America.* Upper Saddle River, NJ: Prentice Hall.

Dye, T. R., Greene, L. S., & Parthemos, G. S. (1980). *Governing the American democracy.* New York: St. Martin's.

Dye, T. R., & Zeigler, H. (2000). *The irony of democracy: An uncommon introduction to American politics.* Fort Worth, TX: Harcourt Brace College Publishers.

Dyer, W. W., & Vriend, J. (1977). *Counseling techniques that work.* Alexandria, VA: American Association for Counseling & Development.

Economic growth and planning. (1997). In *The new encyclopaedia Britannica* (Vol. 17, pp. 878–907). Chicago: Encyclopaedia Britannica.

Edwards, D. W. (1974). Blacks versus Whites: When is race a relevant variable? *Journal of Personality and Social Psychology, 29*(1), 39–49.

Edwards, R. (1995, May). Is self-esteem really all that important? *Monitor,* 44–44.

Eisenman, R. (1970) Birth order, sex, self-esteem, and prejudice against the physically disabled. *Journal of Psychology, 75*(2), 147–155.

Enchautegui, M. E., Fix, M., Loprest, P., von der Lippe, S. C., & Wissoker, D. (1997, December). *Do minority-owned businesses get a fair share of government contracts?* Washington, DC: Urban Institute. (Online). Retrieved July 5, 2000, from the World Wide Web: http://www.urban.org/civil/civil1.htm.

Encyclopaedia Britannica. (1973). Mercantile system. In *Encyclopaedia Britannica* (Vol. 15, p. 175). Chicago: Encyclopaedia Britannica.

Encyclopaedia Britannica. (1990). The mathematic theory of optimization. In *The new encyclopaedia Britannica* (Vol. 25, pp. 217–226). Chicago: Encyclopaedia Britannica.

Encyclopaedia Britannica. (1997). Minority. In *The new encyclopaedia Britannica* (Vol. 8, pp. 169–170). Chicago: Encyclopaedia Britannica.

Encyclopedia Britannica. (2002). Human evolution: Culturally patterned behaviour and evolution. In *The new encyclopedia Britannica* (Macropaedia) (Vol. 18, pp. 803–854). Chicago: Encyclopedia Britannica.

Esser, A. H., & Deutsch, R. D. (1977). Private and interaction territories on psychiatric wards: Studies on verbal communication of spatial needs. In M. T. McGuire & L. A. Fairbanks (Eds.), *Ethological psychiatry: Psychopathology in the context of evolutionary biology.* New York: Grune & Stratton.

Eysenck, H. J. (1952). The effects of psychotherapy: An evaluation. *Journal of Consulting Psychology, 16,* 319–324.

Fabrega, H. (1997). *Evolution of sickness and healing.* Berkeley: University of California Press.

Feagin, J. R. (1991, February). The continuing significance of race: AntiBlack discrimination in public places. *American Sociological Review, 56*(1), 101–116.

Feagin, J. R., & Feagin, C. B. (1978). *Discrimination American style: Institutional racism and sexism.* Englewood Cliffs, NJ: Prentice Hall.

Feagin, J. R. & Sikes, M. P. (1994). *Living with racism: The Black middle-class experience.* Boston, MA: Beacon.

Feierman, J. R. (1994, September–November). A testable hypothesis about schizophrenia generated by evolutionary theory. *Ethology & Sociobiology, 15*(5–6), 263–282.

Feldman, R. S. (1992). *Applications of nonverbal behavioral theories and research.* Hillsdale, NJ: Erlbaum.

Feldman, S. (1997, May). The Fort Bragg demonstration and evaluation. *American Psychologist, 52*(5), 560–561.

Fernando, S. (1984). Racism as a cause of depression. *International Journal of Social Psychiatry, 30*, 41–49.

Fisher, S., & Greenberg, R. P. (Eds.). (1989). *The limits of biological treatments for psychological distress: Comparison with psychotherapy and placebo*. Hillsdale, NJ: Erlbaum.

Fiske, S. T. (1998). Interpersonal power: New principles of stereotypes and stereotyping. *Science Agenda* (American Psychological Association), *11*(4), 8–10.

Fogarty International Center. (2000). *Strategic plan: Fiscal years 2000–2003. Executive summary. Reducing disparities in global health*. Bethesda, MD: National Institutes of Health. (Online). Retrieved March 20, 2002, from the World Wide Web: http://www.nih.gov/fic/about/summary.html.

Forbes, J. D. (April, 1990). Undercounting Native Americans: The 1980 census and the manipulation of racial identity in the United States. *Wicazo SA Review, 6*(1), 2–26.

Ford, D. Y. (1997). Counseling middle-class African Americans. In C. C. Lee (Ed.), *Multicultural issues in counseling: New approaches to diversity* (2nd ed., pp. 81–107). Alexandria, VA: American Counseling Association.

Fortson, S. B. (1997, September). An evaluation of a program to influence academic self-concept among African American male college students. *Journal of Employment Counseling, 34*(3), 104–107.

Foxhall, K. (2000, April). A renaissance for all? *APA Monitor, 32*(4), 32–34.

Frank, J. D. (1991). *Persuasion and healing: A comparative study of psychotherapy*. Baltimore: Johns Hopkins University Press.

Frazer, J. G. (1998). *The golden bough: A study in magic and religion*. Oxford, UK: Oxford University Press.

Fretwell, K. L. (1990, Fall). The pressures of diversity. *College Review Board, 157*, 2–5.

Friedman, R. C., & Rogers, K. B. (Eds.). (1998). *Talent in context: Historical and social perspectives on giftedness*. Washington, DC: American Psychological Association.

Frijda, N. H., & Mesquita, B. (1994). The social roles and functions of emotions. In S. Kitayama & H. R. Markus (Eds.), *Emotion and culture: Empirical studies of mutual influences* (pp. 23–50). Washington, DC: American Psychological Association.

Fromm, E. (1969). *Escape from freedom*. New York: Holt, Rinehart, & Winston.

Fuchs, W. R. (1971). *Cybernetics for the modern mind*. New York: Macmillan.

Gabrielidis, C., Stephen, W. G., Ybarra, O., Pearson, V. M., & Villareal, L. (1997, November). Preferred styles of conflict resolution. *Journal of Cross-Cultural Psychology, 28*(6), 661–677.

Gallagher, R. P. (1995). *National survey of counseling center directors*. Alexandria, VA: International Association of Counseling Services.

Gallo, J. J., Marino, S., Ford, D., & Anthony, J. C. (1995). Filters on the pathway to mental health care, II. Sociodemographic factors. *Psychological Medicine, 25*, 1149–1160.

Garfield, S. L., & Bergin, A. E. (1986). *Handbook of psychotherapy and behavior change*. New York: Wiley.

Garn, S. G. (1981). Races of mankind. In *The new encyclopaedia Britannica* (Macropaedia) (Vol. 15, pp. 348–356). Chicago: Encyclopaedia Britannica.

Garner, D. M., & Bemis, K. M. (1985). Cognitive therapy for anorexia nervosa. In D. M. Garner & P. E. Garfinkel (Eds.), *Handbook of psychotherapy for anorexia nervosa and bulimia* (pp. 107–146). New York: Guilford.

Garner, D. M., Garfinkel, P. E., Schwartz, D., & Thompson, M. (1980). Cultural expectations of thinness in women. *Psychological Reports, 47*, 483–491.

Garrett, M. T., & Pichette, E. F. (2000, Winter). Red as an apple: Native American acculturation and counseling with or without reservation. *Journal of Counseling & Development, 78*(1), 3–13.

Gary, G. E. (1991). Mental health of African Americans: Research trends and directions. In R. L. Jones (Ed.), *Black psychology* (pp. 727–745). Berkeley, CA: Cobb & Henry.

George, F. H. (1977). *The foundations of cybernetics.* New York: Gordon & Breach Science.

Gergen, K. J., Gulerce, A., Lock, A., & Misra, G. (1996, May). Psychological science in cultural context. *American Psychologist, 51*(5), 496–503.

Gerzina, G. (1999). Racism. In *Encyclopaedia Americana* (Vol. 23, pp. 125–126). Danbury, CT: Grolier.

Gibbs, J. T. (1985). *City girls: Psychosocial adjustment of urban Black adolescent females* (pp. 28–36). Thousand Oaks, CA: Sage.

Gibson, R. (1982). Blacks at middle and late life: Resources and coping. *Annals of the American Academy of Political and Social Science, 464*, 79–90.

Gladieux, L. E. (2000, November). Global online higher education: New engine for inequality? *On Campus*, 10.

Global Policy Forum. (2001). *Inequality of wealth and income distribution: Articles from 1998–99.* New York: Global Policy Forum. (Online). Retrieved September 20, 2001, from the World Wide Web: http://www.globalpolicy.org/socecon/inequal/indinq99.htm.

Gold, E. M. (1965). A formal theory of problem-solving. In M. Maxfield, A. Callahan, & L. J. Fogel (Eds.), *Biophysics and cybernetic systems.* London: Macmillan.

Goldberg, L. R. (1959). The effectiveness of clinicians' judgments: The diagnosis of organic brain damage from the Bender-Gestalt Test. *Journal of Consulting Psychology, 23*, 25–33.

Goldner, D., & Smith, M. (2000, March 13). Some minorities fear they will be left out. *Daily News* (New York), 6.

Gollub, E. L. (1999). Human rights is a U.S. problem, too. The case of women and HIV. *American Journal of Public Health, 89*, 1479–1485.

Good, B. J., & Good, M. D. (1986). The cultural context of diagnosis and therapy: A view from medical anthropology. In M. R. Miranda & H. H. L. Kitano (Eds.), *Mental health research and practice in minority communities: Development of culturally sensitive programs* (pp. 1–27). Rockville, MD: National Institute of Mental Health.

Goodnow, J. J. (1976). The nature of intelligent behavior: Questions raised by cross-cultural studies. In L. B. Resnick (Ed.), *The nature of intelligence.* Hillsdale, NJ: Erlbaum.

Gordon, M., & Grantham, R. (1979) Helper preference in disadvantaged students. *Journal of Counseling Psychology, 26*(4), 337–343.

Goslee, S. (1998). *What's going on—losing ground bit by bit: Low-income communities in the information age.* Benton Foundation. (Online). Retrieved February 20, 2002, from the World Wide Web: http://www.benton.org/Library/Low-Income/.

Gould, J. L. (1982). *Ethology: The mechanisms and evolution of behavior.* New York: W. W. Norton.

Grandbois, G. H, & Schadt, D. (1994, February). Indian identification and alienation in an urban community. *Psychological Reports, 74*(1), 211–216.

Greenfeld, L. A., & Smith, S. K. (1999). *American Indians and crime* (NCJ 173386). Bureau of Justice Statistics, U.S. Department of Justice (revised 6/18/99). (Online). Retrieved from the World Wide Web on June 20, 2001: http://www.ojp.usdoj.gov/bjs/pub/ascii/aic.txt.

Greenwald, H., & Oppenheim, D. (1968) Reported magnitude of self-misidentification among Negro children—artifact? *Journal of Personality and Social Psychology, 8,* 49–52.

Grieger, I., & Ponterotto, J. G. (1995). A framework for assessment in multicultural counseling. In J. G. Ponterotto, J. M. Casas, L .A. Suzuki, & C. M. Alexander (Eds.), *Handbook of multicultural counseling* (pp. 357–374). Thousand Oaks, CA: Sage.

Groce, N. E., Chamie, M., & Me, A. (2001). Measuring the quality of life: Rethinking the World Bank's Disability Adjusted Life Years. *Rehabilitation International.* (Online). Retrieved January 2001, from the World Wide Web: http://www.rehab-international.org/measuringquality.htm.

Grossman, H. (1984). *Educating Hispanic students.* Springfield, IL: Thomas.

Guimón, J., Berrios, G. E., & Mezzich, J. E. (1989). *Psychiatric diagnosis: Nosological, biological and psychological aspects.* Philadelphia: Saunders.

Gurin, P., Miller, A. H., & Gurin, G. (1980). Stratum identification and consciousness. *Social Psychology Quarterly, 43*(1), 30–47.

Gurung, R. A. R., & Mehta, V. (2001, May). Relating ethnic identity, acculturation, and attitudes toward treating clients. *Cultural Diversity and Ethnic Minority Psychology, 7*(2), 139–151.

Gutierrez, J., Sameroff, A. J., & Karrer, B. M. (1988, February). Acculturation and SES effects on Mexican-American parents' concepts of development. *Child Development, 59*(1), 250–255.

Gynter, M. D., Lachar, D., & Dahlstrom, W. G. (1978). Are special norms for minorities needed? Development of an MMPI F scale for Blacks. *Journal of Consulting and Clinical Psychology, 46*(6), 1403–1408.

Ha, F. I (1995). Shame in Asian and Western cultures. *American Behavioral Scientist, 38*(8), 1114–1131.

Hagen, E. (1999). The functions of postpartum depression. *Evolution and Human Behavior, 20,* 325–359.

Hagen, E. (2002). *Intraspecific exploitative mimicry in humans.* (Online). Retrieved February 25, 2002, from the World Wide Web: http://www.anth.ucsb.edu/faculty/hagen/dd.html.

Hagen, M. (1997). *Whores of the court: The fraud of psychiatric testimony and the rape of American justice.* New York: Regan.

Hakuta, K., & Garcia, E. E. (1989). Bilingualism and education. *American Psychologist, 44,* 374–379.

Hale-Benson, J. E. (1986). *Black children: Their roots, culture, and learning styles.* Baltimore, MD: Johns Hopkins University Press.

Hall, C. S., Lindzey, G., & Campbell, J. B. (1998). *Theories of personality.* New York: Wiley.

Hammerstein, P., & Selten, R (1994). Game theory and evolutionary biology. In R. J. Aumann & S. Hart (Eds.), *Handbook of game theory, Vol. II.* North Holland, Amsterdam.

Harrison, C. (2000, October, 8). Catering to banks and financial institutions—Marketing to minorities bigger priority for firms. *Dallas Morning News,* October 8, 2000. (Online). Retrieved February 25, 2001, from the World Wide Web: http://www.dallasnews.com/classifieds/employment/financial/187034_ f1hispanic_08e.html.

Haselow, J. H. (1997, August 8). *Honing your selling skills through better overseas marketing.* International Network of Business Advertising Agencies. (Online). Retrieved February 2001, from the World Wide Web: http://www.inba.org/views/13steps.htm#top.

Hatfield, E., & Rapson, R. L. (1996). *Love and sex: Cross-cultural perspectives.* Boston: Allyn & Bacon.

Hayes, L. (2001, March). Lending a helping hand. *Counseling Today,* 8, 10.

Hayles, R. V. (1991). African American strengths: A survey of empirical findings. In R. L. Jones (Ed.), *Black psychology* (pp. 353–378). Berkeley, CA: Cobb & Henry.

Heath, S. B. (1989). Oral and literate traditions among Black Americans living in poverty. *American Psychologist, 44,* 367–373.

Heiss, J. & Owens, S. (1972). Self-evaluations of Blacks and Whites. *American Journal of Sociology, 78,* 360–370.

Helberg, C. (2000). *Pitfalls of data analysis (or how to avoid lies and damned lies).* (Online). Retrieved from the World Wide Web: http://www.execpc.com/ ~helberg/pitfalls/.

Helfrich, S. (n.d.). *An alternative psychobiological view on mental illness.* (Online). Retrieved June 1, 2002, from the World Wide Web: http://www.xs4all.nl/ ~helfrich/psycho/psycho1.html.

Helms, J. E. (1985). Toward a theoretical explanation of the effects of race in counseling: A black and White model. *The Counseling Psychologist, 12,* 153–165.

Helms, J. E. (1986). Expanding racial identity to cover the counseling process. *Journal of Counseling Psychology, 33,* 62–64.

Henry, F. (Ed.). (1976). *Ethnicity in the Americas.* Chicago: Aldine.

Herbert, J. D., Lilienfeld, S., Kline, J., Montgomery, R., Lohr, J., Brandsma, L., Meadows, E., Jacobs, W. J., Goldstein, N., Gist, R., McNally, R. J., Acierno, R., Harris, M., Devilly, G. J., Bryant, R., Eisman, H. D., Kleinknecht, R., Rosen, G. M., & Foa, E. (2001, November). Psychology's response—Primum non nocere [Letter to the editor]. *Monitor on Psychology, 32*(10).

Hernandez, M. A. (1997). *A is for admission: The insider's guide to getting into the Ivy League and other top colleges*. New York: Warner.

Higginbotham, E. (1995). Getting all students to listen. In J. Banks & C. McGee (Eds.), *Handbook of research on multicultural education*. New York: Macmillan.

High self-esteem can have a dark side too. (1996, March). *Monitor*, 7.

Hirschfeld, L. A. (1996). *Race in the making: Cognition, culture, and the child's construction of human kinds*. Boston: MIT Press.

Hoagwood, K. (1997, May). Interpreting nullity: The Fort Bragg experiment—a comparative success or failure? *American Psychologist, 52*(5), 546–550.

Hochschild, J. L. (1993). Middle-class blacks and the ambiguities of success. In P. M. Sniderman, P. E. Tetlock, et al. (Eds.), *Prejudice, politics, and the American dilemma* (pp. 148–172). Stanford, CA: Stanford University Press.

Hofbauer, J., & Sigmund, K. (1998): *Evolutionary games and population dynamics*. New York: Cambridge University Press.

Hogrefe, C. J. (1988). *Cross-cultural perspectives in nonverbal communication*. Lewiston, NY: C. J. Hogrefe.

Hollingshead, A. B., & Redlich, F. C. (1996, c1958). *Social class and mental illness: A community study*. New York: Wiley.

Holloman, R. E., & Arutiunov, S. A. (1978). *Perspectives on ethnicity*. The Hague: Mouton.

Holzer, C., Shea, B., Swanson, J., Leaf, P., Myers, J., George, L., Weissman, M., & Bednarski, P. (1986). The increased risk for specific psychiatric disorders among persons of low socioeconomic status. *American Journal of Social Psychiatry, 6*, 259–271.

Horney, K. (1939). *New ways of psychoanalysis*. New York: W. W. Norton.

Horwitz, A. V., & Scheid, T. L. (1999). *A handbook for the study of mental health: Social contexts, theories, and systems*. New York: Cambridge University Press.

Howell, L. (1977). Compared attitudinal dimensions: A combined social distance-factor analytic approach. *Ethnicity, 4*, 1–18.

Hui, C. C. H., & Triandis, H. (1986). Individualism-collectivism: A study of cross-cultural researchers. *Journal of Cross-Cultural Psychology, 17*, 225–248.

Huntington, S. (1996). *The clash of civilizations*. New York: Simon & Schuster.

Ibrahim, F. A., & Kahn, H. (1987). Assessment of world views. *Psychological Reports, 60*, 163–176.

Ibrahim, F. A., Ohnishi, H., & Wilson, R. P. (1994). Career assessment in a culturally diverse society. *Journal of Career Assessment, 2*, 276–288.

Ibrahim, F. A., & Owens, S. V. (1992, August). *Factor analytic structure of the scale to assess world view*. Paper presented at the annual meeting of the American Psychological Association, Washington, DC.

Idson, T. L., & Price, H. F. (1992). An analysis of wage differentials by gender and ethnicity in the public sector. *Review of Black Political Economy, 20*, 75–97.

Illovsky, M. (1993). The effects of knowledge of psychology on mental and physical health. *Research Communications in Psychology, Psychiatry and Behavior, 18*(1 & 2), 73–76.

Illovsky, M. (1994). Counseling, artificial intelligence, and expert systems. *Simulation and Gaming, 25*(1), 88–98.

Illovsky, M. (1994b, October). Defining sample in multicultural psychological research. *Journal of Multicultural Counseling and Development, 22*(4), 253–256.

Indian Health Services. (2001, July 23). *Part 2: Population statistics. Trends in Indian health 1998–99. Indian Health Services.* (Online). Retrieved October 20, 2001, from the World Wide Web: http://www.ihs.gov/PublicInfo/Publications/trends98/part2.pdf.

International Journal of Psychosomatics. (1984). Philadelphia: International Psychosomatics Institute.

Internet Business Video Network. (2001). *Marketing to minorities.* (Online). Retrieved February 25, 2001, from the World Wide Web: http://www.infoonline.com/videos2.htm.

Irvine, J. T. (1978). Wolof "magical thinking": Culture and conservation revisited. *Journal of Cross-Cultural Psychology, 9,* 300–310.

Irvine, J. J., & York, D. E. (1995). Learning styles and cultural diverse students: A literature review. In J. Banks & C. McGee (Eds.), *Handbook of research on multicultural education.* New York: Macmillan.

Isajiw, W. (1974). Definitions of ethnicity. *Ethnicity, 1,* 111–124.

Ivey, A. E. (1981). Counseling and psychotherapy. *Counseling Psychologist, 9*(2), 81–98.

Ivey, A. E. (1986). *Developmental therapy.* San Francisco: Jossey-Bass.

Ivey, A. E. (1993). On the need for reconstruction of our present practice of counseling and psychotherapy. *Counseling Psychologist, 21,* 225–228.

Ivey, A. E. (1993, January). *Psychotherapy as liberation.* Presentation to the Round Table on Cross-Cultural Counseling, Columbia University, New York.

Ivey, A. E. (1995). Psychotherapy as liberation: Toward specific skills and strategies in multicultural counseling and therapy (pp. 53–72). In J. G. Ponterotto, J. M. Casas, L. A. Suzuki, & C. M. Alexander (Eds.), *Handbook of multicultural counseling* (pp. 333–356). Thousand Oaks, CA: Sage.

Ivey, M., Ivey, A. E., D'Andrea, M., & Daniels, J. (1997). White privilege: Implications for counselor education multicultural identity. *ACES Spectrum, 57*(4), 3–6.

Jackson, A. P., & Ivanoff, A. (1999). Reduction of low response rates in interview surveys of poor African-American families. *Journal of Social Service Research, 25*(1), 41.

Jackson, D. N. (1989). *Personality research form manual.* Port Huron, MI: Sigma Assessment System.

Jackson, G. G., & Kirschner, S. A. (1973). Racial self-designation and preference for a counselor. *Journal of Counseling Psychology, 20,* 560–564.

Jacobsen, F. M. (1988). Ethnocultural assessment. In L. Comas-Diaz & E. E. H. Griffith (Eds.), *Clinical guidelines in cross-cultural mental health* (pp. 135–147). New York: Wiley.

Janicki, M. (1998). *Definition of evolution psychology.* (Online). Retrieved June 20, 2000, from the World Wide Web: http://www.sfu.ca/~janicki/defn.htm.

Jenkins, S., & Morrison, B. (1978). Ethnicity and service delivery. *American Journal of Orthopsychiatry, 48*(1), 160–165.

Jensen, G. F., White, C. S., & Galliher, J. M. (1982). Ethnic status and adolescent self-evaluations: An extension of research on minority self-esteem. *Social Problems, 30*(2), 226–239.

Jerome, L. E. (1989). *Crystal power: The ultimate placebo effect.* Buffalo, NY: Prometheus.

Jones, A. C. (1992). Self-esteem and identity in psychotherapy with adolescents from upwardly mobile middle-class African American families. In L. A. Vargas, A. Luis, J. D. Koss-Chioino (Eds.), *Working with culture: Psychotherapeutic interventions with ethnic minority children and adolescents,* (pp. 25–42) San Francisco: Jossey-Bass.

Jones, E. E., Farina, A., Hastorf, A. H., Markus, H., Miller, D. T., & Scott, R. A. (1984). *Social stigma: The psychology of marked relationships.* New York: Freeman.

Jones, E. E., & Korchin, S. J. (1982). *Minority mental health.* New York: Praeger.

Jones, E. E., & Thorne, A. (1987). Rediscovery of the subject: Intercultural approaches to clinical assessment. *Journal of Consulting and Clinical Psychology, 55*(4), 488–495.

Jones, S. L. (1997, June). A guide to using color effectively in business communication. *Business Communication Quarterly, 60*(2), 76–89.

Jorgensen, B. W., & Cervone, J. C. (1978). Affect enhancement in the pseudorecognition task. *Personality and Social Psychology Bulletin, 4,* 285–288.

Jospe, M. (1978). *The placebo effect in healing.* Lexington, MA: Lexington.

Judd, D. B., & Wyszecki, G. (1975). *Color in business, science, and industry* (3rd ed.). New York: Wiley.

Kaiser Family Foundation. (2000). *Racial and ethnic disparities in access to health insurance and health care.* Washington, DC, Office. (Online). Retrieved March 20, 2002, from the World Wide Web: http://usnews.about.com/newsissues/ usnews/gi/dynamic/offsite.htm?site=http://www.kff.org/content/2000/1525.

Kalb, C. (2001, January 22). Seeing a virtual shrink. *Newsweek, 54,* 56.

Kamin, L. J. (1977). The politics of I.Q. In P. L. Houts (Ed.), *The myth of measurability* (pp. 45–65). New York: Hart.

Kantor, G. K., Jasinski, J. L., & Aldarondo, E. (1994, Fall). Sociocultural status and incidence of marital violence in Hispanic families. *Violence & Victims, 9*(3), 207–222.

Kantrowitz, B., & Wingert, P. (1992, February 17). An F in world competition. *Newsweek, 57.*

Kardiner, A., & Ovesey, L. (1951). *The mark of oppression: Explorations in the personality of the American Negro.* New York: World.

Karlins, M., Coffman, T., & Walters, G. (1969). On the fading of social stereotypes: Studies in three generations of college students. *Journal of Personality and Social Psychology, 13,* 1–16.

Keever, B. A. D., Martindale, C., & Weston, M. A. (Eds.). (1997). *U.S. news coverage of racial minorities: A sourcebook, 1934–1996.* Westport, CT: Greenwood.

Kelley, H. H. (1972). Attribution in social interaction. In E. E. Jones et al. (Eds.), *Attribution: Perceiving the causes of behavior.* Morristown, NJ: General Learning.

Kelley, H. H. (1973). The processes of causal attribution. *American Psychologist, 28,* 107–128.

Kerwin, C. & Ponterotto, J. G. (1995). Biracial identity development. In J. G. Ponterotto, J. M. Casas, L. A. Suzuki, & C. M Alexander (Eds.), *Handbook of multicultural counseling*. Thousand Oaks, CA: Sage.

Kessler, R. (1994, February). The epidemiology of mental illness. *Medical Sciences Bulletin* (Pharmaceutical Information Associates, Ltd. (Online). Retrieved June 20, 2000, from the World Wide Web: http://pharminfo.com:80/pubs/msb/epimen.html.

Keyes, C. (1976). Towards a new formulation of the concept of ethnic group. *Ethnicity, 3,* 202–213.

Khan, O. (2001). *What is forbidden in Islam—homosexuality or practicing homosexuality?* (Online). Retrieved June 20, 2001, from the World Wide Web: http://members.spree.com/SIP1/omerkhan/islam/islam_1/homosexuality.html.

Kibria, N. (2000, Spring). Race, ethnic options and ethnic binds: Identity negotiations of second-generation Chinese and Korean Americans. *Sociological Perspectives, 43*(1), 77–95.

Kim, H., & Markus, H. R. (1999, October). Deviance or uniqueness, harmony or conformity? A cultural analysis. *Journal of Personality & Social Psychology, 77*(4), 785–800.

King, M. L., Jr. (1999, January). King's challenge to the nation's social scientists. American Psychological Association's *Monitor, 30* (1), pp. 26-29.

Kirmayer, L. J. (1998). Editorial: the fate of culture in *DSM-IV. Transcultural Psychiatry, 35,* 339–342.

Kirsh, D. (Ed.). (1992). *Foundations of artificial intelligence.* Cambridge, MA: MIT Press.

Kiselica, M. S. (1995). *Multicultural counseling with teenage fathers: A practical guide.* Thousand Oaks, CA: Sage.

Kiselica, M. S. (2000, April). *Keynote address: The mental health professional as advocate: Matters of the heart, matters of the mind.* Great Lakes Regional Conference of Division 17 of the American Psychological Association, Muncie, IN.

Kiselica, M. S., & Ramsey, M. L. (2001). Multicultural counselor education: Historical perspectives and future directions. In D. C. Locke, J. E. Myers, & E. L. Herr (Eds.), *The handbook of counseling* (pp. 433–452). Thousand Oaks, CA: Sage.

Kiselica, M. S., & Robinson, M. (2001, Fall). Bringing advocacy counseling to life: The history, issues, and human dramas of social justice work in counseling. *Journal of Counseling and Development, 79*(4), 387–397.

Knapp, M., & Hall, J. (1992). *Nonverbal communication in human interaction.* Orlando, FL: Holt, Rinehart & Winston.

Kobak, K. A., Taylor, L. H., Dottl, S. L., Greist, J. H., Jefferson, J. W., Burroughs, Mantle, J. M., Katzelnick, D. J., Norton, R., Henk, H. J., & Serlin, R. C. (1997, September 17). A computer-administered telephone interview to identify mental disorders. *Journal of the American Medical Association* (JAMA), *287*(11), 905–910.

Krause, E. A. (1977). *Power and illness: The political sociology of health and medical care.* New York: Elsevier.

Krauthammer, C. (1990, February 5). Education: Doing bad and feeling good. *Time,* 78.

Kremers, J. (1960). *Scientific psychology and naïve psychology*. (Trans. L. Grooten). Groningen, Netherlands: Nordhoff.

Krieger, N. (1990). Racial and gender discrimination: Risk factors for high blood pressure? *Social Science and Medicine, 30*, 1273–1281.

Kuhn, H. W., & Nasar, S. (2001). *The essential John Nash*. Princeton, NJ: Princeton University Press.

Kuhn, T. (1970). *The structure of scientific revolutions*. Chicago: University of Chicago Press.

Kundu, M. M., & Dutta, A. (1995, January). Implementation of rehabilitation counselor training programs at historically Black colleges and universities. In S. Walker, K. A. Turner, M. Haile-Michael, A. Vincent, & M. D. Miles (Eds.), *Disability and diversity: New leadership for a new era*. Published by the President's Committee on Employment of People With Disabilities in collaboration with the Howard University Research and Training Center, 136–170. (Online). Retrieved from the World Wide Web: http://www.dinf.org/pres_com/pres-dd/kundu.htm.

Kurth, S. B. (1970). Friendships and friendly relations. In G. J. McCall, M. M. McCall, N. K. Denzin, G. D. Suttles, & S. B. Kurth. (Eds.), *Social relationships* (pp. 136–170). Chicago: Aldine.

Kwan, K.-L. K. (2000, February). The internal-external ethnic identity measure: Factor-analytic structures based on a sample of Chinese-Americans. *Educational & Psychological Measurement, 60*(1), 142–152.

LaFromboise, T. M., Coleman, H. L. K., & Gerton, J. (1993). Psychological impact of biculturalism. *Psychological Bulletin, 114*, 395–412.

Lajos, T. (1997). *Visual mobility: New technologies and internationalization*. (Online). Retrieved June 20, 2000, from the World Wide Web: http://www.eaie.nl/ITHE/lajos.html.

Lambert, M. J. (1983). *Psychotherapy and patient relationships*. Homewood, IL: Dow Jones-Irwin.

Lambert, M. J., DeJulio, S. S., & Christensen, E. R. (1983). *The assessment of psychotherapy*. New York: Wiley.

Landrine, H., & Klonoff, E. A. (1996, May). The schedule of racist events: A measure of racial discrimination and a study of its negative physical and mental health consequences. *Journal of Black Psychology, 22*(2), 144–168.

Laosa, L. M., & Henderson, R. W. (1991). Cognitive socialization and competence: The academic development of Chicanos. In R. R. Valencia (Ed.), *Chicano school failure and success: Research and policy agendas for the 1990s* (pp. 164–199). New York: Falmer.

Lawyer, R. W., & Yazdani, M. (1987). *Artificial intelligence and education, Vol. 1*. Norwood, NJ: Ablex.

Lee, C. C. (1998). Counselors as agents for social change. In C. C. Lee & G. R. Walz (Eds.), *Social justice: A mandate for counselors* (pp. 3–16). Alexandria, VA: American Counseling Association.

Lee, C. C., & Richardson, B. L. (Eds.). (1991). *Multicultural issues in counseling: New approaches to diversity*. Alexandria, VA: American Association for Counseling & Development.

Lefley, H. P. (1999). Mental health systems in cross-cultural contest. In A. V. Horwitz

& T. L. A. Scheid (Eds.), *A handbook for the study of mental health: Social contexts, theories, and systems.* New York: Cambridge University Press.

Leo, J. (1990, April 2). The trouble with self-esteem. *U.S. World and News Report,* 16.

Leong, F. T., & Lau, A. S. (1998). *Barriers to providing effective mental health services to Asian Americans.* Manuscript submitted for publication.

Lewis, Len. (1998, April). Culture shock. *Progressive Grocer, 77*(4), 22–28.

Liar, liar, face on fire. (1999, July). *Discover,* 16–17.

Lief, H. I., Lief, V. F., Warren, C. O., & Heath, R. G. (1961). Low dropout rate in a psychiatric clinic. *Archives of General Psychiatry, 5,* 200–211.

Liem, R., Lim, B. A., & Liem, J. H. (2000). Acculturation and emotion among Asian Americans. *Cultural Diversity and Ethnic Minority Psychology, 6*(1), 13–31.

Lin, K., Inui, T. S., Kleinman, A. M., & Womack, W. M. (1982). Sociocultural determinants of the help-seeking behavior of patients with mental illness. *Journal of Nervous and Mental Disease, 170,* 78–85.

Lin, K. M., Anderson, D., & Poland, R. E. (1997). Ethnic and cultural considerations in psychopharmacotherapy. In D. Dunner (Ed.), *Current psychiatric therapy II* (pp. 75–81). Philadelphia: W. B. Saunders.

Li-Repac, D. (1980). Culture influences on clinical perceptions: A comparison between Caucasian and Chinese-American therapists. *Journal of Cross-Culture Psychology, 11*(3), 327–342.

Locke, D. C. (1992). *Increasing multicultural understanding.* Newbury Park, CA: Sage.

Locksley, A., Borgida, E., Brekke, N., & Hepburn, C. (1980). Sex stereotypes and social judgement. *Journal of Personality and Social Psychology, 39,* 821–831.

Lopez, S. R. (1989). Patient variables bias in clinical judgment: Conceptual overview and methodological considerations. *Psychological Bulletin, 106*(2), 104–203.

Loupe, D., & Wright, M. W. (1993, January 14, Section C). Study sees wide gap in high schoolers' views on race: Black, White youth differ in perceptions. *The Atlanta Journal and Constitution,* 1.

Lu, F. G., Lim, R. F., & Mezzich, J. E. (1995). Issues in the assessment and diagnosis of culturally diverse individuals. In J. Oldham & M. Riba (Eds.), *Review of Psychiatry* (Vol. 14, pp. 477–510). Washington, DC: American Psychiatric Press.

Luft, J. (1951). Differences in prediction based on hearing versus reading verbatim clinical interviews. *Journal of Consulting Psychology, 15,* 115–119.

Lunt, I., & Poortinga, Y. H. (1996, May). Internationalizing psychology. *American Psychologist, 51*(5), 504–508.

Luttwak, E. (1969). *Coup d'état: A practical handbook.* New York: Knopf.

Lutz, C., & LeVine, R. A. (1982). Culture and intelligence in infancy: An ethnopsychological view. In M. Lewis (Ed.), *Origins of intelligence: Infancy and early childhood* (pp. 1–28). New York: Plenum.

Lykes, M. B. (1983). Discrimination and coping in the lives of Black women: Analyses of oral history data. *Journal of Social Issues, 39*(3), 79–100.

MacDonald, K. (1998). Evolution, culture, and the five-factor model. *Journal of Cross-Cultural Psychology, 29*(1), 119–149.

MacLean, P. D. (1975). On the evolution of three mentalities. *Man-Environment Systems, 5,* 213–224.

MacLean, P. D. (1985). Evolutionary psychiatry and the triune brain. *Psychological Medicine, 15,* 21–221.

MacLean, P. D. (1993). On the evolution of three mentalities. In J. B. Ashbrook (Ed.), *Brain, culture, & the human spirit: Essays from an emergent evolutionary perspective* (pp. 15–44). Lanham, MD: University Press of America.

Maher, B. A. (1966). *Principles of psychopathology.* New York: McGraw-Hill.

Malandro, L. A. (1983, 1989). *Non-verbal communication* (2nd ed.). New York: Random House.

Malinowski, B. (1961). *Argonauts of the western Pacific.* New York: Dutton.

Marks, I. M., & Nesse, R. M. (1994). Fear and fitness: An evolutionary analysis of anxiety disorders. *Ethology and Sociobiology, 15,* 247–261.

Marin, G., & Marin, B. (1991). *Research with Hispanic populations.* Newbury Park, CA: Sage.

Marrett, C., & Leggon, C. (Eds.). (1980). *Research in race and ethnic relations* (Vol. 2). Greenwich, CT: Jai Press.

Martin, B. (1994). Merit and power. In J. Curtis & L. Tepperman (Eds.), *Haves and have-nots: An international reader of social inequity.* Englewood Cliffs, NJ: Prentice-Hall.

Martin, C. P. (1956). *Psychology, evolution, and sex.* Springfield, IL: Thomas.

Martinez, R. (1996, May). Latinos and lethal violence: The impact of poverty and inequality. *Social Problems, 43*(2), 131–146.

Matier, M. W., & Larson, O. W., III. (1995). *Using TQM to improve the quality of race/ethnicity reporting.* AIR 1995 Annual Forum Paper (35th, Boston, MA, May 28–31, 1995). Florida State University Tallahassee, FL: Association for Institutional Research. (ERIC Document Reproduction Service No. ED 366 977).

Matte-Blanco, I. (1971, November). A symbolic-logic approach to psychiatry and psychology. *Human Context, 3*(3), 576–589.

Matte-Blanco, I. (1972). A symbolic-logic approach to psychiatry and psychology. II. *Human Context, 4*(1), 72–86.

Masserman, J. (1972). *The dynamics of power.* New York: Grune & Stratton.

Mayall, D. (1994). *The worker traits data book.* Indianapolis, IN: JIST Works.

Maynard Smith, J. (1982): *Evolution and the theory of games.* New York: Cambridge University Press.

Mays, V. M., & Albee, G. W. (1992). Psychotherapy and ethnic minorities. In D. K. Freedheim (Ed.), *History of psychotherapy* (pp. 552–570). Washington, DC: American Psychological Association.

Mays, V. M., Rubin, J., Sabourin, M., & Walker, L. (1996, May). Moving toward a global psychology: Changing theories and practice to meet the needs of a changing world. *American Psychologist, 51*(5), 485–487.

McCarthy, J., & Yancey, W. (1971). Uncle Tom and Mr. Charlie: Metaphysical pathos in the study of racism and personal disorganization. *American Journal of Sociology, 76,* 648–672.

McConahay, J. B., & Hough, J. C. (1976). Symbolic racism. *Journal of Social Issues, 32,* 23–45.

McCrea, R. R., Costa, P. T., Del Pilar, G. H., Rolland, J-P., & Parker, W. D. (January, 1998). Cross-cultural assessment of the five-factor model: The revised NEO personality inventory. *Journal of Cross-Cultural Psychology, 29*(1), 171–188.

McCready, W. C. (Ed.). (1983). *Culture, ethnicity, and identity: Current issues in research.* New York: Academic.

McGrew, W. C., & Feistner, A. T. (1995). Two nonhuman models for the evolution of human food sharing: Chimpanzees and callitrichids. In J. H. Barkow, L. Cosmides, & J. Tooby (Eds.), *The adapted mind: Evolutionary psychology and the generation of culture.* New York: Oxford University Press.

McGuire, M. T., & Fairbanks, L. A. (Eds.). (1977). *Ethological psychiatry: Psychopathology in the context of evolutionary biology.* New York: Grune & Stratton.

McGuire, M. T., Marks, I., Nesse, R. M., & Troisi, A. (1992). Evolutionary biology: A basic science for psychiatry? *Acta Psychiatrica Scandinavica, 86,* 89–96.

McGuire, M., & Troisi, A. (1998). *Darwinian psychiatry.* New York: Oxford University Press.

McNeil, E. B. (1970). *The psychoses.* New Jersey: Prentice-Hall.

McShane, D. A., & Plas, J. M. (1982). Wechsler scale performance patterns of American Indian children. *Psychology in the Schools, 19*(1), 8–17.

Mecca, A., Smelser, N. J., & Vasconcellos, J. (1989). *The social importance of self-esteem.* Berkeley: University of California Press.

Mehan, H. (1979). *Learning lessons: Social organization in the classroom.* Cambridge, MA: Harvard University Press.

Mental health: Does therapy help? (1995, November). *Consumer Reports, 734–739.*

Mezzich, J. E., & Berganza, C. E. (1984). *Culture & psychopathology.* New York: Columbia University Press.

Mezzich, J. E., & von Cranach, M. (1988). *International classification in psychiatry: Unity and diversity.* New York: Cambridge University Press.

Mezzich, J. E., Honda, Y., & Kastrup, M. (1994). *Psychiatric diagnosis: A world perspective.* New York: Springer-Verlag.

Mezzich, J. E., Jorge, M. R., & Salloum, I. M. (1994). *Psychiatric epidemiology: Assessment concepts and methods.* Baltimore: Johns Hopkins University Press.

Mezzich, J. E., Kirmayer, L. J., Kleinman, A., Fabrega, H., Jr., Parron, D. L., Good, B. J., Lin, K.-M., & Manson, S. M. (1999, August). The place of culture in DSM-IV. *Journal of Nervous & Mental Disease, 187*(18), 457–464.

Mezzich, J. E., Kleinman, A., Fabrega, H., & Patron, D. L. (Eds.). (1996). *Culture and psychiatric diagnosis: A DSM-IV perspective.* Washington, DC: American Psychiatric Association.

Mezzich J. E., Kleinman, A., Fabrega, H., Parron, D. L., & Good, B. J. (1997). Cultural issues for *DSM-IV.* In T. A. Widiger, A. J. Frances, H. A. Pincus, R. Ross, M. B. First, & W. Davis (Eds.), *DSM-IV Sourcebook.* Washington, DC: American Psychiatric Association.

Michels, R. (1968). *Political parties: A sociological study of the oligarchical tendencies of modern democracy.* New York: Free.

Miller, C. (1993, May 10). Researcher says U.S. is more of a bowl than a pot. *Marketing News, 27*(10), 6.

Miller-Jones, D. (1989). Culture and testing. *American Psychologist, 44,* 360–366.

Mills, C. W. (1995). The power elite. In S. Teodoulou and M. Cahn (Eds.), *Public policy: The essential readings.* Englewood Cliffs, NJ: Prentice Hall.

Miranda, J., & Green, B. L. (1999). The need for mental health services research focusing on poor young women. *Journal of Mental Health Policy and Economics,* 2, 73–89.

Mischel, W. (1968). *Personality and assessment.* New York: Wiley.

Moll, L. C. (Ed.). (1990). *Vygotsky and education: Instructional implications and applications of sociohistorical psychology.* Cambridge, England: Cambridge University Press.

Monderer, D., & Shapley, L. (1996). Potential games. *Games and Economic Behavior, 14,* 124–143.

Moore, J. W. (1970). Colonialism: The case of the Mexican Americans. *Social Problems, 17,* 463–472.

Moran, J., Fleming, C. M., Somervell, P., & Manson, S. M. (1999, October). Measuring bicultural ethnic identity among American Indian adolescents: A factor analysis study. *Journal of Adolescent Research, 14*(4), 405–426.

Moreland, R. L., & Zajonc, R. B. (1979). Exposure effects may not depend on stimulus recognition. *Journal of Personality and Social Psychology, 37,* 1085–1089.

Moritsugu, J., & Sue, S. (1983). Minority status as a stressor. In R. D. Felner, L. Jason, J. Moritsugu, & S. Farber (Eds.), *Preventive psychology.* New York: Pergamon.

Morrison Institute for Population and Resource Studies. (1999). *Human Genome Diversity Project.* Stanford University, Stanford, California. (Online). Retrieved June 20, 2000, from the World Wide Web: http://www.stanford.edu/group/morrinst/hgdp/faq.html#Q7.

Mukherjee, S., Shukla, S., Woodle, J., Rosen, A. M., & Olarte, S. (1983). Misdiagnosis of schizophrenia in bipolar patients: A multiethnic comparison. *American Journal of Psychiatry, 140,* 1571–1574.

Murray, C. L., & Lopez, A. D. (Eds.). (1996). *The global burden of disease. A comprehensive assessment of mortality and disability from diseases, injuries, and risk factors in 1990 and projected to 2020.* Cambridge, MA: Harvard University.

Murray, C. B., & Peacock, M. J. (1996). A model-free approach to the study of subjective well-being. In H. W. Neighbors & J. S. Jackson (Eds.), *Mental health in Black America* (pp. 14–26). Thousand Oaks, CA: Sage.

Nachbar, J. H. (1990). Evolutionary selection dynamic in games: Convergence and limit properties. *International Journal of Game Theory, 19,* 59–90.

Nairfeh, S., & Smith, G. W. (1985). *Why can't men open up?* New York: Warner.

National Center for Education Statistics. (2001). *Digest of Education Statistics, 2001* (table 321). Washington, DC: Author. (Online). Retrieved May 25, 2002, from the World Wide Web: http://nces.ed.gov/pubs2002/digest2001/list_talbes.asp.

National Center for Health Statistics. (1987). *Minority health statistics grants programs, impact on Black health research.* (Online). Retrieved June 20, 2000 from the World Wide Web: http://www.cdc.gov/nchs/about/grants/minpop/black/black.htm.

National Center for Health Statistics. (2000, February 25). *Puerto Ricans' health fares worse than other U.S. Hispanics.* Hyattsville, MD: U.S. Department of

Health and Human Services, Centers for Disease Control and Prevention, National Center for Health Statistics Division of Data Services. (NCHS 2000 Fact Sheet). (Online). Retrieved May 31, 2001, from the World Wide Web: http://www.cdc.gov/nchs/releases/00facts/hispanic.htm.

National Institute on Alcohol Abuse and Alcoholism. (2000, April 3). *Developmental grants for minority collaborative projects* (PA NUMBER: PA-00-085). (Online). Retrieved April 22, 2001, from the World Wide Web: http://grants.nih.gov/grants/guide/pa-files/PA-00-085.html.

National Institute of Mental Health. (1980). *Hispanic Americans and mental health services: A comparison of Hispanic, Black, and White admissions to selected mental health facilities*, Series CN, No. 3, Rockville, MD: U.S. Department of Health and Human Services.

National Institute of Mental Health. (1981). *Characteristics of admissions to selected mental health facilities, 1975: An annotated book of charts and tables*, Series CN Mental health national statistics, no. 2; DHHS publication no. 2 (ADM 81-1005). Rockville, MD: U.S. Department of Health and Human Services.

National Institute of Mental Health. (1983). *Research highlights: Extramural research.* Washington, DC: U.S. Government Printing Office.

National Institute of Mental Health. (1994, June 10). *Centers for research on services for people with mental health disorders.* (PA NUMBER: PAR-94-073). (Online). Retrieved April 22, 2001, from the World Wide Web: http://grants.nih.gov/grants/guide/pa-files/PAR-94-073.html.

National Institute of Mental Health (1995a, May 12). *Women's Mental Health Research NIH Guide* (PA-95-061), 24(16). Bethesda, MD: National Institute of Mental Health/Office of Extramural Research. (Online). Retrieved June 20, 2001, from the World Wide Web: http://grants.nih.gov/grants/guide/pa-files/PA-95-061.html.

National Institute of Mental Health. (1995b, November 24). *Research on the mental health of minority populations* (PA NUMBER: PA-96-007). (Online). Retrieved April 22, 2001, from the World Wide Web: http://grants.nih.gov/grants/guide/pa-files/PA-96-007.html.

National Institute of Mental Health (2000a, March 6). *Women's mental health and gender differences research.* (PA NUMBER: PA-00-074). Bethesda, MD: National Institute of Mental Health. (Online). Retrieved June 20, 2001, from the World Wide Web: http://grants.nih.gov/grants/guide/pa-files/PA-00-074.html.

National Institute of Mental Health. (2000b, December 8). *NIMH minority research infrastructure support program (R24)* (PA NUMBER: PAR-01-029). (Online). Retrieved April 22, 2001, from the World Wide Web: http://grants.nih.gov/grants/guide/pa-files/PAR-01-029.html.

National Institute of Mental Health. (2001, March 9). *Strategic plan for reducing health disparities* (Draft). (Online). Retrieved April 22, 2001, from the World Wide Web: http://www.nimh.nih.gov/strategic/strategicdisparity.cfm; or http://www.nia.nih.gov/strat-plan/2001-2005/.

National Institute on Aging. (2001a, May 3). *Strategic plan to address health disparities—Fiscal years 2000–2005.* (Online). Retrieved June 20, 2001, from the World Wide Web: http://www.nih.gov/nia/strat-planhd/2000-2005/ or http://www.nia.nih.gov/strat-plan/2001-2005/.

National Institute on Aging. (2001b, May 3). *Draft Strategic plan for fiscal years 2001–2005 (Research Goal C, Subgoal 1a).* (Online). Retrieved June 20, 2001, from the World Wide Web: http://www.nia.nih.gov/strat-planhd/2000-2005/ or http://www.nia.nih.gov/strat-plan/2001-2005/.

National Intelligence Council. (2000, December). *Global trends 2015: A dialogue about the future with nongovernment experts.* (GPO stock number 041-015-00211-2). Washington, DC: U. S. Government Printing Office. (Online). Retrieved May 27, 2002, from the World Wide Web: http://www.cia.gov/cia/publications/globaltrends2015/.

National Rural Health Association. (1999, May). *Mental health in rural America.* Washington, DC: National Rural Health Association. (Online). Retrieved September 22, 2001, from the World Wide Web: http://www.nrharural.org/dc/issuepapers/ipaper14.html.

National Telecommunications and Information Administration. (1995, July). *Falling through the net: A survey of the "have nots" in rural and urban America.* Washington, DC: U.S. Department of Commerce.

National Women's Health Information Center. (1998). *Minority women.* Office on Women's Health in the U.S. Department of Health and Human Services. (Online). Retrieved June 20, 2001, from the World Wide Web: http://www.4woman.gov/faq/minority.htm.

Neff, J. (1985). Race and vulnerability to stress: An examination of differential vulnerability. *Journal of Personality and Social Psychology, 49*(2), 481–491.

Negy, C., & Woods, D. J. (1992, May). A note on the relationship between acculturation and socioeconomic status. *Hispanic Journal of Behavioral Sciences, 14*(2), 248–251.

Neighbors, H. W., Bashshur, R., Price, R., Donavedian, A., Selig, S., & Shannon, G. (1992). Ethnic minority health service delivery: A review of the literature. *Research in Community and Mental Health, 7*, 55–71.

Neighbors, H., Jackson, J. Bowman, P., & Gurin, G. (1983). Stress, coping, and Black mental health: Preliminary findings from a national study. *Prevention in Human Services, 2*, 1–25.

Neighbors, H. W., Jackson, J. S., Campbell, L., & Williams, D.(1989). The influence of racial factors on psychiatric diagnosis: A review and suggestions for research. *Community Mental Health Journal, 25*(4), 301–311.

Nesse, R. (1988). An evolutionary view. *Psychiatric Annals, 18*(8), 478–483.

Nesse, R. (1990). Evolutionary explanations of emotions. *Human Nature, 1*(3), 261–289.

Nesse, R. M. (1991, November/December). What good is feeling bad: The evolutionary benefits of psychic pain. *Sciences*, 30–37.

Nesse, R. M. (1993, January). Evolution, emotions, and mental disorders. *Harvard Mental Health Letter, 9*(7), 5–7.

Nesse, R., & Berridge, K. C. (1997, October 3). Psychoactive drug use in evolutionary perspective. *Science, 278*(3), 63–66.

Nesse, R. M., & Lloyd, A. T. (1992). The evolution of psychodynamic mechanisms. In J. H. Barkow & L. Cosmides (Eds.), *The adapted mind: Evolutionary psychology and the generation of culture* (pp. 601–624). New York: Oxford University Press.

Nesse, R. M., & Williams, G. C. (1997, November). Evolutionary biology in the medical curriculum—What every physician should know. *BioScience, 47*(10), 664–666.

Nobles, W. (1991). African philosophy: Foundations for Black psychology. In R. L. Jones (Ed.), *Black psychology* (pp. 47–98). Berkeley, CA: Cobb & Henry.

Noonan, C. J. (1999). *The CIM handbook of export marketing: A practical guide to opening and expanding markets overseas* (2nd ed.). Oxford, Boston: Butterworth-Heinemann.

Obidinski, E. (1978). Methodological considerations in the definition of ethnicity. *Ethnicity, 5*, 213–228.

Oboler, S. (1995). *Ethnic labels, Latino lives: Identity and the politics of (re)presentation in the United States*. Minneapolis: University of Minnesota Press.

Office of Ethnic Minority Affairs. (2000). *Guidelines for research in ethnic minority communities*. Washington, DC: American Psychological Association.

Office of Women's Health. (2000, May). *The health of minority women*. Washington, DC: Department of Health and Human Services. (Online). Retrieved June 20, 2001, from the World Wide Web: http://www.4woman.gov/owh/pub/minority/index.htm.

Office of Women's Health. (2000a, May). *The health of minority women: Minority women's health concerns*. Washington, DC: Department of Health and Human Services. (Online). Retrieved June 20, 2001, from the World Wide Web: http://www.4woman.gov/owh/pub/minority/concerns.htm.

Office of Women's Health. (2000b, August 22). *America's health policies are failing women, finds most comprehesive women's health study ever—In-depth analysis of federal and state health care policies & status of women's health reveals massive gaps in research & policy*. Washington, DC: Department of Health and Human Services. (Online). Retrieved June 20, 2001, from the World Wide Web: http://www.4woman.gov/owh/pub/factsheets/makingthegrade.htm.

Office of Women's Health. (2000c, May 20). *Making the grade on women's health: A national and state by state report card*. Washington, DC: Department of Health and Human Services. (Online). Retrieved February 20, 2002, from the World Wide Web: http://www.nwlc.org/pdf/2001ReportCardExecutive summary.pdf.

Office of Women's Health. (2000d, May 20). *Barrier limiting access to health care*. Washington, DC: Department of Health and Human Services. (Online). Retrieved June 20, 2001, from the World Wide Web: http://www.4woman.gov/owh/pub/minority/barriers.htm.

Olsen, M. (1970). *Power in societies*. New York: Macmillan.

Orlandi, M. A., Weston, R., & Epstein, L. G. (Eds.). (1992). *Cultural competence for evaluators: A guide for alcohol and other drug abuse prevention practitioners working with ethnic/racial communities*. DHHS Publication No. ADM 92-1884). Washington, DC: U.S. Government Printing Office.

Orlans, H. (1989, May–June). The politics of minority statistics. *Society, 26*(4), 24–25.

Orlinsky, D. E., & Howard, K. I. (1986). Process and outcome in psychotherapy. In S. L. Garfield & A. E. Bergin (Eds.), *Handbook of psychotherapy and behavior change*. New York: Wiley.

Ottavi, T. M., Pope-Davis, D. B., & Dings, D. B. (1994). Relationship between White racial identity attitudes and self-reported multicultural counseling competencies. *Journal of Counseling Psychology, 41*, 149–154.

Ozer, M. N. (Ed.). (1979). *A cybernetic approach to the assessment of children: Toward a more humane use of humane beings.* Boulder, CO: Westview.

Padilla, A. M. (Ed.). (1980). *Acculturation: Theory, models and some new findings.* Boulder, CO: Westview.

Pan American Health Organization. (2000, December). United States of America. *Epidemiology Bulletin, 21*(4). (Online). Retrieved March 20, 2002, from the World Wide Web: http://www.paho.org/english/sha/prflusa.htm#socioecon.

Pandered, J. G., & Casas, J. M. (1991). *Handbook of racial/ethnic minority counseling research.* Springfield, IL: Thomas.

Paniagua, F. A. (1994). *Assessing and treating culturally diverse clients.* Thousand Oaks, CA: Sage.

Pargament, K. I. (1997). *The psychology of religion and coping: Theory, research, practice.* New York: Guilford.

Parham, T. A., & Helms, J. E. (1981). The influence of Black student identity attitudes on preference of counselor's race. *Journal of Counseling Psychology, 28*, 250–257.

Parker, W. S. (2002). *The berdache spirit.* Nu-Woman Transgender Cabaret. (Online). Retrieved February 27, 2002, from the World Wide Web: http://www.nu-woman.com/berdache.htm.

Pawlik, K., & d'Ydewalle, G. (1996, May). Psychology and the global community: Perspectives of international psychology. *American Psychologist, 51*(5), 488–495.

Pedersen, P. B. (1985). *Handbook of cross-cultural counseling and therapy.* Westport, CT: Greenwood.

Pedersen, P. B. (1988). *A handbook for developing multicultural awareness.* Alexandria, VA: American Association for Counseling and Development.

Pedersen, P. B. (1997, Winter). The cultural context of the American counseling association code of ethics. *Journal of Counseling & Development, 76*, 23–28.

Pedersen, P., & Ivey, A. (1993). *Culture-centered counseling.* New York: Greenwood.

Peng, K., & Nisbett, R. E. (1999, September). Culture, dialectics, and reasoning about contradictions. *American Psychologist, 54*(9), 741–754.

Peng, K., Nisbett, R. E., & Wong, N. Y. C. (1997, December). Validity problems comparing values across cultures and possible solutions. *Psychological Methods, 2*(4), 329–344.

Pennebaker, W. (Ed.) (1995, September). *Emotion, disclosure, and health.* Washington, DC: American Psychological Association.

Perez, R. M., Constantine, M. G., & Gerard, P. A. (2000). Individual and institutional productivity of racial and ethnic minority research in the *Journal of Multicultural Counseling and Development. Journal of Multicultural Counseling and Development, 47*, 223–228.

Perkins, L. A. Thomas, K. M., & Taylor, G. A. (2000, March). Advertising and recruitment: Marketing to minorities. *Psychology & Marketing, 17*(3), 235–255.

Peterson, C., Maier, S. F., & Seligman, M. E. P. (1993). *Learned helplessness: A theory for the age of personal control.* New York: Oxford University Press.

Pettigrew, T. (1959). Regional differences in anti-Negro prejudice. *Journal of Abnormal and Social Psychology, 59,* 28–36.

Peterson, B., West, J., Tanielian, T., & Pincus, H. (1998). Mental health practitioners and trainees. In R. W. Manderscheid & M. J. Henderson (Eds.), *Mental health United States 1998* (pp. 214–246). Rockville, MD: Center for Mental Health Services.

Pfenning. D. W., & Sherman, P. W. (1995, June). Kin recognition. *Scientific American, 272*(6), 98–103.

Phelps, R. E., Taylor, J. D., & Gerard, P. A. (2001, Spring). Cultural mistrust, ethnic identity, racial identity, and self-esteem among ethnically diverse Black university students. *Journal of Counseling and Development, 79*(2), 209–216.

Phinney, J. S. (1992, April). The Multigroup Ethnic Identity Measure: A new scale for use with diverse groups. *Journal of Adolescent Research, 7*(2), 156–176.

Pinderhughes, E. B. (1988). Treatment with Black middle-class families: A systemic perspective. A. F. Coner-Edwards & J. Spurlock (Eds.). *Black families in crisis: The middle class* (pp. 215–226). Philadelphia, PA: Brunner/Mazel.

Pinker, S., & Bloom, P. (1990). Natural language and natural selection. *Behavioral and Brain Sciences, 13,* 707–784.

Plotkin, H. C. (Ed.). (1988). *The role of behavior in evolution.* Cambridge, MA: MIT Press.

Poll: Minorities find Whites insensitive, bossy. (1994, March 4). *USA Today,* 3A.

Poll: Minorities see Whites as bossy, bigots. (1994, March 3,). *St. Petersburg Times,* 1A.

Polson, M. C., & Richardson, J. J. (1988). *Foundations of intelligent tutoring systems.* Hillsdale, NJ: Erlbaum.

Ponterotto, J. (1988). Racial/ethnic minority research in the *Journal of Counseling Psychology:* A content analysis and methodological critique. *Journal of Counseling Psychology, 35*(4), 410–418.

Ponterotto, J. G., & Casas, J. M. (1991). *Handbook of racial/ethnic minority counseling research.* Springfield, IL: Thomas.

Ponterotto, J. G., Casas, J. M., Suzuki, L. A., & Alexander, C. M. (1995). *Handbook of multicultural counseling.* Thousand Oaks, CA: Sage.

Pope-Davis, D. B. (Ed.). (2001, July). Psychological nigresence revisited (Special issue). *Journal of Multicultural Counseling and Development, 29*(3).

Pope-Davis, D. B., Ligiero, D. P., Liang, C., & Codrington, J. (2001, October). Fifteen years of the *Journal of Multicultural Counseling and Development:* A content analysis. *Journal of Multicultural Counseling and Development, 29*(4), 226–238.

Port, R. E., & Samovar, L. A. (1993). *Communication between cultures* (2nd ed.). Albany, NY: Wadsworth.

Powers, W. T. (1979). A cybernetic model for research in human development. In M. N. Ozer (Ed.), *A cybernetic approach to the assessment of children: Toward a more humane use of human beings* (pp. 11–66). Boulder, CO: Westview.

President's Commission on Mental Health. (1978). *Report to the president.* Washington, DC.: U.S. Government Printing Office.

Price, L. L., & Arnould, E. J. (1999, October). Commercial friendships: Service provider-client relationships in context. *Journal of Marketing.* (Online).

Retrieved March 20, 2002, from the World Wide Web: http://www.cba.unl. edu/faculty/earnould/friendsoct.pdf.

Priest, R. (1991). Racism and prejudice as negative impacts on African American clients in therapy. *Journal of Counseling and Development, 70,* 213–215.

Prilleltensky, I. (1997, May). Values, assumptions, and practices: Assessing the moral implications of psychological discourse and action. *American Psychologist, 52*(5), 536–540.

Procidano, M. E., Busch-Rossnagel, N. A., Reznikoff, M., & Geisinger, K. F. (1995, May). Responding to graduate students' professional deficiencies: A national survey. *Journal of Clinical Psychology, 51*(3), p. 426–433.

Racial and ethnic classifications used in Census 2000 and beyond. (2000). U.S. Census Bureau, Population Division (Online). Retrieved June 20, 2000, from the World Wide Web: http://www.census.gov/population/www/socdemo/race/ racefactcb.html.

Ramírez, J. D., Yuen, S. D., Ramey, D. R., Pasta, D., & Billings, D. (1991). *Final report: longitudinal study of structured immersion strategy, early-exit, and late-exit transitional bilingual education programs for language-minority children: Executive summary.* San Mateo, CA: Aguirre.

Ramirez, M., & Castaneda, A. (1974). *Cultural democracy, bicognitive development, and education.* New York: Academic.

Ramseur, H. P. (1991). Psychologically healthy Black adults. In R. L. Jones (Ed.), *Black psychology* (pp. 353–378). Berkeley, CA: Cobb & Henry.

Rashid, L. (2001). *What is Islam's view of homosexuality?* Muslim Unity.net. (Online). Retrieved June 20, 2001, from the World Wide Web: http://www.islamic.org.uk/homosex.html.

Reese, S. (1997, August). A world of differences. *Marketing Tools.* (Online). Retrieved February 25, 2001, from the World Wide Web: http:// www.marketingtools.com/publications/mt/97_mt/9708_mt/mt970822.htm.

Regeser-Lopez, S., & Guarnaccia, P. J. (2000, Annual). Cultural psychopathology: Uncovering the social world of mental illness. *Annual Review of Psychology, 51,* 571–599. (Online). Retrieved December 2000, from the World Wide Web: http://www.findarticles.com/cf_0/m0961/2000_Annual/61855637/ print.jhtml.

Regier, D. A., Farmer, M. E., Rae, D. S., Myers, J. K., Kramer, M., Robins, L. N., George, L. K., Karno, M., & Locke, B. Z. (1993). One-month prevalence of mental disorders in the United States and sociodemographic characteristics: The Epidemiologic Catchment Area study. *Acta Psychiatrica Scandinavica, 88,* 35–47.

Regier, D. A., Narrow, W. E., Rae, D. S., Manderscheid, R. W., Locke, B. Z., & Goodwin, F. K. (1993b). The de facto US mental and addictive disorders service system. Epidemiologic Catchment Area prospective 1-year prevalence rates of disorders and services. *Archives of General Psychiatry, 50,* 85–94.

Reminick, R. (1983). *Theory of ethnicity: An anthropologist's perspective.* New York: University Press of America.

Revised Standard Version of the Bible. (1971). (English). Riverside Drive, NY: Division of Christian Education of the National Council of the Churches of Christ in the United States of America.

Reynolds, P. C. (1981). *On the evolution of human behavior.* Berkeley: University of California Press.

Richards, P. S., & Bergin, A. E. (Eds.). (2000). *Handbook of psychotherapy and religious diversity.* Washington, DC: American Psychological Association.

Riche, M. F. (1997). United States population: A profile of American's diversity— The view from the Census Bureau, 1996. In R. Famighetti (Ed.), *The World Almanac 1997* (pp. 377–379). Mahwah, NJ: World Almanac Books.

Rist, C. (2000, December). Computers that talk. *Discover, 21*(12), 68–73.

Rogler, L. H., Malgady, R. G., & Rodriguez, O. (1989). *Hispanics and mental health: A framework for research.* Malabar, FL: Krieger.

Rogoff, B., & Chavajay, P. (1995). What's become of research on the cultural basis of cognitive development? *American Psychologist, 50*(10), 859–877.

Root, M. P. P. (1985). Guidelines for facilitating therapy with Asian-American clients. *Psychotherapy, 22,* 349–356.

Rosier, B. (1999, March). Putting colour into PC sales. *Marketing,* 18.

Ross, H. (1999, October/November). President's committee addresses unemployment. *Closing the Gap* (published by the Office of Minority Health, U. S. Department of Health and Human Services), p. 11.

Rothwell, N. V. (1977). *Human genetics.* Englewood Cliffs, NJ: Prentice-Hall.

Rouse, B. A. (1995). Substance abuse and mental health statistics sourcebook. Washington, DC: U.S. Government Printing Office; DHHS Publication Number (SMA) 95-3064.

Royce, A. P. (1982). *Ethnic identity.* Bloomington: Indiana University Press.

Rozner, E. (1998). *Haves, have-nots, and have-to-haves: Net effects of the digital divide.* (Online). Retrieved June 20, 2001, from the World Wide Web: http://cyber.law.harvard.edu/is98/final_papers/Rozner.html.

Rushton, J. P. (1995). *Race, evolution, and behavior.* New Brunswick, NJ: Transaction.

Russell, B. (1986) *The collected papers of Bertrand Russell. Vol. 8: The philosophy of logical atomism and other essays 1914–19.* London: Allen and Unwin.

Russell, G. L., Fujino, D. C., Sue, S., Cheung, M-K., & Snowden, L. R. (1996, September). The effects of therapist-client ethnic match in the assessment of mental health functioning. *Journal of Cross-Cultural Psychology, 27*(5), 598–615.

Sabnani, H. B., & Ponterrotto, J. G. (1992). Racial/ethnic minority instrumentation in counseling research: A review, critique, and recommendations. *Measurement and Evaluation in Counseling and Development, 24,* 161–187.

Saegert, S., Swap, W., & Zajonc, R. B. (1973). Exposure, context, and interpersonal attraction. *Journal of Personality and Social Psychology, 25,* 234–242.

Sampson, W. A., & Milam, V. (1975, December). The intraracial attitudes of the Black middle class: Have they changed? *Social Problems, 23*(2), 153–165.

Sandhu, D. S. (1997, January). Psychocultural profiles of Asian and Pacific Islander Americans: Implications for counseling and psychotherapy. *Journal of Multicultural Counseling and Development, 25*(1), 7–22.

Sandlund, C. (1999, April). There's a new face to America. *Success, 46*(4), 38, 40+.

Santos, R. (1992). US and foreign born Mexican American youth: A socioeconomic comparison. *International Journal of Adolescence & Youth, 3*(3–4), 319–331. (A B Academic Publishers, United Kingdom).

Sarbin, T. R., Taft, R., & Bailey, D. E. (1960). *Clinical inference and cognitive theory.* New York: Holt, Rinehart & Winston.

Sata, L. (1973). Musing of a hyphenated American. In S. Sue & W. Wagner (Eds.), *Asian Americans: Psychological perspectives* (pp. 150–156). Ben Lomond, CA: Behavioral Books.

Sawyer, D. (1991). Native learning styles: Shorthand for instructional adaptations? *Canadian Journal of Native Education, 18*(1), 99–104.

Saxe, L., & Cross, T. P. (1997, May). Interpreting the Fort Bragg children's mental health demonstration project: The cup is half full. *American Psychologist, 52*(5), 553–556.

Scheffler, R. M., & Miller, A. B. (1991). Differences in mental health service utilization among ethnic subpopulations. *International Journal of Law and Psychiatry, 14,* 363–376.

Schimel, J. L. (1972). The relevance of power: An introduction. In J. Masserman (Ed.), *The dynamics of power* (pp. 14–15). New York: Grune & Stratton.

Schwartz, R. C., Barrett, M., & Saba, G. (1985). Family therapy and bulimia. In D. M. Garner & P. E. Garfinkel (Eds.), *Handbook of psychotherapy for anorexia nervosa and bulimia* (pp. 280–307). New York: Guildford.

Sciences. (1992, March/April). Peer review: Letters from readers—The evolution of feelings. *Sciences,* 4–5, 55.

Scott, J. P. (1989). *The evolution of social systems.* New York: Gordon and Breach Science.

Sears, D. O. (1991). Symbolic racism. In P. A. Katz & D. A. Taylor (Eds.), *Eliminating racism: Profiles in controversy* (pp. 53–84). New York: Plenum.

Sechrest, L., & Pion, G. (1990). Developing cross-discipline measures of clinical competencies in diagnosis, treatment, and case management. In D. Johnson (Ed.), *Service needs of the seriously mentally ill: Training: Implications for psychology.* Washington, DC: American Psychological Association.

Sechrest, L., & Walsh, M. (1997, May). Dogma or data: Bragging rights. *American Psychologist, 52*(5), 536–540.

Sedlacek, W. E., & Kim, S. H. (1995). *Multicultural assessment.* (Eric Document Reproduction Services No. EDO-CG-95-24).

Segal, S. P., Bola, J. R., & Watson, M. A. (1996, March). Race, quality of care, and antipsychotic prescribing practices in psychiatric emergency services. *Psychiatric Services, 47,* 282–286.

Segerstrale, U., & Molnar, P. (1997). *Nonverbal communication where nature meets culture.* Mahwah, NJ: Erlbaum.

Serpell, R. (1982). Measures of perception, skills and intelligence. In W. W. Hartup (Ed.), *Review of child development research* (Vol. 6, pp. 392–440). Chicago: University of Chicago Press.

Shade, B. J. (1982). Afro-American cognitive styles: A variable in school success? *Review of Educational Research, 52*(2), 219–244.

Shade, B. J. (1989a). Afro-American cognitive patterns: A review of the research. In B. J. Shade (Ed.), *Culture, style, and the educative process* (pp. 94–115). Springfield, IL: Thomas.

Shade, B. J. (1989b). The influence of perceptual development on cognitive style: Cross ethnic comparisons. *Early Child Development and Care, 51,* 137–155.

Sharf, S. R. (1985). Artificial intelligence: Implications for the future of counseling. *Journal of Counseling and Development*, 16, 34–37.

Shirai, Y., & Tsujii, J. I. (1984). *Artificial intelligence: Concepts, techniques, and applications.* New Yotk: Wiley.

Siess, T. F., & Jackson, D. N. (1967). A personological approach to the interpretation of vocational interests. *Proceedings of the Annual Convention of the American Psychological Association*, 2, 353–354.

Siess, T. F., & Jackson, D. N. (1970). Vocational interests and personality: An empirical integration. *Journal of Counseling Psychology*, 17, 27–35.

Siller, J., Chipman, A., Ferguson, L. T., & Vann D. H. (1967). *Attitudes of nondisabled toward the physically disabled. Studies in reactions to disability.* New York: School of Education.

Simmons, J. (2001, August). Flower power. *Counseling Today*, 10–11.

Singularity Institute of Artificial Intelligence, Inc. (2001). *SIAI guidelines on friendly AI.* Author. (Online). Retrieved February 20, 2002 from the World Wide Web: http://www.singinst.org/friendly/guidelines.html

Small Business Administration. (2000). *The new majority marketing to minorities.* Washington, DC. (Online). Retrieved February 20, 2001, from the World Wide Web: http://www.sba.gov/gopher/Business-Development/Success-Series/Vol6/mktg.txt.

Small Business Administration. (2001). *Ethnic marketing turning obstacles into opportunities.* Washington, DC: Author. (Online). Retrieved February 25, 2001, from the World Wide Web: http://www.sba.gov/gopher/Business-Development/Success-Series/Vol8/obstacle.txt.

Smart, D. W., & Smart, J. F. (1997, May/June). DSM-IV and culturally sensitive diagnosis: Some observations for counselors. *Journal of Counseling and Development*, 75, 392–398.

Smith, H. (1986). *The religions of man.* New York: Perennial Library.

Smith, K.U., & Smith, M.F. (1966). *Cybernetic principles of learning and educational design.* New York: Holt, Rinehart, & Winston.

Smith, T. (1980). Ethnic measurement and identification. *Ethnicity*, 7, 78–95.

Smith, V. G., & Wang, X. (1997, December). *Survey of statistical methods used in minority health research.* Presented to the Department of Biostatistics, University of North Carolina at Chapel Hill. (Online). Retrieved June 2000, from the World Wide Web: http://www.google.com/search?q=cache: www.minority.unc.edu/Other_abst/vgsab1.html+minority+statistical+analyzing&hl=en.

Snowden L. R. (1998). *Barriers to effective mental health services for African Americans.* Manuscript submitted for publication.

Social Audit Gallup News Service. (2001). *Haves and have nots.* Princeton, NJ: The Gallup Organization. (Online). Retrieved September 20, 2001, from the World Wide Web: http://www.gallup.com/poll/socialaudits/have_havenot.asp.

Social Capital Interest Group. (2002). *Social capital: A position paper.* (Michigan State University). (Online). Retrieved February 20, 2002. from the World Wide Web: http://www.ssc.msu.edu/~internat/soccap/position.htm.

Soska, M. (1994, Winter). An introduction to educational technology. *Directions in Language and Education 1*, 1. Washington, DC: National Clearinghouse for Bilingual Education.

Southern Poverty Law Center. (2002). *Hidden bias: A primer.* (Online). Retrieved February 20, 2002, from the World Wide Web: http://www.tolerance.org/hidden_bias/tutorials/06.html.

Soskin, W. F. (1954). Bias in postdiction from projective tests. *Journal of Abnormal Social Psychology, 49,* 69–74.

Soskin, W. F. (1959). Influence of four types of data on diagnostic conceptualization in psychological testing. *Journal of Abnormal Psychology, 58,* 69–74.

Specialty Equipment Market Association. (2000). *Auto aftermarket confab to conduct workshops on marketing to minorities.* (Online). Retrieved February 25, 2001, from the World Wide Web: http://www.sema.org/pressreleases/minor.cfm.

Spriggs, W. A. (1998). *What is evolutionary psychology?* (Online). Retrieved June 20, 2000, from the World Wide Web: http://evoyage.com/Whatis.html.

Steele, R. E. (1978, February). Relationship of race, sex, social class, and social mobility to depression in normal adults. *Journal of Social Psychology, 104*(1), 37–47.

Steen, R. G. (1996). *DNA and destiny: Nature and nurture in human behavior.* New York: Plenum.

Stern, S. (1984, April). Professional training and professional competence: A critique of current thinking. *Professional Psychology—Research & Practice, 15*(2), 230–243.

Stevens, A., & Price, J. (1996). *Evolutionary psychiatry: A new beginning.* New York: Routledge.

Steward, J. H. (1955). *Theory of culture change.* Urbana: University of Illinois Press.

Steward, R. J., Morales, P. C., Bartell, P. A., Miller, M., & Weeks, D.(1998, January). The multiculturally responsive versus the multiculturally reactive: A study of perceptions of counselor trainees. *Journal of Multicultural Counseling and Development, 26,* 13–27.

Sue, D. (1997, May). Multicultural training. *International Journal of Intercultural Relations, 21*(2), 175–193. (Elsevier Science Inc., US).

Sue, D. W. (1990). Culture specific techniques in counseling: A conceptual framework. *Professional Psychology, 21,* 424–433.

Sue, D. W. (1995a). Toward a theory of multicultural counseling and therapy. In J. Banks & C. McGee (Eds.), *Handbook of research on multicultural education* (pp. 647–659). New York: Macmillan.

Sue, D. W. (1995b). Multicultural organizational development: Implications for the counseling profession. In J. G. Ponterotto, J. M. Casas, L. A. Suzuki, & C. M. Alexander (Eds.), *Handbook of multicultural counseling.* Thousand Oaks, CA: Sage.

Sue, S. (1977). Community mental health services to minorities: Some optimism, some pessimism. *American Psychologist, 32,* 616–624.

Sue, S., & Zane, N. (1987). The role of culture and cultural techniques in psychotherapy. *American Psychologist, 38,* 37–45.

Suler, J. (2002). *Computerized psychotherapy.* (Online). Retrieved January 20, 2002, from the World Wide Web: http://www.rider.edu/users/suler/psycyber/eliza.html.

Surgeon General's Report on Mental Health. (1999). *Mental health: A report of the*

Surgeon General—Overview of cultural diversity and mental health services. Rockville, MD: U.S. Department of Health and Human Services, Substance Abuse and Mental Health Services Administration, Center for Mental Health Services, National Institutes of Health, National Institute of Mental Health. (Online). Retrieved January 20, 2001, from the World Wide Web: http://www.surgeongeneral.gov/library/mentalhealth/chapter2/ sec8.html

Surgeon General's Report on Mental Health. (1999a). *Mental health: A report of the Surgeon General—Executive summary.* Rockville, MD: U.S. Department of Health and Human Services, Substance Abuse and Mental Health Services Administration, Center for Mental Health Services, National Institutes of Health, National Institute of Mental Health. (Online). Retrieved March 20, 2002, from the World Wide Web: http://www.surgeongeneral.gov/library/mentalhealth/ summary.html.

Surgeon General's Report on Mental Health. (1999b). *Mental health: A report of the Surgeon General—Chapter 8: A vision for the future.* Rockville, MD: U.S. Department of Health and Human Services, Substance Abuse and Mental Health Services Administration, Center for Mental Health Services, National Institutes of Health, National Institute of Mental Health. (Online). Retrieved March 20, 2002, from the World Wide Web: http://www.surgeongeneral.gov/library/ mentalhealth/chapter8/sec1.html.

Surgeon General's Report on Mental Health. (1999c). *Epidemiology of mental illness.* Rockville, MD: U.S. Department of Health and Human Services, Substance Abuse and Mental Health Services Administration, Center for Mental Health Services, National Institutes of Health, National Institute of Mental Health. (Online). Retrieved January 20, 2001, from the World Wide Web: http://www.surgeongeneral.gov/library/mentalhealth/chapter2/sec2_1.html.

Surgeon General's Report on Mental Health. (1999d). *Overview of cultural diversity and mental health services.* Rockville, MD: U.S. Department of Health and Human Services, Substance Abuse and Mental Health Services Administration, Center for Mental Health Services, National Institutes of Health, National Institute of Mental Health. (Online). Retrieved January 20, 2001, from the World Wide Web: http://www.surgeongeneral.gov/library/mentalhealth/ chapter2/sec8.html#introduction.

Sussman, L. K., Robins, L. N., & Earls, F. (1987). Treatment-seeking for depression by Black and White Americans. *Social Science and Medicine, 24,* 187–196.

Swanson, L. L. (Ed.). (1996, August). *Racial/ethnic minorities in rural areas: Progress and stagnation, 1980–90.* Washington, DC: U.S. Department of Agriculture (Rural Economy Division, Economic Research Services): Agricultural Economic Report No. 731.

Swisher, K., & Deyhle, D. (1989). The styles of learning are different but the teaching is just the same. *Journal of American Indian Education* (Special issue), 1–13.

Sykes, C. J. (1995). *Dumbing down our kids: Why American children feel good about themselves but can't read, write, or add.* New York: St. Martin's.

Szasz, T. S. (1974). *The myth of mental illness: Foundations of a theory of personal conduct.* New York: Harper & Row.

Szasz, T. S. (1978). *The myth of psychotherapy: Mental healing as religion, rhetoric, and repression.* Garden City, NY: Anchor Press/Doubleday.

Taft, R. (1955). The ability to judge people. *Psychological Bulletin, 52,* 1–23.

Tajfel, H. (1970, November). Experiments in intergroup discrimination. *Scientific American,* 96–102.

Tajfel, H. (1981). *Human groups and social categories: Studies in social psychology.* London: Cambridge University Press.

Tajfel, H. (1982). Social psychology of intergroup relations. *Annual Review of Psychology, 33,* 1–39.

Tajfel, H., & Billig, M. (1974). Familiarity and categorization in intergroup behavior. *Journal of Experimental Social Psychology, 10,* 159–170.

Takeuchi, D. T., & Uehara, E. S. (1996). Ethnic minority mental health services: Current research and future conceptual directions. In B. L. Levin & J. Petrila (Eds.), *Mental health services: A public health perspective* (pp. 63–80). New York: Oxford University Press.

Takeuchi, D. T., Uehara, E. S., & Maramba, G. (1999). Cultural diversity and mental health treatment. In A. V. Horwitz & T. L. A. Scheid (Eds.), *A handbook for the study of mental health: Social contexts, theories, and systems.* New York: Cambridge University Press.

Taylor, R. J. (1986). Religious participation among elderly Blacks. *Gerontologist, 26,* 630–636.

Taylor, R. L. (1976). Psychosocial development among Black children and youth: A reexamination. *American Journal of Orthopsychiatry, 46*(2), 4–19.

Tefft, S. K. (1980. *Secrecy: A cross-cultural perspective.* New York: Human Sciences.

Tharp, R. G. (1989). Psychocultural variables and constants: Effects on teaching and learning in schools. *American Psychologist, 44*(2), 349–359.

Thompson, C. E., Neville, H., Weathers, P. L., Poston, W. C., & Atkinson, D. R. (1990, March). Cultural mistrust and racism reaction among African-American students. *Journal of College Student Development, 31*(2), 162–168.

Tokar, D. M., & Fischer, A. R. (Oct. 1998). Psychometric analysis of the racial identity attitude scale—long form. *Measurement and Evaluation in Counseling and Development, 31*(3), 138–149.

Toonies, F. (1957). *Community and society: Gemeinschaft and Gesellschaft* (C. P. Loomis, Ed. & Trans.). New York: Harper and Row.

Tremblay, P. J., & Ramsay, R. (2000, March). *Gay/bisexual male youth suicide problems.* Paper presented at the 11th Annual Sociological Symposium, San Diego, CA. (Online). Retrieved May 1, 2001, from the World Wide Web: http://www.virtualcity.com/youthsuicide/d-gay-male-youth-suicide.htm.

Triandis, H. (Ed.). (1980). *Handbook of cross-cultural psychology.* Boston: Allyn & Bacon.

Trimble, J. E. (2000). Social psychological perspectives on changing self-identification among American Indians and Alaska Natives. In R. H. Dana (Ed.), *Handbook of cross-cultural and multicultural personality assessment.* Mahwah, NJ: Erlbaum.

Trivers, R. (1985). *Social evolution.* Reading, MA: Benjamin/Cummings.

Trull, T. J., & Geary, D. C. (1997, October). Comparison of the five-factor structure across samples of Chinese and American adults. *Journal of Personality Assessment, 69*(2), 324–341.

Tsai, J. L., & Levenson, R. W. (1997, September). Cultural influences on emotional responding. *Journal of Cross-Cultural Counseling, 28*(5), 600–625.

Tsai, J. L, Ying, Y.-W., & Lee, P. A. (2000, May). The meaning of "being Chinese" and "being American": Variation among Chinese American young adults. *Journal of Cross-Cultural Psychology, 31*(3), 302–332.

Tuckett, L. (1999). Reaching the new American mosaic—non-Whites comprise a $1 trillion opportunity for advertisers. *Ad/Insight.* (Online). Retrieved February 25, 2001, from the World Wide Web: http://www.channelseven.com/adinsight/commentary/1999comm/comm19990408.shtml.

Tuller, R. M. (1977). *The human species: Its nature, evolution, and ecology.* New York: McGraw-Hill.

Turner, J. L., Gallimore, R., & Fox-Henning, C. (1980). *An annotated bibliography of placebo research.* Washington, DC: American Psychological Association.

Tyler, F. B., Brome, D. R., & Williams, J. E. (1991). *Ethnic validity, ecology, and psychotherapy.* New York: Plenum.

Uba, L. (1994). *Asian Americans: Personality patterns, identity, and mental health.* New York: Guilford.

Ullman, L. P., & Krasner, L. (1975). *A psychological approach to abnormal behavior.* Englewood Cliffs, NJ: Prentice-Hall.

United States Dept. of Agriculture. (1991). *What every exporter should know: A guide to international food marketing* (4 sound cassettes, analog). Washington, DC: United States Dept. of Agriculture, Foreign Agricultural Service.

United States Department of Commerce v. United States House of Representatives, No. 98-404: Amici curiae filed to the U.S. Supreme Court (1998)—by *American Civil Liberties Union.* (Online). Retrieved June 20, 2000, from the World Wide Web: http://www.aclu.org/court/usdcvhouse.html.

University of Northern Iowa Business Communication. (2002). *Body language.* (Online). Retrieved February 20, 2002, from the World Wide Web: http://www.cba.uni.edu/buscomm/nonverbal/Body%20Language.htm.

U.S. Census. (2000, March). *Poverty 1999.* (U.S. Census Bureau, Current Population Survey). (Online). Retrieved October 20, 2001, from the World Wide Web: http://www.census.gov/hhes/poverty/poverty99/table5.html.

U.S. Census. (2000a). *Index of/population/estimates/nation/.* (Online). Retrieved July 14, 2000 from the World Wide Web: http://www.census.gov/population/estimates/nation/intfile3-1.txt.

U.S. Census. (2000b). *Race data.* (Online). Retrieved June 20, 2000, from the World Wide Web: http://www.census.gov/population/www/socdemo/race.html.

U. S. Census Bureau. (2001, January). *Minority links.* (Online). Retrieved January 20, 2001, from the World Wide Web: http://www.census.gov/pubinfo/www/hotlinks.html

U.S. Department of Commerce. (1997a). *Department of Commerce Strategic Plan for 1997–2002 (September, 1997).* (Online). Retrieved May 25, 2002, from the World Wide Web: http://www.osec.doc.gov/bmi/budget/strtgc/strtoc.htm.

U.S. Department of Commerce. (1997b). *Department of Commerce Strategic Plan for 1997–2002 (September, 1997). Appendix. Authorities for commerce economic infrastructure, science/technology/information, and resource and asset management and stewardship activities*, p. 135. (Online). Retrieved May 25, 2002, from the World Wide Web: http://www.osec.doc.gov/bmi/budget/strtgc/Appendix.pdf.

U.S. Department of Commerce. (1997c). *Department of Commerce Strategic Plan for 1997–2002 (September, 1997). Appendix. Authorities for commerce economic infrastructure, science/technology/information, and resource and asset management and stewardship activities*, p. 163. (Online). Retrieved May 25, 2002, from the World Wide Web: http://www.osec.doc.gov/bmi/budget/strtgc/Appendix.htm.

U.S. Department of Commerce. (1999). *Appendix. Authorities for commerce economic infrastructure, science/technology/information, and resource and asset management and stewardship actitivies.* (Online). Retrieved June 20, 2000, from the World Wide Web: http://www.doc.gov/bmi/.

U.S. Department of Health and Human Services. (2000, November). *Healthy People 2010. (2nd ed.). With understanding and improving health and objectives for improving health. (Vol. 2). 18: Mental health and mental disorders.* Washington, DC: U.S. Government Printing Office. (Online). Retrieved July 20, 2001, from the World Wide Web: http://www.health.gov/healthypeople/document/HTML/Volume2/18Mental.htm.

U.S. Department of Health and Human Services. (2001, January). *Directory of minority health and human services data resources.* (Online). Retrieved January 20, 2001. from the World Wide Web: http://www.hhs.gov/progorg/aspe/minority.

U.S. Library of Congress. (1999). *Ethnic groups.* (Online). Retrieved June 20, 2000, from the World Wide Web: http://lcweb.loc.gov/lexico/liv/e/Ethnic_groups.html.

U.S. Public Health Service (2000). *Report of the Surgeon General's conference on children's mental health: A national action agenda.* Washington, DC: Department of Health and Human Services. Document can be obtained from: Pittsburgh, PA: Superintendent of Documents, Stock No. 017-024-01659-4. (Online). Retrieved June 20, 2001, from the World Wide Web: http://www.surgeongeneral.gov/cmh/childreport.htm.

Van den Berghe, P. L. (Ed.). (1972). *Intergroup relations.* New York: Basic.

Van Hoof, K. (1994, July 18). Surveys point to group differences. *Brandweek, 35*(29), 32–33.

Vargas, M. F. (1986). *Louder than words—an introduction to nonverbal communication.* Ames: Iowa State University Press.

Vega, W. A., & Kolody, B. (1998). *Hispanic mental health at the crossroads.* Manuscript submitted for publication.

Vega, W. A., Kolody, B., Aguilar-Gaxiola, S., Alderete, E., Catalano, R., & Caraveo-Anduaga, J. (1998a). Lifetime prevalence of *DSM-III-R* psychiatric disorders among urban and rural Mexican Americans in California. *Archives of General Psychiatry, 55*, 771–778.

Vega, W. A., & Rumbaut, R. G. (1991). Ethnic minorities and mental health. *Annual Review of Sociology, 17*, 351–383.

Velez, W. Y. (1999, August 27). Minority data. *Science, 285*, 1357–1358.

Veroff, J., Douvan, E., & Kulka, R. A. (1981). *The inner American: A self-portrait from 1957–1976.* New York: Basic.

Vogel, G., & Motulsky, A. G. (1979). *Human genetics.* New York: Springer-Verlag.

Voland, E., & Voland, R. (1989, April). Evolutionary biology and psychiatry: The case of anorexia nervosa. *Ethology & Sociobiology, 10*(4), 223–240.

Vontress, C. E. (1969). Cultural differences: Implications for counseling. *Journal of Negro Education, 38*, 266–275.

Vontress, C. (1971). Racial differences: Impediments to rapport. *Journal of Counseling Psychology, 18*(1), 7–13.

Vontress, C. E., & Epp, L. R. (1997, July). Historical hostility in the African American client: Implications for counseling. *Journal of Multicultural Counseling and Development, 25*(3), 170–184.

Vygotsky, L. S. (1978). *Mind in society: The development of higher psychological processes.* Cambridge, MA: Harvard University Press.

Wallich, P. (1999, November). Who needs Berlitz? *Discover, 20*(11), 55–17.

Walters, K. L. (1999). Urban American Indian identity attitudes and acculturation styles. *Journal of Human Behavior in the Social Environment, 2*(1–2), 163–178.

Washington, E. D. (1994). Three steps to cultural awareness: A Wittgensteinian approach. In P. Pedersen & J. C. Carey (Eds.), *Multicultural counseling in schools: A practical handbook* (pp. 81–102). Boston: Allyn & Bacon.

Waters, M. (1999, March). College students' racial attitudes may be linked to academic success. *APA Monitor,* 6.

Watkins, C. E., & Terrell, F. (1988, April). Mistrust level and its effects on counseling expectations in Black client-White counselor relationships: An analogue study. *Journal of Counseling Psychology, 35*(2), 194–197.

Webster's ninth new collegiate dictionary. (1990). Springfield, MA: Merriam-Webster.

Weibull, J. W. (1995). *Evolutionary game theory.* Cambridge, MA: MIT Press.

Weil, N. (1999, October 21,). Computers will feel your pain: Intuitive future PCs will react to users' moods, averting "computer rage." *IDG News Service.* (Online). Retrieved Febuary 20, 2001, from the World Wide Web: http://www.pcworld.com/news/article.asp?aid=13393.

Weinberger, J. (1993). Common factors in psychotherapy. In G. Stricker & J. R. Gold (Eds.), *Comprehensive handbook of psychotherapy integration* (pp. 43–56). New York: Plenum.

Weiner, B., Perry, R. P., & Magnusson, J. (1988). An attributional analysis of reactions to stigmas. *Journal of Personality and Social Psychology, 55*, 738–748.

Weisfeld, G. E. (1977). A sociobiological basis for psychotherapy. In M. T. McGuire & L. A. Fairbanks (Eds.), *Ethological psychiatry: Psychopathology in the context of evolutionary biology.* New York: Grune & Stratton.

Weizenbaum, J. (1966, March). ELIZA—a computer program for the study of natural language of communication between man and machine. *Communications of the ACED, 6*(3).

Westbrook, M. T., Varoe, L., & Pennay, M. (1993). Attitudes toward disabilities in a multicultural society. *Social Science Medicine, 36*(5), 615–623.

Wester, S. R., & Vogel, D. L. (2002, April). The emperor's new clothes: Sociopolitical diversity in psychology. *American Psychologist, 57*(4), 295–296.

Westermeyer, J. (1987). Cultural factors in clinical assessment. *Journal of Consulting and Clinical Psychology, 55*(4), 471–478.

Whaley, A. L. (1997, March). Ethnicity/race, paranoia, and psychiatric diagnoses:

Clinician bias versus sociocultural differences. *Journal of Psychopathology & Behavioral Assessment, 19*(1), 1–20.

Whaley, A. L. (1998, January). Racism in the provision of mental health services: A social-cognitive analysis. *American Journal of Orthopsychiatry, 68*(1), 47–57.

Whaley, A. L. (2000). Sociocultural differences in the developmental consequences of the use of physical discipline during childhood for African Americans. *Cultural Diversity and Ethnic Minority Psychology, 6*(1), 5–12.

What makes you Black. (1982, January). *Ebony,* 115–118.

When the category totals more than 100 percent. (1991, February 27). *The San Francisco Chronicle,* 1/Z1.

White, J. E. (1999, March 8). Prejudice? Perish the thought: The most insidious racism is among those who don't think they harbor any. *Time Magazine, 153*(9), 36.

White, L. A. (1959a). *The evolution of culture.* New York: McGraw-Hill.

White, L. A. (1959b). The concept of culture. *American Anthropologist, 61,* 227–251.

White, L., & Parham, T. (1990). *Psychology of Blacks: An African American perspective.* Englewood Cliffs, NJ: Prentice-Hall.

White, L., Tursky, B., & Schwartz, G. E. (Eds.). (1985). *Placebo: Theory, research and mechanisms.* New York: Guilford.

Widman, L. E., Loparo, K. A., & Nielson, N. R. (1989). *Artificial intelligence, simulation, and modeling.* New York: Wiley.

Wiese, M. R. (1992, July). Racial research in school psychology. *Psychology in the Schools, 29*(3), 267–272.

Wiggins, J. S. (Ed.). (1996). *The five-factor model of personality.* New York: Guilford.

Wilder, D. (1981). Perceiving persons as a group: Categorization and intergroup relations. In D. L. Hamilton (Ed.), *Cognitive processes in stereotyping and intergroup behavior.* Hillsdale, NJ: Erlbaum.

Wilkinson, S. M., & Burke, J. P. (1984, December). Ethnicity, socioeconomic status, and self-concept: Effects on children's academic performance. *Journal of Instructional Psychology, 11*(4), 203–210.

Williams, D. R., Yu, Y., Jackson, J. S., & Anderson, N. B. (1997, July). Racial differences in physical and mental health: Socio-economic status, stress and discrimination. *Journal of Health Psychology, 2*(3), 335–351.

Wilson, E. O. (1975). *Sociobiology: The new synthesis.* Cambridge, MA: The Belnap Press of Harvard University.

Wittgenstein, L. (1969). *On certainty.* Oxford: Blackwell.

World Bank. (1993). *World development report 1993: Investing in health.* New York: Oxford University Press.

World Health Organization. (1992). *International statistical classification of diseases and related health problems* (10th revision, ICD-10). Geneva: Author.

World Health Organization. (2000). *World Health Report 2000,* WHO, Geneva. (Online). Retrieved Febuary 20, 2001, from the World Wide Web: http://www.who.int.

Wresch, W. C. (1996). *Disconnected: Haves and have nots in the information age.* New Brunswick, NJ: Rutgers University.

Wright, B. A. (1960). *Physical disability—A psychological approach.* New York: Harper and Brothers.

Wright, J. H., Salmon, P., Wright, A. S., & Beck, A. T. (1998). *Cognitive therapy: A multimedia learning program* (Multimedia computer program). Mindstreet. (Online). Retrieved January 2001, from the World Wide Web: http://mindstreet.com/mindstreet.html.

Wright, J. W. (Ed.). (2000). *The New York Times almanac*. New York: Penguin Putnam.

Wu, I.-H., & Windle, C. (1980). Ethnic specificity in the relative minority use and staffing of community health centers. *Community Mental Health Journal, 16*(2), 156–168.

Yamamoto, F. X., & Acosta, J. (1982, October). Treatment of Asian Americans and Hispanic Americans: Similarities and differences. *Journal of the American Academy of Psychoanalysis, 10*(4), 585–607.

Yazdani, M., & Narayanan, A. (1984). *Artificial intelligence: Human effects*. New York: Wiley.

Yetman, N. (1985). Introduction: Definitions and perspectives. In N. Yetman (Ed.), *Majority and minority: The dynamics of race and ethnicity in American life* (4th ed., pp. 1–20). Boston: Allyn & Bacon.

Ying, Y.-W., Lee, P. A, & Tsai, J. L. (2000, July). Cultural orientation and racial discrimination: Predictors of coherence in Chinese American young adults. *Journal of Community Psychology, 28*(4), 427–442.

Yuker, H. E. (1994). Variables that influence attitudes toward people with disabilities. *Journal of Social Behaviour and Personality, 9*, 3–22.

Yuker, H. E., Block, J. R., & Campbell, V. (1960). *A scale of measuring attitudes towards disabled persons*. Albertson, NY: Human Resource Center.

Zajonc, R. B. (1968). Attitudinal effects of mere exposure. *Journal of Personality and Social Psychology, 9*, 1–27.

Zehler, A. M. (1995). *The uses of communications technology for language proficiency assessment and academic assessment*. Arlington, VA: Development Associates.

Zhang, A. Y., Snowden, L. R., & Sue, S. (1998). Differences between Asian and white Americans' help-seeking patterns in the Los Angeles area. *Journal of Community Psychology, 26*, 317–326.

Zsembik, B. A., & Beeghley, L. (1996, February). Determinants of ethnic group solidarity among Mexican Americans: A research note. *Hispanic Journal of Behavioral Sciences, 18*(1), 51–62.

Zweigenhaft, R. L., & Domhoff, G. W. (1982). *Jews in the Protestant establishment*. New York: Praeger.

Zweigenhaft, R. L., & Domhoff, G. W. (1998). *Diversity in the power elite: Have women and minorities reached the top?* New Haven, CT: Yale University Press.

Index